D0176308

HARD CHOICES

**California Series on
Social Choice and Political Economy**
Edited by Brian Barry and Samuel L. Popkin

HARD CHOICES

How Women Decide about Work, Career, and Motherhood

KATHLEEN GERSON

UNIVERSITY OF CALIFORNIA PRESS   *Berkeley / Los Angeles / London*

University of California Press
Berkeley and Los Angeles, California

University of California Press, Ltd.
London, England

© 1985 by
The Regents of the University of California

Printed in the United States of America
1   2   3   4   5   6   7   8   9

Library of Congress Cataloging in Publication Data

Gerson, Kathleen.
    Hard choices.

    Bibliography: p.
    Includes index.
        1. Women—United States—Social conditions.
2. Mothers—United States—Social conditions.   3. Women—
Employment—United States—History.   4. Mothers—Employ-
ment—United States—History.   5. Family size—United
States—History.   6. Women—United States—Psychology.
I. Title.
HQ1420.G4   1985   305.4'0973   84-8602
ISBN 0-520-05174-2

CONTENTS

LIST OF FIGURES

LIST OF TABLES

Appendix A: Tables

Appendix C: Sample Characteristics

PREFACE

Two concerns motivated me to write this book. The first was personal. The issues explored here are among the most important in my own development. As the research took shape, however, I realized that many, perhaps most, women in my generation share the same concerns. Although their responses vary, they face similar dilemmas, risks, and choices. Thus, a sustained analysis of these "personal" decisions seemed useful practically and politically, as well as intellectually, to a broad group of people.

Second, the book emerged from a growing dissatisfaction with prevailing theories of gender. Despite enormous intellectual advances in recent decades, neither established theories nor emerging feminist alternatives convincingly explained the changes currently taking place in women's social position and personal experiences. Whether these theories stressed hormones, psychological predispositions, capitalist economic arrangements, or male oppression, they tended to focus almost exclusively on forces beyond women's ultimate control. Although all these factors surely constrain women's lives to varying degrees, they alone do not provide a satisfying account of women's place. A full analysis of the active role women play as partially "knowledgeable agents" (as Anthony Giddens proposes) in the construction of their lives is also needed. This book proceeds from the belief that, in the context of structural constraint, women actively build their lives out of the materials provided by larger social forces. In so doing, they in turn shape and under propitious circumstances reshape the world that has shaped them.

This starting point led me to build my analysis around three orienting assumptions. First, this study stresses variation among women. It argues that the psychological and social differences among women are large, significant, and consequential. Indeed, they may well be as significant as those between women and men. The theoretical and empirical focuses of most earlier analyses of gender have centered upon the differences between women and men and thus, at least by implication, have underplayed the differences among women. Although this approach has made major contributions, it has also had some unfortunate consequences. The search for gender differences, with the accompanying tendency to lump all women together, has often led to generalizations about women, and men, that apply to at most a sizeable proportion of them.

The focus on female-male differences has also promoted the tendency among both feminists and nonfeminists to conclude implicitly (and sometimes explicitly) that one sex excels in specified ways. This view is dangerous no matter which sex is judged to be "better." If men are judged more rational, aggressive, task-oriented, or morally developed, as a number of traditional theories argue, then women's subordinate position is justified in obvious ways. But even if women are judged superior (for example, in their interpersonal, emotional, or nurturant capacities), the analysis places women on a pedestal, putting them in a position that can be and has been used against them.

It is necessary but not sufficient to argue, as many feminists do, that many women's skills are unfairly undervalued. Social theory also needs to recognize that women, like men, vary in their orientations, capacities, and abilities to integrate the parts of their selves. By examining differences among women, this study views them not as members of a homogeneous group, but rather as social science has always viewed men: as individuals situated in variable social contexts who bring differing resources and degrees of power to their situations. By examining the processes of negotiation *between* women and men, this study views women not as separated from men by an unbridgeable temperamental gulf, but rather as social actors motivated by similar processes and forces, but responding to different dilemmas and constraints.

This book also proceeds from the belief that it is important to understand the nature of recent changes in women's social position. Much of the literature stresses how and why gender inequality has been reproduced over time. This is certainly an important research focus, but over the last thirty years, and especially over the last fifteen years, important changes have occurred in the degree and type of gender inequality. It is as important to specify and explain these changes as it is to document and account for the persistence of inequality. By looking at the intersection of biography, history, and social structure (what C. Wright Mills called the orienting framework of social science), this book offers a method for studying the role of human action in social change.

Through the analysis of in-depth interviews with both domestic and nondomestic women from a variety of social and economic backgrounds, I have tried to cast light on women's diverse situations, worldviews, and concerns. Although the topics explored in these interviews are the subject of considerable controversy, I am not concerned with evaluating the desirability of one choice over another. The aim here is to explain, not pass judgment.

Finally, this analysis is based on the belief that social science knowledge can contribute to human freedom. Although social scientists tend to look for the causes of individual and social outcomes in preexisting structural and psychic arrangements, this insight need not imply that human beings have no control over their fate. Those who would choose their fate, however, must first understand the forces that would, were they to remain unaware, determine it. By identifying these constraints and by illuminating the points at which meaningful choice is possible, this book seeks to expand the range of human action.

ACKNOWLEDGMENTS

Writing a book is a solitary, often lonely, experience; yet there are few tasks that require the help of so many. This book, like most, could not have been written without the support, advice, encouragement, and criticism of many people.

First, I owe a great intellectual debt to my years of training at the University of California at Berkeley and to the committee that oversaw this project when it began as a dissertation. As committee chair, Hal Wilensky performed above and beyond the call of duty. From the early stages of research design to reading the final draft, he provided that difficult combination of support and criticism. Although he never withheld his enthusiasm, he nevertheless demanded the highest standards of scholarship and sought relentlessly to uncover weaknesses of design, analysis, or presentation.

Claude Fischer, Arlie Hochschild, and Karen Paige also served as members of the dissertation committee. Claude Fischer taught me how to translate an interesting question into a researchable study and more than once rescued me from the trap of trying to do too much in too little time with too few resources. Arlie Hochschild helped keep my sociological imagination alive when the demands of normal science threatened to overwhelm the creative urge. Karen Paige provided critical aid in thinking through the logic of the research and grounding it in an empirical base. As much by example as by direct intervention, all these people taught me two lessons about the sociological enterprise: First, it is more important to ask the right question than to find the right answer; second, large issues are often best illuminated by small, well-crafted studies.

The most valuable resources in graduate school are one's fellow students. I was fortunate to participate in a dissertation study group, where friends and colleagues not only forced me to confront my own demons, but, by facing their own, also showed me how. My deep thanks go to Joyce Bird, Jane Grant, Sydney Halpern, David Hummon, Robert Jackson, Robert Mayer, and Ann Stueve. Happily, the completion rate among this group is approaching 100 percent.

Others also helped in concrete ways at critical points. Guy Swanson and John Clausen awarded me an N.I.M.H. predoctoral fellowship in personality and social structure to support the year of interviewing. The "Rose Blum Foundation" provided additional financial aid for interview transcription. Charlotte Coleman of the Berkeley Survey Research Center helped transform a rambling interview schedule into a first-rate instrument. This schedule, which provided the central structure to the study, reflects her painstaking attention and considerable interviewing skills. Kristin Luker, whose work on women's contraceptive decisions inspired me to forsake the computer for the field, helped resolve what at the time seemed an irresolvable sampling problem. Susan Miller Lowe offered herself and a long list of names when people were needed to pretest the interview. Ann Van de Pol pointed me in the right direction to locate an appropriate working-class sample. University and community college officials, whose names must remain anonymous, generously provided lists of names from which the sample was chosen. Elinor Bernal was a gifted observer as well as the best transcriber anyone could want. As the only other person to listen to all of the interviews verbatim, her perceptive reactions fueled my confidence in and understanding of the material.

The book that developed out of the dissertation was revised and restructured several times in response to the critical readings of a number of colleagues. Brian Barry, Eugenie Ladner Birch, Richard Busacca, Arlene Kaplan Daniels, Glen Elder, Jr., Barbara Heyns, Robert Jackson, Samuel Popkin, Susan Shapiro, Ann Stueve, Norma Wikler, and two anonymous reviewers read all or parts of earlier drafts. Their collective suggestions made this a much better book than it otherwise would have been.

Grant Barnes, formerly of the University of California Press, and Sheila Levine and Mary Renaud, both currently of the University of California Press, handled the publication process with the high level of professionalism for which the press is known. They also made this process remarkably pleasant for me. Sylvia Stein's editing significantly improved the manuscript. Famah Andrew produced beautifully typed manuscripts more times than I care to admit or she cares to remember.

There are some people whose basic support makes work possible. The contributions of Linda Gerson, Rose and George Blum, and Ron Spinka go beyond words. Robert Jackson has influenced my understanding of analytic and social processes so thoroughly that it is sometimes difficult to separate his ideas from my own. As a colleague and constant friend, he has taught me to value the work that sociologists do, to persevere despite the internal and external obstacles, and to try not to settle for less than the best from myself. As a friend, companion, editor, intellectual confidant, and loyal supporter, John Mollenkopf gave me the will to start, to keep going, and finally to end this project. His belief in the study and his own commitment to the sociological endeavor kept this project alive through good times and bad. His nurturing disposition and culinary skills not only kept me well fed and cared for; they also served as reminders of one of the study's major goals: to rethink theoretical and working assumptions about women, men, and the human capacities of both.

Finally, my deep appreciation goes to the women who generously shared their lives with me. Their struggles, hopes, and strength sustained the study when I needed bolstering. What follows is about them, is for them, and could not have been written without them. My hope is that they will benefit from it in some way.

This book is dedicated to John, who above all others made its writing possible, and to Emily, whose birth was made possible by my writing it.

1 | *Women's Work and Family Decisions*

The "Subtle Revolution" in Historical Perspective

We are in the midst of a "subtle revolution." Even seasoned observers, armed with statistics, are pointing to changes in women's behavior so vast as to warrant this label (Smith, 1979a). Current concerns about "the new working woman" and "the new choice of motherhood" reflect a growing awareness among experts and lay observers alike of the far-reaching changes taking place in the work and family patterns of American women.

The rising number of female workers is the most obvious indication of the changing position of women.[1] The 1970s witnessed a veritable explosion in the number of women working for pay outside the home. The percentage of women at work rose from 43.3 percent in 1970 to an unprecedented high of 51.2 percent in 1980 (U.S. Department of Labor, 1980:3). For the first time in American history, more women are in the labor force than out of it, and women are likely to continue to stream into the workplace in the coming years. Recent predictions suggest that by 1990 around 70 percent of all women of working age will be employed or looking for a job. For younger groups, this figure

---

1. I use the term "work" to refer specifically to work performed outside the home for pay. Whether or not they are paid for what they do, all women (except for a small group of "leisure class" members) work in some way. The significant question is not whether they work, but how they work.

is likely to rise even higher (Masnick and Bane,1980; Smith, 1979b). The scale has thus tipped in favor of the employed woman.

A dramatic drop in women's fertility has accompanied this trend. Despite fears of a population explosion when the children of the baby boom reached childbearing age, the 1970s brought a "baby bust" instead. Although the fertility rate among baby boom mothers rose as high as 3.7 births per woman in the 1955–1959 period, it dropped to about 1.8 births per woman in the 1975–1980 period (Alonso, 1980; Sternlieb et al., 1982).[2] As women's workplace participation reached a historic high, the birthrate also dropped below the replacement rate to a historic low.[3] If current trends continue, the generation now in its prime childbearing years will not bear enough offspring to reproduce itself.

That the rise in the number of women workers occurred alongside a sharp decline in women's fertility is no coincidence. Women's work and family decisions have always been closely connected, and recent changes simply underscore the interactive, indeed inseparable, quality of this relationship.

This book explores the relationship between women's work and family decisions by taking a close look at the women most responsible for recent changes in female work and childbearing patterns. It examines the lives of a strategic group of women now in their prime childbearing years, all members of a generation in which large numbers have departed from the well-worn paths of their forebears. As the generation whose own life choices are most responsible for dramatic demographic shifts, this group is especially well positioned to illuminate the causes, consequences, and meaning of the subtle revolution now under way.

Examining the forces that have shaped these women's decisions clarifies the more general process by which women choose between work and family commitments as their work aspirations interact with their desires to bear and rear children. The experiences of these women also show how work and family decisions emerge from the broader social context in which they occur. Proceeding from the lives of this strategically placed group, this study thus presents a model for understanding general processes of human development and a method for analyzing the link between human action and social change.

2. The fertility rate refers to the number of births a woman would have in her lifetime if she kept pace with the age-specific birthrates for the given period (Sternlieb et al., 1982).

3. The birthrate refers to the number of births per 1,000 population.

Changing Work and Family Patterns

In important respects, American women have often diverged from the model of the homebound, domestic mother. The child-centered housewife is actually a relatively recent historical development and is a social position that has generally been reserved for the more privileged members of the female population.

The rise of the factory system in the nineteenth century promoted the physical, social, and economic separation of the home and the workplace and thus ultimately relegated women to the private sphere. Yet throughout the early stages of industrialization, women contributed directly to the economic support of their families in a variety of ways. In the beginning years of industrial capitalism, many women and children worked alongside men in the factories, withdrawing from the industrial workplace only after male workers fought for and secured a "living" or "family wage" upon which the entire household could depend (Hartmann, 1976; Oakley, 1974b; Smelser, 1959). Many women were never able to withdraw completely from the paid labor force; sizeable segments of working-class and poor women have always worked outside the home for pay (Kessler-Harris, 1981; Tilly and Scott, 1978). Even though most nineteenth-century women did not participate in the paid work force, many took in boarders and lodgers to supplement the family income (Modell and Hareven, 1973).

Early nineteenth-century families were not especially child-centered. Instead, they generally operated as small businesses, looking to all household members, including women and children, to contribute to the "family economy." In order to sustain an acceptable standard of living for the family as a whole, children were often treated in ways that appear decidedly "adult" to modern eyes. Many left home to become apprentices long before the age we now consider appropriate for children to live on their own (Modell et al., 1976). Those who remained at home were expected to fend for themselves without the benefit of doting mothers such as those modern children are believed to need.

A lengthy, leisurely childhood and prolonged adolescence are thus modern inventions that came into existence only after the rise of the mass system of education (Demos, 1970; Kett, 1977). If the modern family is expected to gear itself toward the child's needs, then the preindustrial family expected the child to orient himself or herself to its needs (Hareven, 1977). As industrialization proceeded, motherhood only gradually came to assume the idealized, almost mystical, aura that captured the American imagination throughout most of the twentieth century.

The first half of the twentieth century witnessed two paradoxical developments in the position of women. First, after the turn of the century, the size of the female labor force began to grow at a faster pace. In the hundred years between 1800 and 1900, the percentage of women in the paid labor force rose only from about 5 to 20 percent. Yet between 1900 and 1945, the female labor force grew to slightly over 38 percent, gaining 18 percentage points in only fifty years (Blau, 1979:271; Brownlee and Brownlee, 1976:3). During this period, women poured into the workplace both to occupy jobs vacated by men away at war and to fill the expanding job pool in the "pink-collar" service sector so central to postindustrial capitalism (Howe, 1977; Oppenheimer, 1970).

Along with the steady rise in the number of working women, this period saw the consolidation of the ideology of female domesticity. This ideology originated in the nineteenth-century notion of "true womanhood," which argued that women are uniquely endowed with the emotional qualities necessary to oversee the private sphere and thus to safeguard society's moral fabric from the corrupting influence of industrialism (Welter, 1966). This ideal of femininity and woman's "proper place" was translated into the belief that mothering is every woman's ultimate fulfillment and should be every woman's highest priority. Ironically, women were encouraged to embrace motherhood just as the birthrate began to plunge and they began to move out of the home in substantial numbers.[4] Thus, Hareven (1977:69) concludes that

> motherhood as a full-time vocation has emerged only since the middle of the 19th century. Ironically, its glorification as a lifelong pursuit for women began to emerge at a time when demographic and social factors were significantly reducing the total proportion of a woman's life actually needed for it.

During the middle decades of the twentieth century, the domestic, nuclear household, whose cornerstone is the housewife-mother, captured the popular imagination as an ideal, if not always the reality. The economic prosperity of the immediate post–World War II era finally enabled large numbers of middle-class and working-class women to attain this domestic ideal. This period spawned the baby boom, promoted the child-centered household, and raised the full-time

---

4. For a full consideration of the history of the practice and ideology of "mother love" and its relation to social circumstances, see Badinter (1981). For an analysis of the emergence of the bourgeois, child-centered household in the nineteenth century, see Ryan (1981). Oakley (1974b) presents a historical overview of the rise of the housewife. Ryan (1979) presents a similar overview for American women from colonial times to the present.

housewife-mother to a predominant place in American culture. After a long, steady decline dating back well before 1800, the birthrate turned upward in the mid-1930s and then rose even more sharply after World War II. Similarly, after rising sharply during the war, women's labor force participation dropped precipitously immediately thereafter, reaching wartime levels again only in the mid-1960s.

Figure 1 outlines the major contours of women's fertility and work patterns since the turn of the century. Except during the mid-1930s and mid-1950s, the birthrate has declined steadily since well before the turn of the century. In contrast, except for a brief period immediately following World War II, women's labor force participation has either risen or remained constant over this same time period. The two trends tend to be interactive and inversely related. Since the mid-1950s especially, the birthrate has tended to go down as women's labor force participation has gone up. The figure thus reveals a long-term trend toward women's movement out of the home in the twentieth century. The post–World War II period of resurgent domesticity, and not current patterns, appears to be "a conspicuous and unusual departure" from this overall direction of change (Alonso, 1980:37).

Women's declining fertility and growing ties to the workplace are thus not new developments, but rather extensions of trends that have long been in the making. The roots of recent changes in women's commitments to work and family are deeply embedded in the structure of American society, as well as in virtually all the other advanced industrial nations. Cross-national studies attest to the nearly universal movement of women out of the home under conditions of advanced industrialism. (See, for example, Land, 1979; Lapidus, 1978; Sullerot, 1971; Wilensky, 1968.) Only from the perspective of the immediate post–World War II period do these recent changes appear unexpected. From the perspective of long-term historical change, the 1950s appear more aberrant than typical.

Since the 1950s, the pace of change has quickened dramatically. In slightly more than thirty years, women's labor force participation has risen more than 20 percentage points, from a low of 30.8 percent in 1947 to an all-time high of 51.2 percent in 1980. Similarly, over the last twenty-five years, the birthrate has dropped from an average of 25 children per 1,000 population in 1955 to an average of only 15 in the late 1970s. Notably, this drop has occurred despite the fact that the exceptionally large cohorts of "baby boomers" entered adulthood during the 1970s, placing an especially large number of women in their prime childbearing years. Current patterns in women's work and fertility behavior stand in sharp contrast to the model of female domesticity that attracted so many adherents in the 1950s. Daughters have increasingly departed from their mothers' paths.

Figure 1 *Comparisons Between the U.S. Birthrate and the Female
Labor Force Participation Rate, 1890–1980*

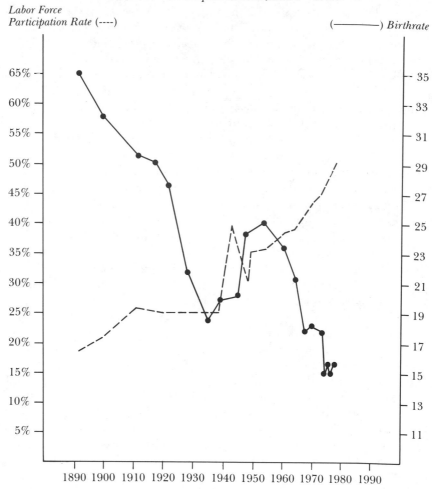

*Labor Force
Participation Rate (----)*   (———) *Birthrate*

SOURCES: Brownlee and Brownlee (1976:3); Moore and Hofferth (1979:127); U.S.
Department of Labor (1980:3).

The 1950s thus provide the contrast that makes the reemergence
of long-gathering trends in the last two decades so striking. Yet recent
changes in women's behavior stand out in bold relief not simply because
we tend to compare them to the somewhat atypical patterns of the
1950s. Women's current work and family patterns differ qualitatively,
and not just quantitatively, from past developments.

First, alterations in the kinds of women who work have accompanied the recent explosion in the proportion of women workers. Historically, the typical woman worker was young, single, and childless. For most, paid employment represented a temporary commitment that ended or was substantially curtailed with marriage and the arrival of children. This is no longer the case. Rather, as Table A.1 demonstrates, the biggest increase in women workers since 1950 has occurred among married women, mothers with children (and especially preschool children) in the household, and women aged twenty-five to forty-four. (See Appendix A.) There has also been a notable rise in the percentage of women workers who work full-time, year-round. An increasing proportion of women workers are married, rearing young children, working throughout the middle adult years, and working full-time throughout the year.

Women today have not simply joined the work force in historically high numbers; they have also shown a growing commitment to steady, long-term, full-time workplace attachment. In these important respects, women workers have begun to resemble male workers.[5] Like men, women of all ages and family statuses, and not simply those with few family responsibilities, are building strong work ties. Few, including men and children, have failed to feel the impact of these changes.

Second, the recent sharp drop in the birthrate appears to reflect more fundamental changes in women's orientations toward childbearing and mothering. The decline in the birthrate in the early decades of the twentieth century did not signal a rise in the rate of childlessness or one-child families, as it appears to do today. Historically, the birthrate decline resulted from a drop in average family size, not a rise in childlessness (Bane, 1976; Hofferth and Moore, 1979; Masnick and Bane, 1980). To the contrary, the percentage of ever-married women remaining childless or bearing only one child has also declined until recently—probably because of improved health and increased fecundity among women of childbearing age. Thus, in this earlier period, average family size dropped, but the proportion of women remaining childless or bearing only one child also decreased (Masnick and Bane, 1980).

Recent trends suggest that this historical aversion to childlessness and only children is declining. The cohorts of women now in their

---

5. The reverse is also true. Men's labor force participation has dropped from 86.4 percent in 1950 to 77.2 percent in 1980 (U.S. Department of Labor, 1980:3). In addition, men tend to work shorter hours and switch careers more often than they did thirty years ago (Hirschhorn, 1977). Men's work patterns thus increasingly resemble the part-time, interrupted model once reserved primarily for women.

prime childbearing years have shown a marked lack of enthusiasm for childbearing, as shown by their increased propensity to remain child-less or to have fewer children later in life. Although their ultimate decisions remain an open question, so far these women have exhibited notably higher rates of childlessness than most cohorts of the same age range born earlier in the twentieth century.

Among women born between 1935 and 1939, 80.7 percent had their first child by age twenty-nine, and only about 10 percent remained permanently childless. Only 63 percent of those born between 1950 and 1954 had had a child as they neared thirty. This trend appears to be more than just a preference among younger cohorts for postponed childbearing. When asked in 1979 to report their lifetime birth expec-tations, almost a quarter of the women between ages eighteen and thirty-four said they expected to have either no children or only one child (U.S. Bureau of the Census, 1980a). (Also see Table A.2, Appen-dix A.)

Although the link between predictions and actual future behavior is tenuous at best, these forecasts indicate that children are assuming a far less central position in many women's lives than they did thirty years ago. There is considerable controversy among informed analysts concerning the future. Some argue that the voluntary childless rate is declining and that an "echo baby boom" may soon occur as the bio-logical clock runs out on this generation (Houseknecht, 1982). Others are convinced that low birthrates are here to stay and that a sizeable proportion (perhaps as large as 20 to 30 percent) of women currently in their prime childbearing years will remain permanently child-less (Bloom and Pebley, 1982; Ryder, 1979; Westoff, 1978). Whatever these women finally do, their current behavior signals significant social change. So many women postponing motherhood and acknowledging the possibility of childlessness is in itself consequential. At the very least, as one analyst puts it, we can expect rates of childlessness "con-siderably higher than the 10 percent rates that prevailed throughout most of the century" (Bloom, 1981:16A).

Since the 1950s, the nondomestic woman has emerged to challenge the predominance of the homemaker-mother. The traditional house-hold composed of a breadwinning husband and homemaking wife dropped from 59.4 percent of all American households in 1950 and 51.2 percent in 1960 to only 30.3 percent in 1980. (When the presence of children in the household is also taken into account, this figure dips even lower.) Increasing numbers of dual-earning couples (with and without children), single-parent households (overwhelmingly headed by women), and single adults living alone or with other unrelated persons (primary individuals) have steadily eroded the dominance of the "traditional" household.[6] The greatest growth has occurred among married couples with a working wife and primary individuals, most of whom live alone (Gerson, 1983:140).

The domestic woman who builds her life around children and home-making persists, but she now coexists with a growing number of working mothers and permanently childless women. The nondomestic woman, whether she combines work and motherhood or eschews motherhood altogether, is no longer a statistical, social, or psychological anomaly. Instead, a variety of life patterns more accurately describes the current situation of American women.

Cohorts and Social Change

Recent changes in work and mothering patterns are not distributed equally across the population of women. Rather, these changes have occurred primarily through the aging of successive cohorts, whose decisions have differed in important respects from those made by the generations that preceded them.

Table A.3 shows that younger cohorts of women are much more likely than older cohorts to work. The rise of the woman worker has thus resulted not so much from changes in the behavior of all women, but from the progressive entrance of younger cohorts into the labor force as they reached working age. Women born after 1940, most of whom are now in their twenties and thirties, are most responsible for the steep rise in the percentage of women workers.

Table A.4 shows a similar pattern for changes in women's child-bearing patterns. Cohorts born after 1944 largely account for the recent sharp decline in the birthrate. Because these women are still moving through their prime childbearing years, their final rates are subject to change. When compared with older cohorts at a comparable age, however, they display notably lower propensities for childbearing.

Table A.5 offers an additional perspective on the fertility patterns of different generations by comparing the percent remaining childless

6. I use the term "traditional" to refer to women whose primary commitments and orientations are to the home and the domestic sphere. Female domesticity is not a consistently dominant historical pattern. As used here, the term "traditional" thus refers to the type of female homemaker and mother who gained ascendency in the mid-twentieth century, and not to an idealized image that probably never predominated in the more distant past. (See Scott and Tilly, 1975; Tilly and Scott, 1978.)

among different cohorts at different ages. This table reveals an interesting difference between the baby boom mothers born between 1930 and 1940 and the baby boom offspring born between 1945 and 1959. Although only about 20 percent of the women in the older group were childless by the time they reached their late twenties, well over 30 percent of the younger group remained childless throughout their twenties. Among those born between 1945 and 1949, almost 20 percent were childless well into their thirties; for those born between 1950 and 1954, over 35 percent were still childless as they approached thirty. Thus, despite improved health standards that helped lower the rate of childlessness throughout the first half of the twentieth century, recent female cohorts have returned to the high childlessness rates that characterized the earlier part of the century.[7]

In sum, younger female cohorts are most responsible for the rise in the percentage of women workers, the decline in the birthrate, and the increasing proportion of childless women in the later stages of their reproductive lives. The personal decisions of young adult women, most of whom came of age in the 1970s, underlie these rapid social changes.

This generation reached adulthood during a period of accelerated social change. Born in the aftermath of World War II, most of its members grew up in so-called traditional households. Ironically, the mothers of this generation are the women who vacated the workplace in large numbers to devote themselves to home and family. Yet the world this generation has inherited, and helped as adults to create, differs greatly from the world it knew as children. As members of a generation on the cutting edge of social change, they have collided with social institutions in flux. They have become both the recipients and the agents of far-reaching changes in work and family life.

Recent demographic changes in women's position can thus be best understood by examining the forces that have shaped the work and family decisions of that generation of women currently in its prime childbearing years. These women's lives offer especially rich clues to understanding the sources, contours, and likely future implications of the subtle revolution in women's behavior.

---

7. It is difficult to disentangle voluntary and involuntary childlessness. Aside from those with infertility problems, most women who have postponed or rejected motherhood have found the option of childbearing difficult to implement *and* have found other options more attractive. Their choices thus reflect both constraints on their fertility behavior and opportunities to pursue other goals. There is, furthermore, an uneven distribution of fertility as economically disadvantaged women with fewer attractive alternatives to motherhood tend to have more children than educationally advantaged women.

Alternative Paths in Adult Development

Despite the rising number of women who appear to be breaking from former patterns, those who constitute this strategic generation have not made uniform choices. This group displays a varied range of responses to the structural dilemmas facing all women. Indeed, the experiences encountered by women of all generations may be found to some degree within its ranks.

Many have embraced the patterns of their predecessors; they have married, borne children, and settled down to full-time mothering; they have worked outside the home only intermittently, if at all. Yet a sizeable number of women have departed from this "traditional" path. These women have postponed, and even foresworn, motherhood; they have developed ties to the workplace that resemble the committed, permanent pattern once reserved for men; and they have rejected the domestic path that places children, family, and home above all else. In short, they have moved through their young adult years in markedly different ways from earlier generations. There have always been some women who fit this emerging pattern, but today their numbers are growing on a scale never seen before.

Consider, for example, the diverse paths taken by the following women drawn from the larger group interviewed in this study:

Laura grew up in a "typical" middle-class family. Her father, a middle-level manager for a large utilities company, was happy in his work and able to support his wife and three children with ease. Her mother never worked for pay, devoting herself instead to caring for her family and managing their comfortable suburban home.

Laura never gave much thought to the future when she was young; she always "just assumed" that she would become a wife and mother much like her mother before her. Because there were ample financial resources, she also planned for college. She looked upon this period as a chance to train for a profession, such as teaching or nursing, that would mesh with homemaking. College would also provide the perfect setting, she reasoned, for meeting a man who would support her domestic aspirations.

For Laura, things turned out much as she expected. After two years of post–high school training, she went to work as a nurse. She met her husband, Steve, on the job, and two years later they were married. Because her work did not offer the pay or advancement opportunities that Steve enjoyed as a physician, she began to look forward to trading the long, late hours of nursing for what she imagined would be the more rewarding work of parenting. Because Steve's income rose rapidly, she did not feel financially obligated to remain at a job that had grown tedious. She soon became pregnant and withdrew from the workplace.

Since the birth of her first child, Laura has stayed home with few, if any, regrets. Although she plans to return to work part-time when her two children are older, she states firmly that her family "will always come first." She also resents the undertones of disapproval she senses when she tells inquirers that being a mother is her "career."

■ ■ ■

Joanne's childhood was not filled with the same advantages as Laura's, but she did grow up with similar expectations. As a repairman, her father struggled to make ends meet. Her mother nevertheless did not work outside the home until Joanne was in the eighth grade. Both parents agreed that the children should have a full-time mother, even if this arrangement entailed forgoing material luxuries. Despite their limited finances, they hoped Joanne would attend college to prepare herself for a "better life" than either of them had achieved.

Joanne, however, did not share her parents' aspirations. She was more interested in dating than in schoolwork and was not inspired by her part-time job as a waitress in a fast-food chain. Thus, when she became pregnant at seventeen, she did not greet this news with disappointment or panic. Instead, much to her parents' chagrin, she married her high school boyfriend and settled down to full-time mothering.

Two children, several sales jobs, and ten years later, Joanne still prefers domesticity to her other options. She occasionally feels social and financial pressure to forsake her domestic commitments for paid work. However, her husband earns enough money as a mechanic to "make ends meet." And every time she searches the want ads, she remembers how much she disliked the few temporary jobs she has held over the years. She then promptly turns her attention back to her children and her home. She is even considering having another child.

These two life histories illustrate the *traditional model* of female development in which an adult woman chooses the domestic life for which she prepared emotionally and practically as a child. Although they have disparate social backgrounds, Laura and Joanne share a similar life course trajectory. For each, adult life went according to plan. Neither experienced a substantial change in life goals or emotional priorities as she moved into and through adulthood. Both were also insulated from events that might have caused them to veer off their expected life paths: They were neither pushed out of the home by economic necessity or marital instability nor pulled into the workplace by expanding opportunities. They thus remained committed to the domestic path they assumed was a woman's proper place. In its essentials, these life histories fit well the traditional model of female domesticity that gained momentum during the late nineteenth and twentieth centuries and reached a peak during the post–World War II period.

In contrast, consider the life paths of Elizabeth and Jane:

Elizabeth, like Laura, grew up in a traditional, comfortable, middle-class home. As a lawyer, her father took great pride in supporting his family in style. Indeed, he vetoed the few attempts his wife made to find work outside the home, arguing that children need their mother at home and her working would reflect badly upon both parents. Similarly, he expected his daughter to go to college not to prepare for an occupation, but rather to find a suitable mate. Adopting the messages she received, Elizabeth grew up believing a woman's place is in the home.

Elizabeth, the dutiful daughter, thus married a young engineer soon after college graduation. Within a few years, however, the marriage began to sour. Before she could fully assimilate the implications of her situation, she was divorced and out on her own for the first time in her life. Desperate for a paycheck, she wandered into an employment agency looking for a job, any job. They placed her in a small company, where she started as a receptionist and office manager. She quickly made herself indispensable and over a period of about five years worked her way up the organization to her present position of executive vice-president.

Elizabeth is now in her mid-thirties, and there appear to be few limits on how high she can rise. Rearing a child could, of course, conflict with her career goals. There is little chance that motherhood will interfere with her work, however, for she has foresworn marriage forever and probably childbearing as well. Despite her childhood expectations, home and family just do not fit with the commitments she has developed as an adult. As she looks back over this chain of events, she wonders how she could have come so far from where she began.

■ ■ ■

Like Laura, Joanne, and Elizabeth, Jane also assumed when she was growing up that she would marry, have many children, and live "happily ever after," just as her parents before her. Her father, a Southern European immigrant, worked day and night to support his large family. Her mother clung tightly to the "old country" ways, which included loyalty to her husband and an almost total devotion to her children. Jane harbored a hidden desire to go to college, but her father opposed such pursuits for women and could not have underwritten the expense in any case.

Jane worked for a short time after high school as a filing clerk. She married two years later and was pregnant within six months of the ceremony.

Shortly after the birth of her daughter, however, she became bored and dissatisfied. Taking care of a baby was not the ultimate fulfillment she had anticipated. Instead, she found motherhood to be a decidedly mixed experience—alternately rewarding and frustrating, joyful and depressing. Although she was reluctant to admit these feelings to herself or others, a growing sense of emptiness plus the need for additional household income spurred her to look for a paid job.

Thus, to keep herself busy and help with the family finances, she took a job as a bank teller. She expected this situation to be temporary, but the appropriate time to leave work never arrived. Her husband, Frank, could not seem to "make it" as a salesman working on commission, and his income consistently fell short of their needs. As time passed, the marriage began to falter. Frank's work difficulties, coupled with his growing desire to have another child, left Jane feeling that she might be happier without Frank than with him.

Just when it seemed that the marriage had become unbearable, Jane's boss offered her a promotion into management, including higher pay, increased responsibility, and more respect from peers and co-workers. The bank was facing affirmative action pressures and had responded by initiating a program designed to advance women who lacked college degrees. Jane was initially worried about the increased pressures the new job would entail, but she was also eager to move ahead. Not coincidentally, she also divorced Frank.

Today, Jane is dedicated to her job, aspires to upper-level management, and has no plans to expand her family beyond her only child. She is convinced, moreover, that her daughter is better off because she left the bulk of child care to someone else who enjoyed the work more than did she.

These lives illustrate an emerging and increasingly common pattern among both middle-class and working-class women that involves *rising work aspirations* and *ambivalence toward motherhood*. Elizabeth and

Jane grew up wanting much the same things in life as Laura and Joanne, but adult experiences intervened to push them off their expected life courses. Despite their contrasting class backgrounds, both Elizabeth and Jane experienced similar constraints and opportunities as adults. Not only did their early marriages deteriorate over time, but unanticipated work advancement opportunities also opened to both. Growing work ambitions and a diminishing interest in mothering thus eventually replaced their early domestic aspirations. These examples illustrate the developmental path taken by an increasing proportion of women from both the middle and working classes who grew up believing in the "feminine mystique," only to find that adult life offered a very different set of alternatives.

The next four lives begin from notably different starting points than the first four stories. First, there are the cases of Gail and Mary:

Gail was not attracted to motherhood as a child, but rather hoped to avoid it. Her mother had relinquished a promising career as an artist to raise three children and never seemed to recover from this sacrifice. As her children grew, Gail's mother slipped deeper into depression and frustration.

Gail's father, in contrast, seemed to thrive on both his work and his children. As a successful businessman who had pulled himself out of poverty after the Depression, he encouraged his children, all girls, to aim for whatever they wanted in life. It is not altogether surprising, therefore, that for as long as she could remember Gail wanted to be a lawyer. She knew this was an unusual desire for a girl, but the prohibition against it only fueled her determination.

In major respects, Gail has not waivered from her early plans. She went to college, graduated in the top third of her class, and entered law school, where she was surprised to find that over 30 percent of her classmates were women. After receiving her law degree, she joined a small law firm and was eventually made a partner. Throughout this period, she never found the time or felt the inclination to marry or have a child.

Now secure in her career, Gail has begun to view children as an option she can afford to consider. Time is running out, however, and no partner is in sight. There have been a few serious relationships with men, but they have all ended badly. She is fast losing confidence that she will find a suitable partner for the joint enterprise of child rearing and has reluctantly concluded that an exclusive commitment to one person for life may not be possible anymore. Because having a child outside of marriage seems unfair to herself and the child, the chances are high that she will never have children. She acknowledges this probability with mild regret.

■ ■ ■

Mary, like Gail, yearned from an early age for a life beyond the boundaries of home, children, and family. As the oldest of six children in a strict Catholic family, she had few illusions about the constant, often thankless task of rearing children. Her father worked hard as an electrician to keep his children clothed and fed. Her mother also worked hard cooking, washing, cleaning, and generally making sure her numerous children stayed out of trouble. Although Mary remembers her mother as devoted to her duties, she also remembers never wanting to follow her example. Her mother's life seemed stifling, and children seemed more a burden than a fulfillment.

Although she harbored vague ambitions for the independence work could offer, she married within a year of high school graduation. She now admits her primary motivation was to escape her parents' home and the confining atmosphere of her family. Unlike many of her friends, however, she did not rush into motherhood, but instead went to work for a mid-sized corporation.

The work was frustrating at first, but every time she quit, she found staying home was worse. From time to time, she considered starting a family; but both she and her husband had become dependent on her income, and she still viewed children as something she was supposed to but did not want. Rather than getting pregnant, she took a series of clerical jobs. Eventually her persistence paid off, and in her late twenties, she was promoted into the lower level of management at a major corporation.

Today Mary is just past thirty. She is more committed to work than ever and still has strong misgivings about becoming a mother, but she also feels the biological clock ticking away. Her husband, who loves young children, is growing impatient to have a child of his own. Mary is beginning to fear that never having a child might condemn her to loneliness later in life. She has recently decided that having one child might be the perfect compromise. With one child, she reasons, she can pursue her growing work ambitions without sacrificing completely the pleasures of building a family.

Despite their divergent class and family backgrounds, neither Gail nor Mary found domesticity an appealing option. Even as children, they viewed motherhood apprehensively and hoped for something different out of life. Although Gail formed clear career goals early in childhood and Mary's goals remained vague well into her twenties, both saw children as a potentially dangerous obstacle to achieving other desired life endeavors. For these women, mothering did not represent the ultimate fulfillment to which they could happily devote their lives; rather, it threatened to be a trap they wished to avoid.

Like Laura and Joanne, Gail and Mary realized their early life goals and did not substantially change direction over the course of their lives. Because their goals were different from those of traditional women, however, Gail's and Mary's lives developed in a different direction: out of the home, away from motherhood, and toward committed work ties. These women met a set of circumstances in adulthood that enabled them to travel a *nontraditional path*. Their original nondomestic aspirations were supported by the people and institutions they encountered as adults.

In an earlier historical period, these women would have been more likely to have succumbed to the pressures to foreswear career ambitions in favor of childbearing. Today, however, women's social environment is more likely to nurture their work aspirations. Similarly, women today who experience deeply felt ambivalence toward mothering are less likely to repress, deny, or ignore these misgivings than they were in the past, when the sanctions against antimaternal feelings were strong.

The next two women shared Gail's and Mary's high work ambitions and early apprehensions about parenthood. Unlike Gail and Mary, however, they did not meet felicitous circumstances in adulthood that supported these early goals. They thus experienced a marked change of life direction as they turned toward home and children over time:

Susan grew up in a middle-class home, but it was not a happy one. Her parents, who eventually divorced, fought often. Her father worked for an airline and was absent from their home much of the time. Her mother, whom she remembers fondly, worked part-time as a door-to-door saleswoman and occasionally took Susan on these outings. The money her mother received from this intermittent work helped the family over occasional economic rough spots. With her husband generally gone, Susan's mother doted on her two children and wished for them the education and opportunities she never received.

Susan shared her mother's hopes and earned a scholarship to college. She attended college with optimism, but a number of factors ultimately thwarted her career ambitions. First, she met and married John in her senior year. His education required her economic support as well as her attention to the household tasks. Because his career needs collided with hers, she dropped her plans for a business degree and earned a teaching credential instead. She did not particularly like the idea of working with children, but a teaching degree on the primary school level could be earned quickly and promised her job security—or so she thought.

As it turned out, she had a difficult time finding a job and eventually settled for preschool teaching. Despite the low salary, economic constraints have kept her in teaching ever since. She has, not surprisingly, grown steadily weary of the demanding work and lack of chances for advancement.

In contrast, John is beginning to make progress in his architectural career and has begun to complain that he wants more of her attention directed to their life together. Susan can now depend on John for financial support; so she plans to resign and start a family. Ironically, she now looks forward to motherhood as her best chance to escape from the world of children that defines her job.

■ ■ ■

Vicki's childhood was marked by difficulty. Her father supported his wife and four children on a janitor's salary. Her mother provided little in the way of emotional or economic help, for she was in and out of mental hospitals throughout many of Vicki's early years.

Vicki was never especially oriented toward motherhood. Instead, since she was old enough to know who the police were, she wanted to be a policewoman. She was attracted to the excitement of life on the streets, to the physical and mental challenge. An exciting career also offered the hope of leaving behind her parents' poor existence.

Forced to take the best job she could find after high school, Vicki became a secretary-clerk. She also took the qualifying exam for police work and passed with high marks. No jobs were available, however, and she returned to her desk job, still hoping for "bigger things."

In the meantime, she met and married Joe. Joe's job as a construction worker required that they move a lot. Vicki found herself changing jobs often for the sake of Joe's "career." Once she even turned down the chance to advance because Joe's work came first. She ultimately grew to hate working, for it usually involved taking orders from bosses she did not respect.

Joe also began to pressure her to have children. Children were very important to Joe, for he had been orphaned and wanted to give his children the love he never received. Vicki viewed children as a burden she could do without, but Joe even threatened to leave her if they did not start a family soon. She decided that losing Joe was too heavy a price to pay for her fears and became pregnant in her late twenties.

After the birth of her first child, Vicki discovered that staying home to rear a child was more rewarding than her succession of boring, dead-end jobs. By her mid-thirties, she was a full-time mother of two.

Today she has given up hope of becoming a policewoman, but in return for this sacrifice she feels she has gained the secure home life she never knew as a child. She occasionally considers taking a part-time job, but she hopes she will never have to return to the full-time work she grew to abhor. She worries that, if something ever happened to Joe or the marriage, she would be forced out of the home again.

Susan and Vicki represent a fourth pattern for women that has probably long been in existence but only recently recognized: a woman who harbors deep-seated ambivalence toward mothering and domesticity but over time experiences *falling work aspirations* and begins to see *the home as a haven*. As children, neither Susan nor Vicki identified with the ideal of feminine domesticity, but as adults, they did not meet the supportive environment that greeted Gail and Mary. They ventured into the workplace with high hopes, only to find thwarted opportunities and stifling experiences. In time, work became burdensome, not fulfilling, to these women. They also came to perceive work as a threat to securing the intimacy and support they depended on at home.

Susan and Vicki thus ultimately concluded that mothering was preferable to the frustration of paid work and that it also promised to cement a cherished relationship at home. Despite their early work ambitions and persistent ambivalence toward child rearing, they eventually opted for domesticity over strong work ties.

These two women may seem out of step with their age peers who have found a more supportive environment for rising work aspirations, but they represent a growing group forced into jobs and occupations they find stultifying in order to earn a living. These women also resemble men who find themselves in jobs they would prefer to leave, except for one important difference: Men can weigh the relative costs of remaining in an unsatisfying job versus finding a new one, but few men enjoy the traditional, although shrinking, female option of trading paid work for domestic work. This group of women ultimately reaches occupational roadblocks that lead them to view domestic pastures as greener.

These two examples also demonstrate three important aspects of female development. Many women choose motherhood not to fulfill deep-seated emotional needs, but rather as the best option among a number of unappealing alternatives. Second, an apparent lack of ambition may actually be a well-founded concern for preserving a stable private life. Finally, the erosion of the domestic option, although no loss to women like Gail and Mary who secure work that is rewarding, is perceived as an understandable threat to women like Susan and Vicki who find work a dead-end street. Unlike most men, many women have traditionally had the option *not* to earn a paycheck. As this option erodes, some women's gains are inevitably offset by others' losses.

Each of these eight life histories illustrates the powerful, interactive link between women's work and family decisions. As a group, they also illustrate the varied paths women negotiate through adulthood. Although these are only eight cases amid considerable diversity, they demonstrate four general patterns that a woman's life course can assume, whether she was born into the working or the middle class.

These four patterns are based on two especially important dimensions around which distinct groups of women form. First, women differ in their early expectations about the goals they plan to pursue as adults. Exposed to a diverse, complex set of experiences as children, women, like men, develop a variety of conscious and unconscious aspirations long before they are able to test these wishes as adults. For some, these early images take the shape of well-formed plans in which the future appears as certain as the past. For others, these goals are more amorphous, assuming the form of vague hopes that may or may not be realized.

However misty or clear, these early desires form the baseline for adult life. Some plan to build their lives around the traditional feminine commitments to home, husband, and children; these women expect their own lives to resemble the domestic model that has been so prevalent in the recent past. Others view marriage and motherhood with trepidation and aspire to the less traditionally feminine pursuits of work advancement. Because their numbers have been few in the past, members of this latter group may be less convinced that their life choices are guaranteed than are those who start with domestic aspirations. Their lack of certainty, however, in no way diminishes the power of their feelings. The aspirations that women take into adulthood may thus center around domestic or nondomestic goals.

Once established, these early orientations are subjected to the real constraints and opportunities encountered in adulthood, the second dimension that distinguishes groups of women from each other. The social circumstances adults confront can support or undermine their original goals. Initial goals can prove viable, leading one down a life path wholly consistent with early expectations, or these early plans can ultimately turn out to be uninviting or even impossible, encouraging or perhaps requiring individual change. Unexpected events can lead adults to reevaluate their past assumptions and reorient themselves toward the future. Thus, pathways through adulthood may either follow or diverge from one's beginning baseline.

People differ in the extent to which they are exposed to change-inducing experiences. They consequently vary in the degree to which change characterizes their developmental path. When the pace of historical change is slow, most people are insulated from events that might shake up their views of the world or their proper place in it. Under these circumstances, most people tend to assume that their lives are preordained and rooted in the natural order of things. Even during periods of accelerated social change, many are able to move stably through life without veering significantly from an expected path.

Periods of rapid change increase the likelihood of exposure to triggering events that promote and sometimes force individual change. At these times, people who might otherwise assume that the order of their lives is given find that they must undergo personal change in order to adapt to changing social circumstances. These people experience turning points when they abandon old assumptions and confront new possibilities.

In the following pages, I will examine these four groups of women and delineate the forces that have impelled each along its divergent path. Each group can be distinguished by its initial orientation toward work and family (determined primarily by early childhood experiences) and the subsequent experience of stability or change in adulthood. Some of those who began adulthood wanting to become mothers and homemakers stayed on the domestic path; others veered away from the private sphere and into the workplace. Among those who entered adulthood ambivalent toward motherhood and aspiring for workplace accomplishments, some remained on this nondomestic path, and others moved toward domesticity over time. Those whose initial life plans did not change enjoyed supportive circumstances that sheltered them from challenges to their goals or from enticements to new directions. In contrast, unexpected obstacles or opportunities faced those who did change as they moved through the early stages of adulthood. Figure 2 illustrates these alternative pathways.

To understand the subtle revolution, we must determine why women born into the same historical period and confronting similar life cycle deadlines make different choices and orient themselves toward different goals as their lives proceed. By distinguishing divergent pathways, we can answer this larger question by looking at a number of smaller ones: How are the baseline orientations set? Why do some women proceed smoothly down their initially chosen path and others veer away, particularly from domesticity toward nondomestic pursuits? When women hold nondomestic orientations at the outset, why do some sustain them and others forsake them in favor of mothering

Figure 2 *Alternative Adult Pathways*

Baselines	*Present Work-Family Orientation*
(childhood goals and expectations)	(present situation combined with future plans)

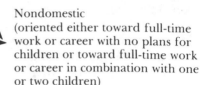

Domestic	Domestic
(expected to marry, bear children, and either be a homemaker or work intermittently in a traditionally female occupation)	(is or expects soon to be a homemaker or mother with loose, if any, ties to work)
Nondomestic	Nondomestic
(oriented toward full-time work or career, not oriented toward bearing and rearing children, or both)	(oriented either toward full-time work or career with no plans for children or toward full-time work or career in combination with one or two children)

and homemaking? What social forces pull some women out of the home and push others into it? What social-psychological processes render a structured potential into an individual fact? Answers to these questions will help explain the subtle revolution currently under way in women's behavior and the larger process by which women choose between work and family commitments.

2 | *Explaining Women's Behavior*

A Theoretical Overview

To explain why women take the variety of pathways outlined in Chapter One, we must first address the underlying causes of women's behavior. Two general models for understanding women's behavior currently prevail: One stresses the role of social-structural coercion, and one stresses processes of early childhood socialization.[1] These approaches parallel two of the dominant approaches in social theory generally, but neither is ultimately sufficient.

Theories that stress the importance of external structural constraints follow in the tradition of conflict theory, and especially Marxian class (or interest) analysis.[2] Childhood socialization theories trace their roots to the psychoanalytic revolution, although most of these ideas were first introduced into sociological analysis by Parsons and

---

1. I do not consider theories that posit biological influences as the cause of women's behavior because their theoretical status in sociology is weak. For excellent critiques of this approach, see Chodorow (1978), Pleck (1981), and Rosaldo (1974). For a more sympathetic point of view, see Rossi (1977, 1984). I am concerned with differences among women, and biological influences shared by all women obviously cannot explain the phenomena under analysis here.

2. Some of the first, most influential works to take this approach include Mitchell (1973), Rowbotham (1973), and Zaretsky (1976).

the early functionalists.[3] Neither perspective logically excludes the other; there have, indeed, been numerous attempts to synthesize the two.[4] Similarly, there is considerable variety within each perspective. Both feminist and conservative theories, for example, can fall under either rubric. Distinctions between traditional and feminist theories of women's behavior often lie more in the *value* each places upon gender differences than in the hypothesized causes or nature of these differences.[5]

Taken alone, neither structural coercion theories nor socialization theories can successfully explain the divergent pathways that form the focus of this book. It is thus necessary to develop a third approach that incorporates aspects of the other two, but focuses more directly on the variety of developmental paths women take.

The Structural Coercion Approach

The structural approach stresses the ways in which social institutions created and controlled by men shape women's options and thus coerce their behavior. It begins with the assumption that men as a group dominate women as a group; there may be isolated individual exceptions to the rule of male domination, but these anomalies do not invalidate the general principle. Given this generally indisputable assumption, the structural approach posits that women's behavior results from male domination. The central problem of understanding women thus becomes locating the causes of male domination—determining under what social conditions female oppression emerges and how it is perpetuated.

3. See especially Parsons (1942, 1950, 1954, 1958), and Parsons and Bales (1955) for some of the earliest sociological applications of Freudian theory to gender differences in social position. We will see that these early works interpret Freudian theory in functionalist terms. Later critiques (including this one) argue that Freud more fundamentally laid the groundwork for analyses that stress intrapsychic and interpersonal conflict.

4. See especially Firestone (1970), Mitchell (1974), and Zaretsky (1973).

5. Feminist theorists who stress psychological processes, for example, do not reject the notion of a distinct feminine personality. They disagree, however, with more conventional psychological theory about the social value of these gender differences or the inherent superiority of masculine personality traits. See, for example, Chodorow (1978) and Gilligan (1982).

Feminists have suggested two probable "causes" for women's subordination vis-à-vis men. Some locate the source of gender inequality in patriarchy, which Hartmann (1976:138) defines as

a set of social relations which has a material base and in which there are hierarchical relations between men, and solidarity among them, which enable them to control women. Patriarchy is thus the system of male oppression of women.

This patriarchal system predates industrial capitalism, tends to transcend historical and cross-cultural variations in economic, political, and cultural systems, and persists to the present. This analysis thus emphasizes the role of "ordinary men, men as men, men as workers— in maintaining women's inferiority in the labor market" and elsewhere (Hartmann, 1976:139).

This approach's appeal rests with its ability to "explain" the apparently universal quality of female subordination, to which there have been disturbingly few, if any, exceptions throughout human history. The problem is that patriarchy as a system of male control does not apply to all settings and is especially ill suited to modern ones. Rubin (1975:145) notes that the specific form of male dominance known as patriarchy "is more properly confined to pastoral nomads and other such groups where one old man holds absolute dominance over wives, children, herds, and dependents as an aspect of the institution of socially defined fatherhood." The modern sources of male dominance stem only partially and incompletely from patriarchal authority or the father's power, which has declined sharply in strength since the advent of industrialism.

The theory of patriarchy is not really a theory. It lacks the necessary specification of causal relations. Causes are not carefully delineated from effects, and the theory fails to show the mechanisms by which the system is created and reproduced. Instead, it indicts "ordinary men," who eagerly and almost unanimously oppress their female counterparts. Zaretsky (1982:217) points out that it is insufficient to equate

patriarchy with men and then [argue] that men did as much as employers (who were anyway men) to relegate women to a secondary status in the workforce. . . . That men oppress women is an empirical observation that needs to be explained. Giving it a name—"patriarchy," "male supremacy," the "sex-gender system"—may be temporarily useful, but it is no substitute for an explanation.

Structural analysis turns to the system of capitalism to provide the historically grounded causal model that the concept of patriarchy lacks. This account argues that the economic system of capitalism causes the particular form of female subordination found in the modern world.

The capitalist organizaton of labor creates and reinforces the conditions under which women are exploited as unpaid workers at home and as paid workers in the labor force. In the domestic sphere, women provide services that are necessary for the survival of the family unit and thus ultimately the larger economic system but that do not directly generate income. They command "use" but not "exchange" value in Marx's terms (Benston, 1969). Industrial capitalism thus relegates women to the position of domestic servants and makes them asymmetrically dependent on men, who are able to exchange their labor for wages in the marketplace.

Capitalism also exploits women as paid workers in two somewhat contradictory ways. Capitalists treat women as a "reserve army" of labor that can be used to keep wages low when male workers threaten to improve their position vis-à-vis owners or to take up the slack when there is a shortage of male workers, such as during World War II. Women workers are expected to enter and leave the paid labor force according to the needs of male workers and employers.

Second, the capitalist system segments the labor market by sex, relegating women to a set of jobs that offers low wages, prestige, and advancement opportunities compared with those awarded men. These female-dominated occupations span the class structure from working-class service and clerical jobs to the so-called middle-class female professions such as nursing, child care, and elementary school teaching.

Workers in these occupations do not constitute a reserve labor army, for there is nothing "surplus" about the market work women do in advanced industrial societies. To the contrary, postindustrial capitalism requires the legions of clerks, typists, saleswomen, teachers, and child-care workers that keep male-dominated work organizations running. Most of the jobs in this growing "service" sector are reserved for women (Oppenheimer, 1970). Occupational sex segregation consigns women to the bottom rungs of most hierarchical organizations and ensures male supremacy in both the public and private spheres of modern society. Some argue that, despite the movement of women into the labor force, "women's defining role is a domestic one" (Oakley, 1974b:73). According to this analysis, women's work ties remain tenuous, their family responsibilities still take precedence, and the kinds of paid labor they perform are usually extensions of their domestic caretaking duties. These arguments, however, obfuscate important changes in women's position. Women today tend to spend a smaller percentage of their adult lives bearing and rearing children than did their nineteenth-century counterparts and a larger percentage of their adulthood working for pay outside the home (Modell et al., 1976; Neugarten and Datan, 1973). Indeed, to define women's work in the office as essentially domestic reinforces the ideology, rather than the fact, of women's domesticity. As Milkman (1980:102) notes,

> The link between women's domestic labor and their wage labor, to which Marxist-feminists attribute the allocation of women to specific jobs, is actually an ideological link. There is nothing intrinsically "feminine" about the jobs women do as wage workers.

Marxist feminists argue that women as a group form an underclass of exploited workers in the home and the workplace. Industrial capitalism makes all women, regardless of their husbands' or fathers' class positions, economically, socially, politically, and ultimately psychologically dependent upon men.

This analysis provides the specificity that analyses based solely on patriarchy do not; it outlines a model of cause and effect grounded in a specific set of social relations. This very specificity, however, poses problems for the theory. Gender inequality not only emerged well before the development of capitalism; it also transcends economic and political variations among industrial nations. Communist and socialist countries have fared slightly better than capitalist ones, but even among these nations, gender equality has proved an elusive goal (Lapidus, 1978; Scott, 1974; Stacey, 1983; Sullerot, 1971).[6] There are thus too many instances of women's subordination in noncapitalist contexts to make the capitalist system per se the single most compelling cause of women's inferior position. There is, moreover, no logically necessary

---

6. Some argue that all modern societies are capitalist, that no true socialist societies currently exist. Those nations labeling themselves socialist are thus mere pretenders, and women will not be free until a true socialist society is achieved. But this argument does more than beg the question. It denies there are meaningful differences between modern nations and changes the definition of capitalism from a specific economic system based on the accumulation and investment of private capital to the more general process of industrial production. If distinctions cannot be drawn among modern nations, then no test of the capitalist exploitation of women is possible. The only contrasts remaining among societies that have actually existed would be among preindustrial, industrial, and postindustrial social systems. Few would argue, given these choices, that women would be better off returning to an earlier period.

Finally, there remains the option of comparing existing capitalist societies with some future, as yet undetermined, social system. It is, of course, vitally important to think about and aim toward future social forms that would be far more humane and egalitarian than those existing today, whether capitalist or socialist. Indeed, this should be the goal and purpose of sound social policy. But just as we have to take account of women's own experiences and actions in explaining their current situation, so women themselves will have to play a major role in opposing subordination in the context of any future economic system.

link between the needs of capitalism and universal female subordination. Even if capitalists must resort to exploitation to produce profits, there is no inherent reason they must exploit women more than men. There are many ways besides gender to segment a labor force. Whatever capitalism's ills, its decline does not ensure gender equality or female liberation. There have been and continue to be many ways to keep women subordinate. The destruction of the capitalist economic system will not necessarily dissolve female subjugation, any more than did the destruction of precapitalist economic and social forms.

One obvious solution to the problems with theories that stress patriarchy or capitalism alone is to incorporate them both into a single analysis. An increasingly popular perspective thus argues that capitalist exploitation combines with patriarchy to produce the conditions for female oppression in the modern context (Eisenstein, 1979; Hartmann, 1976; Sokoloff, 1980). But two inadequate theories do not add up to a single adequate one. The problems of each are too embedded in the logical character of their arguments. They stem more from how the question is posed than from how it is answered.

Whether structural approaches stress patriarchy, capitalism, or both, they tend to focus on factors of external coercion to the exclusion of other forces. The problem of motivation, of what women want and why they want it, thus plays no independent causal role in these analyses. Women either are coerced to comply with male-dominated capitalist institutions or become victims of "false consciousness." Women who support the structure of female domesticity or prefer their position to that of men fail to perceive their true interests and instead maintain a mistaken allegiance to an ideology propagated by men and designed to maintain male dominance.

The unfortunate implication of these analyses is that women are so victimized as to lack either the intelligence to see their situation accurately or the strength to do anything about it. This is undoubtedly so in many cases. But what about the woman who wishes to protect interests she perceives to be grounded in the status quo or who prefers her position to that of a man's, despite his overall privilege?

In fact, women, like men, do not share a set of unified, internally consistent interests. Women vary in their social positions, their personal preferences, and much, much more. Their "interests" thus vary as well. Any individual woman is more likely to face a package of diverse, cross-cutting, partial interests than a consistent, unified whole. The problem is not one of false consciousness versus straightforward coercion, but of understanding why women perceive their situation as they do and how they decide *among* the conflicting interests they confront.

Because structural theories focus on the similarities among women (and among men), they are ill equipped to explain the variation among women (or men) in behavior, mental states, or social circumstances. Yet as more women move out of the home, while others remain in more traditional positions, differences among women—not only in class position, but in their work-family situations and psychological orientations as well—are growing. These deepening divisions among women have important consequences for how they perceive their situation and what political stances they adopt.

Finally, structural approaches depend on a less than convincing psychology of the individual, whether male or female. However much some men may benefit from and enjoy dominating women, surely not all men do so all the time. However powerful men as a group may be, domination exhausts neither the range of existing male-female relationships nor the range of motives of individual men. Most men, like most women, depend on the other sex for emotional as well as material sustenance that cannot be entirely coerced. Because support is among the strategies most likely to secure support in return, men's relationships with women are likely to include concern (at least to some degree) as well as control. Thus, in a number of cases too large to be ignored, the need for mutual support mutes men's motivation to dominate women completely and produces a tension between their efforts to protect their own privileged status and their affirmation of women's empowerment. As Goode (1982:132) points out, "there are inherent *emotional* contradictions in any effort to achieve full domination in that intimate sphere. . . . [These contradictions] reduce the degree to which men are willing to exploit their wives, mothers, and sisters."

Even more important, the stress on capitalism or male domination ultimately underestimates women's *active* role in creating their own lives. Some women are passively coerced; some women conform actively to traditional social arrangements; others contribute to social change by refusing to acquiesce. The full range of women's behavior cannot be completely understood as the result of external coercion alone. If men make history, but not under conditions of their own choosing, then surely women do also.

The Voluntarist Approach

If the structural approach lacks an adequate theory of motivation, then the childhood socialization approach helps provide a missing link. Socialization theories focus on the process by which female and male personalities are created, as children internalize the capacities, values, and motivations appropriate to their gender role. A number of distinct theories are housed within this general approach. Psychoanalytic models, which stress unconscious processes of development, differ in important respects from role learning models, which stress how children learn from the models and messages of their immediate social environment. Each, nevertheless, argues that the most important causes of adult gender differences are located in early childhood experiences, and especially those that take place within the nuclear family.

Talcott Parsons was one of the earliest and perhaps most influential proponents of the socialization approach; he argued that the gender socialization process provides the key link between society's functional needs and people's personalities.[7] By combining elements of the psychodynamic and social-learning models of personality development, Parsons constructed a general paradigm upon which much subsequent analysis, including feminist analysis, has drawn.

Parsons begins with the assumption that the survival of the social system requires "individual personalities [who are] trained to be motivationally and technically adequate to the performance of adult roles" (1959:297). The socialization process accomplishes this task in two ways: It instills in children the capacities necessary to perform the tasks that will be required of them as adults and ensures that they develop a desire to perform these adult tasks.

In the case of gender differentiation, Parsons argues that boy and girl children become both motivated and able to conform to the "role expectations" others will hold of them as adult men and women through a largely unconscious developmental process worked out first in relation to their mothers, who are the earliest and most important objects of attachment for all children, and later as members of the whole nuclear family. Through identification, children internalize (or incorporate into their personalities) the norms of the larger society they will join and the "need dispositions" appropriate to the sex roles they will assume. In this way, children become social participants.

The logic of development, however, differs in important ways for males and females. Although children of both sexes begin with a strong attachment to their mother, each ultimately identifies with the parent of his or her own sex. For girls, the process is comparatively smooth; because mothers are presumed to be close and continuously available throughout childhood, a girl easily learns how to be a woman—that is, a wife and mother. Boys, however, must transfer from their original object of attachment, their mother, to an identification with a more

---

7. See Parsons (1942, 1943, 1950, 1954, 1958); Parsons and Bales (1955); Parsons and Shils (1951).

appropriate, but also more distant object, their father. According to Parsons and Bales (1955:101), this developmental asymmetry between boys and girls ensures that the "masculine personality tends more to the predominance of instrumental interests, needs, and functions . . . while the feminine personality tends more to the primacy of expressive interests, needs, and functions." The socialization process creates women who are prepared to perform "the maternal function" and men who are prepared to participate "in the wider society—economic, political, or otherwise" (Parsons, 1958:333).

Gender personality differences thus grow out of early childhood experiences within the family. These personality differences lead adult men and women to choose (and prefer) different roles in the social system: Men become breadwinners; women become wives and mothers. The socialization process ensures that society's needs for a stable family system in which one partner oversees the private sphere and one the public meshes conveniently with individual desires.[8] The social order thus survives intact and reproduces itself over time, as psychological sex differences are passed from one generation to the next via the production of children who are motivated to behave much as their same-sex parents.

Despite the conservative implications of Parsons's approach, feminist theory has recently returned to a perspective that emphasizes early childhood development and gender differences in personality. Drawing heavily on psychoanalytic theory, and especially the object-relations school of psychoanalysis, Chodorow (1978) examines women's mothering as a central factor in the creation of gender differentiation. She argues that the sexual division of labor is rooted in women's mothering and results largely from unconscious psychodynamic processes that take place between mother and child in the earliest stages of development:

> the contemporary reproduction of mothering occurs through social structurally induced psychological processes. It is neither a product of biology nor of intentional role training. I draw on the psychoanalytic account of female and male personality development to demonstrate that women's mothering reproduces itself cyclically. Women, as mothers, produce daughters with mothering capacities and the desire to mother. These capacities and needs are built into and grow out of the mother-daughter relationship itself. By contrast, women as mothers (and men as not-mothers) produce sons whose nurturant capacities and needs have been systematically curtailed and repressed. This prepares men for their less affective later family

8. There is, of course, no logically necessary reason that a stable family system requires a breadwinner-father and homemaker-mother. Many structures may fulfill the same function. A family structure based on co-parenting and dual earning may work as well, if not better, than this traditional model.

role, and for primary participation in the impersonal extra-familial world of work and public life. The sexual and familial division of labor in which women mother and are more involved in interpersonal, affective relationships than men produces in daughters and sons a division of psychological capacities which leads them to reproduce this sexual and familial division of labor (1978:7).

According to Chodorow, a wide range of psychological and social gender differences results from women being the primary caretakers of children. Because women are the first and most significant object of attachment for all children, males and females have different experiences of the world from infancy on. Mothers enter into a closer, less bounded relationship with daughters than with sons. Maturing girls identify with their mothers and acquire the relational needs and capacities to become mothers themselves. Maturing boys, excluded from an equally close, intimate relationship with their primary caretaker, do not develop mothering capacities. Instead, they repress their relational needs, develop strong ego boundaries, and are left with only weakly developed capacities to nurture, love, and share intimacy.

Once instilled in childhood, motivations and capacities either for or against mothering lead adult men and women to recreate their parents' pattern in their own lives. Little girls become women who enthusiastically pursue and capably assume child-rearing responsibilities, and little boys become men whose underdeveloped desires and capacities for emotional attachment lead them to shun parenting in favor of more impersonal work attachments. According to Chodorow (1978:209), the sexual division of labor thus passes from generation to generation through women's mothering:

> Because women are themselves mothered by women, they grow up with the relational capacities and needs, and psychological definition of self-in-relationship, which commits them to mothering. Men, because they are mothered by women, do not. Women mother daughters who, when they become women, mother.

Although feminists dislike the outcome and functionalists applaud it, feminist and functionalist socialization theories use a similar approach to explaining gender differences. Both emphasize the importance of early childhood experience for adult behavior; both stress the mother's role in personality formation; and both focus upon the causal role of personality in creating social arrangements and overlook the ways that social institutions outside the family help form personalities and channel behavior. These approaches may thus be fairly criticized for the common ground on which they stand.

First, socialization theories oversimplify the psychoanalytic notion of socialization. Wrong (1961:187) points out that the common sociological use of "internalization" is based on a misinterpretation of its original meaning:

> Thus when a norm is said to have been "internalized" by an individual, what is frequently meant is that he habitually both affirms it and conforms to it in his conduct. The whole stress on inner conflict, on the tension between powerful impulses and superego controls the behavioral outcome of which cannot be prejudged, drops out of the picture. And it is this that is central to Freud's view, for in psychoanalytic terms to say that a norm has been internalized, or introjected to become part of the superego, is to say no more than that a person will suffer guilt-feelings if he fails to live up to it, not that he will in fact live up to it in his behavior.

A female child who has internalized a "feminine" psychic structure is thus likely to experience conflict and ambivalence if she fails to conform to the expectations of the female gender role; but she will not necessarily consistently conform in her behavior. Internalized norms and values may shape how people feel about what they do, but they alone do not determine what people will do. Gender socialization theories tend to adopt an "oversocialized" conception of women, and men, because they generally fail to distinguish feelings from behavior.

Chodorow, for example, is vague and inconsistent in defining the term she is trying to explain. "Mothering" can have many meanings, all of which she uses at some point in her argument: (1) the desire to mother (motivation); (2) the capacity to mother (skills); (3) the choice to bear children (behavior); (4) the choice to devote oneself exclusively or primarily to the task of child rearing (behavior); and (5) the derivation of gratification from bearing and rearing children (a psychological state). Chodorow's failure to distinguish among these dimensions of mothering obfuscates some of the central questions that need to be answered about women's orientations and behavior toward children. The analysis of interviews with women in the following chapters shows that behavior, motivation, and skills are separate analytic categories that are related to each other in different ways, depending on the social context.

Second, by postulating that people identify exclusively with their same-sex parent, socialization theories imply that the child acquires an internally consistent set of capacities, motives, and values. But this assumption, too, oversimplifies what can and often does actually happen. Children are exposed to many influences beyond those of their parents, and they can plausibly internalize models and messages from mothers, fathers, and other close nonparental figures. They may receive varied and even inconsistent messages from one or all of these sources, forcing them to choose between competing desires later in life.

The values of the wider society also exert a powerful influence on children. When there is inequality in the rewards associated with masculine and feminine attributes, all children, including girls, are likely to some degree to adopt the more highly valued masculine orientations. As Weitzman (1979:206) points out,

> Without denying the pressures on women to conform to the feminine role, one can see that women are socialized in an ambivalent fashion. At the same time that girls are rewarded for typical feminine behavior, they are also rewarded for some types of "masculine" behavior. This is because what is labeled masculine behavior is generally highly regarded and rewarded in our society. The girl who excels in school, wins the tennis championship, or fixes a broken car receives approval for each of these activities. Although she may be regarded as too aggressive or masculine, she is also admired for her accomplishments. Thus, the feminine role is not consistently reinforced.

If wider social values conflict with feminine attributes, ambivalence is a more likely outcome than unconflicted conformity. Women are thus especially likely to be socialized in ambivalent ways and to develop structurally incompatible goals, needs, and capacities.[9] This process of ambivalent socialization increases the likelihood that trade-offs between desired goals will be necessary in adulthood; it also lessens the degree to which psychic configurations instilled in childhood, whether they are learned or unconsciously acquired, predetermine any specific adult choice.

Third, by postulating that adult behavior results from early childhood experience, socialization theories imply that motives, capacities, and desires do not, perhaps cannot, change over time. Yet adults may face a social context that differs dramatically from the one in which they were raised. If behavioral options change over time, adult experiences may significantly alter a person's goals as well as his or her ability to accomplish them. By focusing upon reproduction processes rather than change, socialization theories underestimate the human capacity for development beyond childhood.

In a related manner, the socialization perspective also assumes that

---

9. In a fascinating article that illustrates vividly the split between feminine attributes and socially valued attributes, Broverman et al. (1970) report that clinical psychologists clearly distinguish between the healthy female and the healthy person. When asked to rank a set of psychological traits according to whether they describe the healthy woman, the healthy man, or the healthy person, these clinicians agreed that a healthy man and a healthy person exhibit the same traits, but a healthy woman is the opposite of a healthy person. In other words, a healthy woman is considered to have the same psychological traits as a neurotic person. This study tells us more about the double binds and dilemmas women face in constructing their lives and selves than it tells us about women's actual personalities.

the opportunity to realize childhood goals will be available to most adults. This assumption requires another assumption: that social institutions, like people, are stable over time. Yet, if social institutions rearrange the options open to individuals, the childhood socialization perspective cannot account for the resulting behaviors. Will people continue to act on the basis of motives, capacities, and values they acquired as children, even when these do not fit their present circumstances and no reasonable way to put them into practice exists? Like an adult trying to squeeze into children's clothing, this is likely to prove an impossible task.

Childhood socialization theories thus offer an especially inadequate set of tools for understanding behavior during periods of accelerated social change. (See Gerth and Mills, 1953, for a thoughtful discussion of this problem.) In fact, this approach cannot account for how social change could occur at all. Ryder (1965:852) notes,

> Any model of individual development which postulates early crystallization (that the core of personality is laid down at the beginning of life) is embarrassing to the person explaining rapid social change. If personality is viewed as a quasi-hereditary phenomenon, the possibilities of change are reduced to evolution . . . a very slow process.

Of course, what constitutes change is debatable and often becomes a matter of whether the glass is perceived to be half full or half empty. A structure such as the institution of motherhood may endure without being reproduced in identical form in the next generation. Because socialization theories emphasize stable processes, however, they have difficulty distinguishing the forms of change, much less isolating their causes.[10]

Fourth, gender socialization theories, like structural theories, focus on differences between men and women, thus implying that differences among women (and among men) are either minimal or theoretically inconsequential. By emphasizing gender differences in instrumental and expressive capacities, the socialization perspective exaggerates the extent to which women share a distinct set of psychological traits that distinguishes them from men.[11] The focus on within-gender uniformity leaves socialization, like structural, theories unable

10. To some extent, Chodorow's model would have it both ways. She argues that women's mothering is a near universal, but also that it is especially well suited to the functional needs of capitalism. In either case, the logic of her analysis does not easily lend itself to the explanation of historical or cross-sectional variation.

11. Although worked out in finer detail and clothed in more elaborate psychoanalytic language, Chodorow's analysis basically extends Parsons's notion of gender differences in instrumental and expressive functions. She adds an ironic twist, however, by implying that, by virtue of their deeper range of emotional capacities, women are actually superior, rather than inferior, to men.

to account for variation in women's psychological orientations, behavioral choices, or developmental paths.

In reality, women vary greatly in their psychological profiles. Taken as a whole, they do not look as vastly different from men as these theories would lead us to believe. Indeed, most measures designed to tap gender-specific personality traits have found much overlap between men and women and much variation within each gender group (Tresemer, 1975). Statistically, gender differences refer only to the fact that male and female curves on any given measure do not share the same mean. But these gender curves overlap so greatly that many men and women share a common central position, with only those at the opposite tails diverging to a consequential extent.

Analyses that postulate a uniform feminine personality that is distinct from a masculine personality thus oversimplify empirical reality, underestimate actual variation, and "grossly exaggerate" (Tresemer, 1975:319) the degree and importance of gender differences in personality. Moreover, they needlessly imply that instrumental and expressive traits are mutually exclusive. They perpetuate an image of women as universally nurturant, oriented toward motherhood, and excelling in expressive capacities and an image of men as disinterested in parenting, incapable of strong emotional attachment, and excelling in instrumental capacities. By emphasizing gender differences in psychological capacities, they also come dangerously close to implying that one gender is somehow "better" than the other, or at least better suited for specific social tasks.

These images fly in the face of recent historical trends. We can no longer assume that all women and only women are especially suited for parenting. Men can certainly no longer claim a special affinity for paid work or a special incapacity for child rearing.[12] The images of both men and women spawned by the socialization approach appear more stereotypic than real and more suited to the social conditions of the 1950s, when this approach gained prominence, than to those of the 1980s. The persistence of these images in the context of widespread social change suggests that they serve more as mechanisms of social control to bolster waning traditional patterns than as accurate descriptions of men's and women's psychological orientations and capacities.

The childhood socialization approach is thus especially ill suited for explaining variations among women or exploring the dynamics of individual and social change. Because it places so much emphasis on

12. For other critiques of Chodorow's approach, see Coser (1981), Lorber (1981), Pleck (1981), and Rossi (1981). Badinter (1981) reports a marked increase in men's participation in child rearing in France in recent years.

the conforming, thoroughly socialized individual, it tends to ignore the roots, processes, and significance of nonconforming behavior. In the end, it lacks a theory of the individual as an *actor* involved in a process of actively constructing her or his life.[13] If coercion approaches sacrifice the actor at the altar of structural determinism, then socialization approaches reduce adult behavior to the results of processes of unconscious internalization that take place long before the individual possesses an awareness of choice or an ability to make decisions. (See DiTomaso, 1982, for a penetrating discussion of the problem of reductionism in Parsonian functionalism and Althusserian Marxism.)

A Developmental Approach

We can ignore neither the subtle ways that childhood experiences influence later life choices nor the structural constraints on women's options. But neither is enough. A complete theory of women's behavior must include how women themselves, as actors who respond to the social conditions they inherit, construct their lives out of the available raw materials.

Childhood experiences provide the context in which personal conflicts are formed, but they do not determine how, or if, these conflicts will be resolved in adulthood. Because women tend to be reared with a number of ambiguous expectations, not all of which they can realize as adults, the relevant question becomes why a woman chooses to affirm one value, norm, or goal over another. To answer this question, we must look at how people's motives, goals, and capacities develop as they move through a series of life stages and confront a series of choices in which they must make consequential life commitments.

Similarly, although social institutions constrain behavior in powerful ways, of which we are often unconscious, they are rarely static or completely unyielding. Social arrangements, like the people who embody them, are constantly being constructed as successive generations inherit

---

13. Giddens (1976:16) states that

Parsons went on to identify voluntarism with the "internalization of values" in personality and hence with psychological motivation ("need-dispositions"). *There is no action in Parsons' "action frame of reference,"* only behavior which is propelled by need-dispositions or role-expectations. The stage is set, but the actors only perform according to scripts which have already been written out for them.

To borrow psychoanalytic language, in Parsons's account of the socialization process, the ego drops out and the superego becomes the behavioral prime mover.

a specific historical context and make their imprint on the social order. Whether social arrangements are reproduced or changed over time depends in part on how new generations process them.

The malleability of individuals and social institutions over the long term has two implications for the study of women. First, to uncover the causes of women's adult behavior, we must not confine ourselves to the study of childhood, but must rather look at female development over the life course. Second, to understand how women's social position is changing, we must look at how new cohorts of women "process" the social structural arrangements they inherit.

Life History Analysis

Life history analysis offers an ideal method for examining the interplay between social constraints, psychological motivation, and the developing actor. Tracing people's paths as they age, face critical choice points, and make consequential decisions focuses attention on what C. Wright Mills calls "the co-ordinate points of the proper study of man . . . [the] problems of biography, of history, and of their intersections within social structures" (1959:143). This method makes it possible to chart the variety of life paths women take and helps uncover the factors, both structural and psychological, that lead them down their divergent paths. It thus focuses on what structural and socialization theories tend to overlook: variation among women as a group and change over time in the lives of individual women.[14]

Cohort Analysis

Everyone's life has potential implications for social theory, but some people are especially well suited to illumine social processes. The generation of women who were young adults during the 1970s is such a group. This generation is on the cutting edge of social change. These women came of age when dramatic changes were occurring in women's options and life patterns; the subtle revolution in women's work

14. A life course, or developmental, perspective is gaining increasing favor in history and social psychology as well as in sociology. Historians, for example, are making good use of a life course framework for charting processes of historical change, especially in family life and household structure (see, for example, Hareven, 1977; Modell et al., 1976). Sociologists and social psychologists are employing a similar approach to analyze the processes of growth and change in adult development (see especially Elder, 1974, 1978a, 1978b). These studies commonly report that psychological change is an integral part of adulthood and that it is closely linked to larger structural forces in the adult environment (see, for example, Gould, 1978; Levinson, 1978).

and family patterns, which had been developing for many decades, surfaced dramatically. Young adult women are most susceptible to and responsible for implementing these changes.

Young adults are the most likely agents in the social change process, for they are old enough to act on their own but young enough not to be irrevocably committed to a way of life or a psychological orientation. They are thus well positioned to respond to structural changes in the social environment. Ryder (1965:844–48) points to the critical role played by young adults in the process of social change:

> Each fresh cohort is a possible intermediary in the transformation process, a vehicle for introducing new postures. The new cohorts provide the opportunity for social change to occur. They do not cause change; they permit it. . . . In particular, the potential for change is concentrated in the cohorts of young adults who are old enough to participate directly in the movements impelled by change, but not old enough to have become committed to an occupation, a residence, a family of procreation, or a way of life. Furthermore, the fact of change facilitates their development of other orientations than those of their parents and their community. . . . Out of the confrontation of the cohort of any year and the societal structures into which it seeks entry, a shape is forged which influences the directions in which the structures will change.

Young adults do not create the underlying conditions of change, but they nevertheless affect how change is implemented, the new social forms it takes, and its limits. Social change takes place not simply through a mass political movement, but even more fundamentally through the personal decisions of many individuals. These choices reflect underlying structural changes and ultimately have structural consequences.

The current generation of young adult women is in an especially good position to expose the causes, contours, and consequences of women's changing life patterns. They are old enough to be nearing or recently past critical choice points in their lives, but young enough to have been exposed to the recent structural changes in work and family arrangements that have fueled the subtle revolution in women's behavior. These social changes—such as expanding job opportunities for women and increasing marital instability—have altered the context in which women make work and family commitments and induced a sizeable proportion of this generation to forge pathways that only dimly resemble those of their parents. (See Chapter Eight for a full discussion of the institutional changes that are both causes and results of women's changing life patterns.)

Young adult women also find themselves at the life stage when the structural conflicts between forging a work identity and creating a family become most acute. They must make initial commitments that will affect both the future contours of their own life paths and the social institutions they join (or fail to join). By providing examples of what is or is not possible, their decisions will probably influence generations of women to follow. Examining the factors that have impelled members of this strategic cohort down their various life paths thus provides a method for understanding changes in women's position more generally.

Cohort Variation

The entry of new cohorts into social institutions makes social change possible, although certainly not inevitable. The delicate balance between stability and change depends on how new cohorts respond to the world they inherit. Social arrangements, however, limit the range of responses open to various cohorts in two ways. Each cohort faces a set of alternatives defined by the specific historical period in which it comes of age. In this way, one generation (or group of cohorts) becomes differentiated from another. Much like Stinchcombe's idea of a paleontology of organizations, there is also a paleontology of age groups. Each cohort reflects and embodies, to some degree, the structure of opportunities that characterized the historical period in which it came of age and made its life commitments. By examining the intersection between history and biography, we can learn much about the organization of institutions and social structures (Stinchcombe, 1965). (See Elder, 1978a, for more on this approach to the study of the family and social change.) But members of the same generation also vary in their social position and thus in the degree and type of constraints they face. A full analysis of the role cohorts play in social change requires examining the full range of situations cohort members encounter.

Young adult women make their family and work decisions in a variety of social contexts, which not only define their options, but also affect how they will evaluate alternative options. Class position exerts a particularly powerful influence upon a woman's choices, shaping her alternatives and defining her constraints and opportunities. A full analysis of women's behavior requires a look at how both middle-class and working-class women build their lives from the varying raw materials they are offered.

The next five chapters chart the life histories of a carefully selected group of women, all members of the generation that came of age during the late 1960s and 1970s. This sample was randomly selected from lists of recent enrollees at a community college in a working-class community and lists of alumnae of a large four-year university in the

San Francisco Bay Area. This procedure yielded a sample within a delimited age range that varied on the critical dimensions of class location, occupation, and current family-work situation. (See Appendixes B and C for details of methodology and sample characteristics.)

All the women interviewed fell between the ages of twenty-seven and thirty-seven. Their average age at the time they were interviewed in 1978 and 1979 was thirty-one, and 78 percent fell between the ages of twenty-eight and thirty-four. This age group includes those cohorts young enough to have been exposed to recent social changes but old enough to be confronting or recently past life cycle deadlines concerning childbearing and work.[15]

These women were selected to reflect the varying class backgrounds of their generation, although as a group they are somewhat better educated than many of their peers. Approximately 55 percent had attended at least two to four years of college and had received some type of college degree (or higher), and most of the remaining 45 percent had completed high school. These latter women had attended four years of high school and had taken a course or two beyond (mostly of a business or technical nature), but none had completed a higher degree. Most left school immediately after high school to marry or join the work force. Educational attainment is, of course, not an exact proxy for class level, but it is closely linked to class background, life chances, and ultimate class position. Even more important, as the most powerful determinant of occupational access, educational level affects the work and thus indirectly the family decisions women make.

The group selected for analysis includes women from a wide variety of working-class and middle-class occupations, including occupations in female-dominated fields such as clerical and secretarial work, nursing, and teaching, as well as occupations in male-dominated fields such as law, medicine, and administration. This variation allows for an analysis of the ways in which occupational structure affects the development of women's work and family careers.

The group was also selected to ensure variation in work and family choices. It thus includes full-time homemakers, working mothers, and childless workers as well as single, divorced, and married women. Variation along this dimension makes it possible to chart the paths and

---

15. "Generation" is a less technical, looser term than "cohort," which refers to a specific year or set of years when an age group was born. A generation usually contains a number of birth cohorts. The particular age group chosen here represents several cohort groups, which combine to make up much, if not most, of a generation. In this study, the term "generation" does *not* refer to a temporal unit of kinship structure, but rather to a broad age span that shares a meaningful sociological identity by virtue of its common historical location. (See Ryder, 1965.)

isolate the factors that led some women toward domesticity and others away from it.

The sample selected underrepresents minority women. Although it includes a small amount of ethnic variation (see Appendix C), no black women were interviewed. The issues under study here are equally consequential for minority women, and a full understanding of women's behavior must ultimately include them. However, the limits of this study made it unwise to include a representative proportion of minority women. This study is exploratory and based on a small sample; the complexities of race threatened to confuse more than they illuminated. The choice was thus made to develop a theory of women's behavior on the basis of a racially homogeneous sample. The ideas developed in this study can then be tested and refined with other racial and socioeconomic groups (see Appendix B).

Through an examination of the life histories of this strategic group of women, I develop an analysis of the logic of women's work and family choices. These women built their life paths out of a series of decisions over the course of their lives in response to the opportunities and constraints posed by their immediate social environments. Some opted for traditional commitments to marriage, motherhood, and homemaking; others chose to follow a less traditional route toward work, career, and in some cases, childlessness. Comparing those who moved toward domestic goals with those who did not will reveal the factors that led these women down their divergent life paths. In so doing, we will also gain insight into how new social forms emerge even as old ones persist and continue to attract adherents.

Children may not devote much time to thinking about their future, but most people, even as children, make both conscious and unconscious assumptions about what they want and will likely be able to get out of life. These early orientations provide a baseline from which adult development proceeds. Looking at childhood baselines shows how, as adults, the women of this study either stayed on course or veered away from their early life goals.[1]

1. The analysis that follows is based wholly on the respondents' retrospective reports. Time series data collected over the respondents' life courses would obviously have provided a more ideal source of data. Unfortunately, as in most research, such material was not available. Indeed, the kinds of questions this book addresses were not being asked when these respondents were young.

The data base for this study is, nevertheless, both reliable and well suited to a study designed to *discover* (rather than verify) theory (see Glaser and Strauss, 1967; Luker, 1975). The interview schedule was carefully constructed and pretested over a six-month period. The interviews were long (three to four hours on the average), carefully administered by the author, and designed to ensure that each respondent was asked the same questions. The respondents were not asked to go back further in their life accounts than they felt comfortable remembering. The interview focused on the recent past and present, and the sampling procedure selected respondents who were relatively close in time to the events they were recounting. For a full description and rationale of the study's methodology, see Appendix B.

Two points emerge from this exercise. First, for both social-structural and psychological reasons, childhood models and experiences are poor predictors of eventual outcomes. Second, although many of the women in this study began adulthood with traditional notions about their lives, simple images of marriage, motherhood, and domesticity capture neither the diversity of their early hopes and aspirations nor the variety of pressures they all experienced as adults.

A clear picture of how the group's baselines varied, where they came from, and how respondents "used" them as their lives proceeded begins to suggest why early life experiences poorly predict adult choices. The respondents' experiences show that early messages were typically ambiguous and often contradictory, that they were often received with ambivalence, and that they were subject to reinterpretation and re-evaluation over time.

Childhood Socialization

The generation of women under study here grew up during a period characterized by two countervailing trends. First, most of their mothers and their mothers' friends stayed home to bear and rear children. Suburbanization and the domestic life-style it fostered developed rapidly after World War II, and Dr. Spock's advice on devoted motherhood and indulgent child rearing was standard bookshelf fare. (See Slater, 1970, for a provocative discussion of the social and psychological implications of "Spockian" child-rearing practices.) For most of these respondents, both the image of female adulthood projected by the media and the reality for the vast majority of their mothers were domestic and child-centered. Thus, as children, these respondents received models of feminine behavior from a world populated largely by adult women who defined themselves primarily as wives and mothers.

But this period was also a time of unprecedented economic growth and rising economic and social expectations. The added stimulus of the Cold War led many parents to view their children as the best hope for the nation's as well as their own future. The combination of a child-centered atmosphere and a rapidly expanding economy promoted the allocation of considerable social and personal resources toward educating the "sputnik" generation, without regard to sex. Young boys and girls alike grew up in an environment that stressed educational accomplishment, promised unbounded opportunities to those who earned such rewards, and provided high quality, mass public education to unprecedented numbers of middle- and working-class children.

The women of this generation thus often received conflicting and confusing messages as children about what was expected of them and what they should aim for in adult life. The adult female images around them were largely domestic; yet, in some important ways, they were also treated as sexual equals to whom the work ethic very much applied—strive for achievement, be successful, and you shall be rewarded. Given this ambiguous context, their childhood socialization experiences could not be expected, at least in a direct sense, to determine their adult choices.

Mother-Daughter Dynamics

Although there were a small number of exceptions, the mothers of most of the women in this study provided traditional images of femininity. Most respondents grew up in large families of three or more children in which their mothers stayed home to care for them and run the household, at least when the children were young. Almost a quarter (24 percent) came from families with four or more children, and an additional 32 percent were from three-child families. Less than half (43 percent) grew up in two-child families, and only one respondent was an only child. Respondents' mothers generally put family first and devoted their early and middle adult years to rearing their children. Only 14 percent of the respondents reported their mothers working while the respondents were in their preschool years; 46 percent said their mothers had never worked between the time the respondents were born and the time they left home for college, work, or marriage. Mothers of the remaining 40 percent had worked, but only after the respondents had started school, and usually in a part-time and temporary capacity even then.

Most respondents recalled that they had perceived their mothers to be satisfied as homemakers. A mother's decision to go to work was almost always triggered by financial need and was usually made with regret. When asked whether their mothers had preferred working or staying home when the children were young, 72 percent replied that they felt their mothers had preferred staying home. Among those whose mothers had never worked, that figure rises to 88 percent. Even among those whose mothers had been employed at some point during the respondent's childhood, the perceived preference for staying home was strong. A full 67 percent of those whose mothers had worked part-time or intermittently felt their mothers would have preferred to stay home. Another 15 percent remembered that their mothers had felt ambivalent about working. Only those few respondents whose mothers had been employed continuously full-time recalled that their mothers had preferred working. Thus, most respondents perceived that their mothers had preferred domestic pursuits to employment outside the home, although a notable, if small, minority felt their mothers either had preferred or would have preferred to work (see Table 1).

Despite perceiving their mothers as "happy homemakers," many respondents did not choose and did not intend to choose the domestic route for themselves. As Tables 2 and 3 indicate, there is no consistent relationship between mothers' work patterns or fertility behavior and their daughters' early orientations or later choices and plans. Table 2 shows that, although there is a slight relationship between mother's work pattern and daughter's baseline orientation, it diminishes and even reverses over time. Among those respondents whose mothers had never worked, only 59 percent stated that they had held domestic aspirations as children. Only 49 percent of this group held domestic

Table 1 *Mother's Attitude Toward Working When Her Children Were Young by Mother's Work Experience*

	Preferred to Work	Preferred to Stay Home	Mixed Feelings	Total N
Mother never worked	12%	88%	—	(25)
Mother was a part-time or intermittent worker	18	67	15%	(33)
Mother was a full-time, continuous worker	100	—	—	(3)
All mothers	20	72	8	(61)[a]

[a]Two missing cases.

Table 2 *Percent Domestic by Mother's Work Pattern*

	Respondent's Baseline Orientation	Respondent's Current Orientation	Total N
Mother never worked when R lived at home	59%	49%	(29)
Mother worked, but after R started school	60	40	(25)
Mother worked when R a preschooler	33	67	(9)
All mothers	52	48	(63)

Table 3   *Percent Domestic by Mother's Fertility Behavior*

	Respondent's Baseline Orientation	Respondent's Current Orientation	Total N
Mother bore 1 child	—	—	(1)
Mother bore 2 children	67%	33%	(27)
Mother bore 3 children	50	58	(19)
Mother bore 4 or more children	47	56	(16)
All mothers	52	48	(63)

aspirations as adults. Among those whose mothers had worked after they started school, 60 percent had held domestic aspirations as children, but only 40 percent did so as adults. Among those few respondents whose mothers had worked before they began school, only 33 percent had held domestic aspirations as children. Since these are the women whose mothers provided nondomestic examples, this finding is not surprising. It is more surprising, however, that 67 percent of this group had developed domestic orientation as adults.

A similarly inconclusive pattern holds for mothers' fertility behavior. There is a slight relationship between the number of children her mother bore and the respondent's childhood orientation, but it is a negative relationship. The more children her mother bore, the less likely a respondent was to be domestically oriented as a child. This relationship reverses with time, however, so that a respondent is less likely to be domestically oriented as an adult if she came from a two-child family. In general, however, there is no consistent link between their mothers' fertility behavior and the respondents' own orientations. Thus, despite the stress both psychoanalytic and role learning theories place on the importance of mothers in transmitting feminine values, needs, and capacities from one generation of women to the next, the behavior and perceived orientations of the mothers of these women are not powerful predictors of their daughters' behavior and orientations.[2]

Of course, these respondents are reporting only what they *perceived* their mothers to feel and experience. Their perceptions might well differ from their mothers' actual feelings toward mothering and work. Despite this possible disparity, the respondents' experiences constitute the critical information. For the child constantly involved in a process

2. Clausen (1968) summarizes the socialization literature. Maccoby (1966) and Maccoby and Jacklin (1974) provide thorough compendiums of studies that examine psychological sex differences. For a consideration of working mothers specifically, see Nye and Hoffman (1963) and Hoffman and Nye (1979).

of interpreting the actions of her adult caretakers, it matters little what these caretakers "actually" feel unless these feelings are adequately and accurately expressed. It is thus the perception, rather than the fact alone, that the child processes and applies to her own life. Moreover, although a child might be expected to see consistency between her outlook and her mother's, these respondents report instead a high degree of inconsistency.

These mothers' actions tell us little about their daughters' ultimate choices because a child will "use" whatever model she is exposed to in ways that parental behavior and values do not predetermine. How a woman interprets and responds to her childhood relationships and models is as important as the content of the models themselves. This process of interpreting mother-daughter dynamics has three major aspects.

First, mothers do not influence their children in any simple, unidimensional sense. Mothers may feel ambivalent about their own choices and their own children; they may also present ambiguous images and provide double, or even negative, messages to their daughters. These mothers are from a generation of women who successfully assumed the technical and supervisory jobs vacated by men during World War II, only to step aside after the war for returning GIs. Although this study cannot directly confirm these mothers' feelings and experiences, temporary success in well-rewarded occupations may have left some with feelings of ambivalence toward work and mothering as they returned home to bear and rear the children of the baby boom generation.

Although in the minority, openly dissatisfied mothers provide a good example of this process of maternal ambivalence. (For discussions of maternal ambivalence, see Coser, 1974, and Rich, 1976.) In these cases, the discrepancies between a mother's choices and her feelings about those choices sowed the first seeds of doubt in a daughter's mind. A childless lawyer in her mid-thirties responded to her mother's frustration at home by wishing her mother had followed a promising career she relinquished in order to raise children:

> A: She's a very talented person, and she didn't get to do what she *could* have done. I believe there was a certain amount of frustration there. As I became older, preadolescent or whatever, I wanted her to pursue her career. I think all of us children would have been better off. Instead, it appeared to me, at least my conscious process was, that I had to make a choice, too . . . that I would be precluded from having a career were I to follow the traditional path. And I knew I was going to have a career.

Daughters can thus evaluate their mothers' behavior positively and seek to emulate it *or* they can evaluate it negatively and use it instead as a warning of what to avoid in their own lives. This respondent, who had recently resigned from her sales job to bear her first child at age thirty-three, spoke of how she would not follow the materialistic values her mother had stressed:

A: I remember hearing what we really gain from our parents are the negative things. Because they stick out so much, we learn not to do those. We learn what we *don't* want to do with our children or in our own lives. But there have been a lot of positive things, too. If I hadn't seen what certain of her priorities did to her and how they made her express herself and conduct her life, I might have those priorities and want those things, and I'm grateful not to.

Daughters, then, do not passively receive and adopt the personalities and orientations of their mothers. They can separate themselves from these examples and make both conscious and unconscious judgments about them.

Over time, daughters choose to confirm or deny particular aspects of their mothers' behavior in their own lives. It is not enough to know what a mother did or how she felt; we must also take into account how a daughter evaluated her mother's behavior when she was young and how she consciously and unconsciously responds to her mother's model as her own life develops. This process can reinforce the emulation of a mother's model, or it can undermine it and even promote an opposite reaction to it. Thus, a domestically oriented and seemingly fulfilled mother does not ensure that her daughter will reproduce her pattern. A thirty-seven-year-old, self-employed mother recounted the differences between her mother and herself and the gap these differences created between them:

Q: Did your mother work when you were young?

A: No. She was very glad to get married and get rid of her job, because she worked up to the age of twenty-eight. She's the type who would go to her home as soon as she got married. She's a real homemaker. We totally disagreed on that. She loved it; it's her whole life. Now her grandchildren are her whole life. That's why I never wanted the same scene. I remember I thought she had an extremely boring life. All it seemed she was ever doing was washing, doing dishes, and scrubbing floors. That used to drive me crazy.

Housewives are not the only models that can trigger a negative reaction. A working mother can also provide a child with an example she would rather avoid. Although this respondent eventually became a working mother, her mother's negative example had made her averse to such an arrangement earlier in life:

> A: When I was a child, I kind of swore I'd never work. I think it was when I dealt with my mother working and not being at home. I wanted her home.

Especially if coupled with an unhappy childhood, a working mother can serve to make a home, a family, and a life of domesticity look more inviting than work to a daughter. In the following instance, a happily married, thirty-four-year-old homemaker with two children reacted against her mother's alcoholism, which had broken apart her childhood home, sending her mother into the work force:

> A: My mother always had a drinking problem. It was really a terrible life for us kids. We all lived in foster homes for not quite two years. . . . I used to think, "God, I'm never going to have a bunch of kids." But I had one at a time, and I enjoyed them so much; they were just so much fun, even as little babies. One at a time, and just watching them grow, it was a pleasure.
>
> Q: And what about working?
>
> A: Maybe because my mother worked and had a lot of children close together, we didn't have a lot of time with our parents; so I always wanted to spend a lot of time with my kids [instead of working].

In sum, whatever model a mother consciously or unconsciously provides, she rarely transmits a simple message. The child may process the model in a variety of ways, both negative and positive. It is far from a forgone conclusion that the daughter will be motivated or able to follow in her mother's footsteps.

The process by which daughters interpret their mothers' models has a second facet as well: Daughters are likely to be attracted to and identify with other models in addition to or in the place of their mothers. When society values other models more highly, the child, male or female, is likely to do so as well. This thirty-six-year-old, childless high school teacher realized early that her employed father was more socially valued than her housekeeping mother:

> A: I never did want to be my mother in there washing those dishes. I wanted to be my father who was reading the paper and just came home from work and was much more important.

A child can "identify with" and feel ambivalent about a number of objects at the same time. These respondents demonstrate the ambiguous messages female children receive. An ambivalent response that includes both attraction to and repulsion from adult models of both sexes is common.[3]

A third aspect of the interpretation process has the greatest significance, however. Regardless of her responses when young, as she ages, a child may reinterpret and reevaluate her initial reactions. Later life experiences can cause her to reexamine, undermine, and eschew her early childhood models. For example, a daughter may conclude when she is older that, although her mother appeared happy with her choices in the short run, they resulted in unpleasant consequences in the long run. Indeed, the story of the aging, unfulfilled mother is a common theme among the respondents:

A: I see a woman like my mom. She's a pretty bright lady, and, when her kids left, her two babies walked out of the house, she had nothing left in her life. It was all she was geared up for, and it came very close to turning into an almost hate kind of thing toward us for taking away the one thing she had. . . . Look what happened to her. That's just terrible that's all she had in life.

The long-run consequences of a mother's choice can ultimately appear disastrous to a grown daughter who once thought she would lead the same kind of life. This thirty-two-year-old, childless social worker attributed her mother's mental collapse to a life of domesticity. Though reared to follow her mother's example, she later vowed to avoid her mother's fate:

A: When I got out of college and started my first job, my mom started a psychotic break which lasted for six years. Then I realized that a middle-age crisis in women comes from having all your eggs in one basket, having low self-esteem. That's what my mother did; that's what my sister's doing. I've convinced myself that it won't happen to me unless I do that, too, unless I also devote my whole life to a family. If I at least balance family and work or something that I

3. Firestone (1970) argues that, to the extent to which it can be said to exist at all, the classic psychoanalytic concept of penis envy is actually based on structural configurations and the social values attached to child rearing versus working. The female child does not envy a man's penis so much as the power, independence, and control that accrue to his social position at home and in the wider world. The penis is merely a physical symbol of men's dominant social position and women's subordinate one; what the female child really wants that men have and women lack is power.

continue for me as a person, something that isn't going to leave at eighteen, then at least I've got a chance. It was a real therapeutic process.

The daughter may also conclude that what she felt was in her best interest as a child might not have been in her mother's best interest. Upon becoming a mother herself, this thirty-one-year-old librarian realized that her desire for a mother at home when she was growing up worked against her mother's long-term needs for sustaining commitments beyond motherhood:

Q: How do you feel about your mother staying home?

A: I feel really ambivalent, because I think I liked having her home and available when we came home from school. On the other hand, I think if she had had some kind of job at the time, it might have been better in the long run.

Respondents tended to become increasingly aware of this clash between the long-term interests of their mothers and their own wishes as children as they moved closer to facing the same dilemma in their own lives. (See Bart, 1970, for an analysis of how full-time motherhood promotes middle-age depression when the children leave home.) Even if the long-term consequences of a mother's choices do not turn out to be negative, a daughter may find that she is different from her mother and wants a different life. She then has difficulty comprehending how her mother could have been happy and may find this happy image oppressive. To this thirty-one-year-old, childless physician, her mother's fulfillment and mothering skills became onerous images that threatened to undermine her own work ambitions:

Q: When you were young, do you think your mother preferred staying home?

A: Yes, I think she did. I think she really enjoyed having children and that being her occupation. She was the typical mad housewife. . . . I really treasure those years when we went to the beach every afternoon in the summer, we went to the library every morning, and we went to the store. She did all this stuff. . . . She can't imagine that a job could be as important as a family. It negates her that I am rejecting or not participating in her sphere of femininity. It's very hard for her.

Q: Are you afraid the same would be expected of you if you had children?

A: That's what I would expect, I think.

When a rift occurs between mother and daughter, the daughter may feel ambivalence and guilt. Such feelings, however, do not determine her behavior. A woman may suffer intensely in the process of rejecting her childhood models, but this will not in itself prevent her from acting in a new way. Although her plans to combine career and motherhood were at odds with the lessons she learned from her mother, this thirty-year-old, childless manager was committed to this course and prepared to confront the psychological struggles it entailed:

A: I still have to reconcile being a working mother with my mother, who was so good to me and never left home until I was thirteen or whatever. But I couldn't stay home just because she devoted her whole life to raising us.

A few years ago I was certain: I will just work until I have a baby and then, of course, I have to stay home. And that's a bunch of bull, but I have to get rid of the guilt feelings that are associated with going back to work.

Women whose lives diverge from their mothers' patterns are more likely to question and reevaluate their mothers' choices than are those whose lives do not. It is not surprising, therefore, that the women who did not follow their mothers into homemaking were the most prone toward reinterpretation. The underlying significance of this pattern applies in all cases, however. Whether a daughter chooses a traditional or nontraditional route, her mother's model does not deterministically "cause" the outcome.

In conclusion, domestic mothers do not necessarily reproduce their own orientation toward mothering and domesticity in their daughters. Nor do nondomestically oriented mothers necessarily produce nondomestically oriented daughters. Although the importance of mothers is undeniable, the *way* in which they are important in shaping their daughters' orientations is complex and open-ended. Daughters may respond to their mothers in a variety of subtle ways that go beyond emulation; they may also be motivated by other factors and other childhood models; and as time passes, they may change their understanding of their mothers' lives and their own experiences as children. In the long run, daughters must make their own way in the world— informed by, but not controlled by, their mothers' decisions and relationships with them as children.

Parental Expectations, Family Dynamics, and the Wider Social Milieu

In addition to focusing on mothers as the vehicles for transmitting feminine capacities and motives from adult women to female children, socialization theories emphasize how parents, as representatives of the wider culture, and siblings to a lesser degree, socialize female children to domesticity. By rewarding their female offspring for sex-appropriate behavior and withholding approval for masculine behavior and orientations, parents transmit and support the larger system of gender differentiation. In order to please their parents, reap the ensuing benefits, and avoid the negative consequences of noncompliance, daughters internalize feminine values and orientations and eventually put them into practice as adults. (Weitzman, 1979, summarizes and critiques the role-learning approach to gender socialization.)

In fact, however, parental attitudes and expectations (at least as experienced by their children) prove just as inadequate as mothers' models in explaining these respondents' adult choices. The messages these women received from their parents were far from uniform or exclusively "feminine" in nature. Nor were these respondents uniformly motivated or able to comply with their parents' expectations. Parental messages were also subject to reassessment and reinterpretation in adulthood.

The respondents' experiences clearly show that parents did not uniformly or unambiguously stress marriage and motherhood to their female offspring. Although 32 percent of the total sample responded that their parents had stressed marriage and family above all else, a surprising 27 percent reported that greater importance had been attached to education, work, or economic self-sufficiency than to the security or joys of marriage and parenting. Another 42 percent received either mixed or weak signals. Of these, 25 percent reported having received mixed messages; the importance of education, work, or economic survival had been stressed while marriage, motherhood, and homemaking had been assumed. The remaining 17 percent had no memory of any strong expectations, traditional or nontraditional, expressed by their parents.

In addition, as Table 4 illustrates, the impact of these messages diminished over time, especially among those whose parents stressed marriage and motherhood. Although 79 percent of this group had expected to become wives, mothers, and homemakers above all else when they were young, only 47 percent retained this domestic orientation at the time of the interview. Change among those whose parents stressed other goals is not as dramatic, but parental impact also diminished as some women opted for domestic goals despite their parents' contrasting hopes. Thirty-eight percent of those whose parents had stressed nondomestic goals were domestically oriented at the time of the interview. Among those who had received mixed or weak messages, 56 percent were domestically oriented as adults.

Table 4 *Percent Domestic by Parental Expectations*

	Respondent's Baseline Orientation	Respondent's Current Orientation	Total N
Parents stressed marriage and family first	79%	47%	(19)
Parents stressed education or work first	31	38	(16)
Parents stressed both (mixed messages) or neither (no strong expectations)	48	56	(25)
All parents[a]	52	48	(60)

[a]Three missing cases.

Parental expectations are poor predictors of daughters' eventual choices for several reasons. First, a woman may be exposed to a web of cultural values that contain a wide-ranging set of implicit expectations, not all of which are congruent. This respondent's experience of conflicting messages was common among the group:

> A: My parents pushed me in a good way. They always gave me mathematical games in the car on long trips; they always did things to put my learning forward. They always told me I should succeed, that I was capable of succeeding, that they expected me to. I didn't get a lot of "act like a girl" kind of stuff from my parents in terms of academic achievement, at least. I'm sure they expected me to marry a nice Catholic Italian boy and settle down and raise a whole bunch of kids. I think it wasn't spoken because it was just assumed.
>
> Q: So, some double messages there?
>
> A: That's right. That's really true. Succeed in school until it's time to stop, and then stop.

Mixed messages can come from a variety of sources. Parents may not agree with each other or they may stress a set of goals divergent from those of the wider culture. The high ambitions these parents held for their daughter stood in contrast to the larger social context to which she was exposed:

> Q: So your family was supportive of all sorts of rather high ambitions?
>
> A: Yes, and expected them. I think I was aware of having a career very early because I think my dad touted that. "You better learn to support yourself. You better think about what you want to do."

Q: What were your parents' attitudes toward marriage and family?

A: That was more a general cultural thing, just something you kind of assumed. Everybody did then. That's what women do in the movies; that's what women do on TV; that's what my mother does; that's what my mother's friends do. I knew no career women.

Such ambiguities are not merely artifacts of a middle-class environment. Working-class parents may not think or talk in terms of professional careers, but they may be even more acutely attuned to the realities of adult life, which often necessitate work and financial self-sufficiency even for their daughters. The following high school–educated respondent, a full-time worker and childless at twenty-nine, reported:

Q: Did your parents express any expectations for you when you were growing up?

A: I guess they expected I would be married and have children. They obviously expected I would be working or they wouldn't have pushed business college so much. I think they wanted to make sure that, if I didn't get married and something ever happened, I could support myself at some point.

Second, whatever parents expect or stress, and whatever messages they consciously or unconsciously convey to their young daughters, children are not always motivated to please their parents or conform to their wishes. Indeed, as age groups become more strictly delineated and the pace of change quickens in modern society, children are as likely to rebel and innovate as to conform to parental expectations.[4] In the case of women, this rift between parents and children often takes the form of parents stressing domestic pursuits while their daughters yearn for something else. This struggle knows no class boundaries. A high school–educated, divorced mother and full-time worker complained:

A: I wanted to go to college very badly, but my father's idea of women was to get an MRS degree.

4. See, for example, Eisenstadt (1956) and Davis (1974) for classic treatments of the question of increasing incidence of youth rebellion and intergenerational conflict in modern societies. Remarkably, this perspective has yet to be applied to women's behavior.

And the father of this thirty-two-year-old, childless administrator with a college degree expressed strong disapproval of her desires to work:

A: Work and career were not acceptable. Maybe they were to my mother, but she was not in a place to encourage it. My father has just now reached the point that he can accept the fact that I am a career woman, but he still considers it not even second place to a wife and mother. It's *way* down.

Moreover, just as mothers can project images that children evaluate negatively, so the whole family environment, including fathers, siblings, and even close friends, can also serve as negative models. A single mother and clerical worker recalled how she reacted against her father's patriarchal household:

Q: Why do you think you didn't want to be married?

A: I don't know if it's just maybe the way my father was raising us or the old-fashioned tradition. Maybe it's just the domineering of a male. Maybe that was it, because brothers never did anything wrong and you were constantly picking up after them, along with your mother picking up after them. Of course, I never felt they had a superiority. I always felt tomboyish and felt like one of the guys in the neighborhood.

A rift between parents' expectations and daughters' preferences is a real, if not always realized, potential and can undermine the impact of parents' goals for their children as time passes. Although a split is most likely to occur when a daughter develops nondomestic ambitions and orientations that clash with her parents' values and life-styles, the process can also operate in the reverse. Despite her father's support for nontraditional goals, this thirty-five-year-old part-time secretary and mother of two opted for motherhood:

A: My father, because his education was so short, had great hopes that I would go ahead and get my college diploma. I have always wanted to get my education completed, but I let outside things influence me. I guess it was the big decision: Am I getting married, or am I going ahead with my career? I decided on marriage instead. At the time it seemed like starting a family and getting in the swing of things was the most important thing. But now I do have moments when I think, "Gee, you could have gotten the education and maybe branched into something more interesting.". . . I feel I'm failing myself and my father because I would like, if there was something I could do, to make him feel like he had given me every chance.

Thus, even though a child may want to please her parents, she may want other conflicting goals as well. Guilt or ambivalence may result from not pleasing them, but such conflicts do not inevitably result in behavioral compliance. Just as traditional parental expectations do not guarantee that daughters will opt for domesticity as adults, neither does parental stress upon achievement guarantee nontraditional choices. Children, although influenced by their parents in ways so subtle they may never be evident, are also separate from them. They are capable of using the information they receive from their childhood environment in a variety of ways. Often they have little motivation to give their parents, or the larger cultural milieu, simply what is wished or requested. And even when children are motivated to please, they also experience other, potentially competing desires and contingencies that may in the long run render their parents' wishes irrelevant.

Finally, as with mothers as models, women reassess parental expectations and cultural values over time. One childless lawyer-in-training, for example, once ruled out as inappropriate for her gender the very occupation she eventually chose:

A: I remember saying out loud that, if I had been a boy, I would want to go to law school. . . . But I didn't really think at all about the future and a career. I didn't plan my future all that much. I just sort of assumed that I would one day get married and have children.

When adult women reassess parental messages, they often feel anger and bitterness toward those authority figures who failed to support their personal childhood hopes. This thirty-six-year-old, childless working woman, for example, resented being channeled away from the things she really wanted as a child. Although she eventually broke with this early channeling, it involved conflicts she was still trying to resolve for herself:

A: I had rather high expectations for myself, higher than other people, I think. I really feel resentment toward people now. I know it's my responsibility, but I also know there was this goddamn [high school] principal telling my father, "Well, she'll get married," instead of somebody saying, "If you want to be a doctor, hey, that's neat!" I feel a lot of resentment somehow, and yet I know you're in charge of your own life.

This woman is expressing a common emotional struggle for women who find their early childhood options and experiences at odds with their emerging adult goals. In their effort to define an independent self and build a nontraditional life, they are caught between the need to take responsibility for their actions and the need to place appropriate blame on external social conditions, both past and present. Whether the resentment that emerges from this difficult process of attribution and reassessment is directed toward parents, other authority figures, or more abstract social institutions, it is an important, perhaps necessary, step in the creation of a more autonomous, more empowered identity.

In sum, like mothers' models, parental behavior and expectations and the historically grounded cultural values they reflect do not determine in any simple, linear way what children will do as adults or how they will do it. When contradictory messages are embedded in the social structure, when avenues for independence and noncompliance are readily available to children, and when social change rearranges options and incentives over time, parental influences are likely to be undermined.

Starting Points

Given their frequent exposure to conflicting and ambiguous messages and their correspondingly ambivalent responses, it is not surprising that these women held childhood expectations about the future that were often confused, vague, and subject to change. More surprising, perhaps, is the degree to which the respondents focused their hopes and fantasies on nondomestic images despite the traditional milieu of their childhood. Although 55 percent reported that they had indeed anticipated a future oriented toward marriage, children, and homemaking when they were growing up, the remaining 45 percent had not.

Domestic Beginnings

To grow up focusing on domesticity implies an orientation toward marriage, home, and children and a concomitant lack of interest in work as a central life concern. Over half the respondents reported such traditional beginnings. For these women, although work may have been part of the anticipated future, it clearly held a secondary position to marriage and family. A thirty-four-year-old, divorced, childless social worker was more definite than most in formulating her childhood plans, but her focus on mothering at the expense of work commitment is representative of this group:

> A: I was going to be a teacher. You were either a teacher or nurse; those were good jobs because they were always around for women. You could be there when the kids came home; you wouldn't work until the kids were in kindergarten, and you could start back. You'd always have something to fall back on if you needed money or if your husband got sick or if he died. I remember that very well. And I liked kids a lot, and it seemed to fit. It wasn't only what you did; it was something that I wanted to do. I would get my degree in education, get married the summer after I graduated. I would have my first child two years after we were married. I would wait four years for the second child. And when the second child was in kindergarten, I would go back and start working again.

For most, these domestic aspirations were vague, and for some, they took on an idealized aura. In these real-life versions of children's fairy tales, attaining home and family was often seen as a romantic ending in which one lived happily ever after. This twenty-nine-year-old, high school–educated mother, surprised to find herself back at work within months of her son's birth, recalled her warm but unrealistic childhood visions of domesticity:

> A: [When I was young,] I didn't think I'd be working at this age. I thought when you got married, everything was nice and rosy. I knew I'd be married and have children, but not anything further than that, than a housewife.

Others equated domesticity—and especially marriage—with normality. For this high school–educated, childless woman in her thirties, any fate other than marriage was considered failure:

> A: Several years ago, a friend of mine said to another friend, "She's not even married," and I said, "Just because you're married, that doesn't make you a whole person." What makes me bring this up is I can remember feeling the exact same way. Oh, I would be married. I didn't know about myself and whether I would be working, but I definitely saw myself in a pretty traditional woman's role.

For many of those with early traditional orientations, the idea of motherhood as a profession was often translated into wanting a large family. Although none of the respondents actually had more than three children at the time of the interview, many remembered dreaming about numerous children when they were younger. A thirty-year-old childless clerk recounted with obvious amazement: "I thought I would have three or four kids and would not be working at this point. I'd be staying home with them [and] married."

But by far the most common response among this group with traditional baselines was that they and everyone around them just assumed marriage and children; to do otherwise was rarely, if ever, entertained and was considered a form of heresy. As one respondent explained, "In those days, that's how you were programmed."

In sum, many respondents assumed as children that their adult lives would closely resemble the domestic models around them. This was so as much for those who well into their thirties were neither wives nor mothers as for those who had married and borne children. Many of these women had developed occupational ties as strong as any man's.

Nondomestic Beginnings

Domestic aspirations were far from universal, however. A full 45 percent of the respondents reported that they had looked on marriage and children with either indifference or disdain as children. Instead, they had given central importance to work.

Many did not find the images of home and family around them inviting. As a result, they were more likely to focus on the costs of domesticity and to use their childhood experiences as lessons about what to avoid in their own lives. As this thirty-year-old librarian explained:

A: I was *never* going to get married; that's the biggest memory.
      I guess because I looked around totally objectively and
      didn't see a happily married couple. Plus children were just
      a pain; that was pretty obvious.

In some cases, prolonged, close exposure to children, and especially to younger siblings, engendered not a maternal response, but a reaction against childbearing. For some, too many responsibilities for younger siblings dampened enthusiasm for motherhood at an early age because resentment could result when fun with dolls gave way to such responsibility:

A: When I was very little and played with dolls, I would think
      of how many [children] I was going to have and name them
      all and go through all these kinds of things in my mind,
      until about sixth grade, and after that it began to change.

Q: What brought about the change?

A: It could have to do with the change in my own family. That was the time when I started having to be more responsible [for my sister]. [I began to see children as] a restriction on one's freedom.

Early exposure to the rigors of child rearing also left this childless clerk hostile to motherhood at twenty-nine:

A: I was the second oldest child and had to help out a lot, and I hated it. I'll never forget how much I hated it. I know that governed very much how I felt about children. I enjoyed them, but I didn't necessarily want my own. When I got married, at eighteen, real young, I said I didn't want children for ten years. I would be married, but I didn't see any children.

Like parents and younger siblings, friends and older siblings can also point out the negative consequences of marriage and childbearing. Having seen the consequences of premature motherhood, this homemaker in her late twenties was determined to avoid a similar fate:

A: One of my best girlfriends became my sister-in-law. She was only thirteen at the time; so I decided at a very young age that that wasn't what it was cracked up to be, especially knowing my brother's attitude toward all my friends. It so happened that he had to marry her, and it didn't work after two years; so I could see what was going on very early. I just thought about having money, working, holding down a job, being independent.

Older siblings, too, can alert women to the dangers of domesticity and lead them to consider other alternatives simply by their own unattractive example. Even when one's own parents fit the ideal image, one can instead select another, less pleasant image to focus on. An older brother's unhappy marriage made all marriages appear undesirable to this thirty-one-year-old, childless real estate agent:

A: My brother's marriage was a very stormy one. I had had such a naive impression, because my parents were so Ozzie and Harriet. We were a little family, and Mother was always preparing breakfast and kissed us goodbye, waved at the window when we came home. Everything worked very much for them, but not for him, unfortunately. When he was married, it was my eighth birthday, and there was lots of anger, emotions, screaming, drinking, irregular hours, bad communication. I had a very split image, but from about twelve on, I was *very* aware that life was not calico curtains and picking out silver patterns, because of all the shit that hit the fan with my brother. I remember saying at twelve that I wouldn't be married before twenty-eight. I made that declaration.

Thus, choosing to emphasize the dangers of domesticity instead of its joys, many respondents developed a childhood aversion to marriage and motherhood.

Although some respondents had focused on the costs of childbearing and marital commitment as children, others had focused on the joys of work, career, or simply adult independence. Just as some found domesticity glamorous, so the life of the single career woman, however vague the image, seemed glamorous to others. Not everyone assumed a husband, a home, and a family; some took work for granted, as this childless, married teacher explained:

A: I thought I'd be a veterinarian. I was certain I'd have a career and a college education. I was very interested in everything I studied in high school, and I just couldn't see getting married and having kids and staying home all the time. It wasn't even a decision I had to think about. It was automatic in my mind.

Indeed, in some cases where work came first, family did not enter into the picture at all. This respondent, childless and in her early thirties, had held high occupational ambitions as a child that left no room for traditional feminine pursuits:

A: When I was in high school, I wanted to be a doctor, and I wanted to be a medical missionary; so I expected I would be on a foreign mission field.

Q: Did you think about marriage or children?

A: No, I really didn't think that would be part of my future.

A middle-class upbringing is more likely than a working-class one to foster visions of a professional future, but childhood fantasies about careers were not confined to the college-educated group. A number of high school–educated women also expressed hopes of training for professional careers such as science or business or choosing a male-dominated, blue-collar occupation requiring extensive training and long-term commitment. This full-time mother in her late twenties had dreamed of moving far beyond the clerical jobs she had held before leaving work to have a child:

A: I had hoped, I was thinking about going to college, and I wanted to have anything to do with the ocean that I could.

> Marine biology was on my mind. When I was a teenager, I
> loved the ocean; so I thought that's what I would like to
> do. . . . Then I realized that I probably wasn't going to be
> able to go to college and switched over to business courses
> and started to prepare myself for work then. In fact, I
> started working before I graduated.

This part-time clerk and mother of two had strong, yet unfulfilled
ambitions for police work:

> A: My goal was to be working for the police department. I
> expected to work.
>
> Q: What made you want to be a policewoman way back then?
>
> A: Well, I guess basically I'm a physical type person who enjoys
> outdoor sports and such, and that just caught my interest.

Thus, early hopes for careers outside the sphere of traditional "wom-
en's work" were not unusual among this sample, irrespective of class
background.

Career can mean a variety of things. Although many hoped to acquire
jobs in male-dominated fields with career ladders and long-term futures,
such as physicians, scientists, and policewomen, some focused on jobs
they considered careers but that tended in the long run to lead to dead
ends. Not surprisingly, these jobs were usually located in the female-
dominated labor markets of the service sector. This twenty-seven-year-
old, full-time mother of two had always wanted a career but discovered
much later her chosen occupation did not offer one:

> Q: Was there ever a time when you thought in terms of a
> career?
>
> A: Always, always. I really thought airline stewardess would be
> the career. When that didn't turn out, I was crushed for a
> while.

Whatever the outcome, however, these respondents had not held
domestic orientations as children. Instead, they had tended to focus
away from the home and traditional feminine concerns and toward
accomplishment and independence in a more public forum. For many
in this career-oriented group, husband and children were also part of
the expected future, but family goals did not preclude or supersede
work goals. Despite the cultural admonition that committed work is
not compatible with responsible motherhood, some respondents, even
in childhood, had dared to aim for both. A biologist and mother of
three recalled:

> A: I wanted to be a medical doctor from age nine or ten. I also
> wanted to be a nurse or a scientist.

Q: What about marriage and children?

A: I wanted that, too. I wanted everything. I did expect to have everything.

Focusing on work and career did not preclude wanting marriage and children as well, but it did involve avoiding a thorough assessment of the contradictions inherent in such desires. For those who wanted "everything," the easiest way to deal with the potential problems of combining career and family was to postpone facing them. An ex-schoolteacher and full-time mother described this common strategy of postponement:

A: I expected to have some kind of career, but I also expected to be starting my family sooner than it worked out I did. My plans were tremendously vague. I really believed that I could have it all. I mean, I was unrealistic about how much time all the various facets of one's life take.

This hospital administrator awaiting the birth of her first child was just beginning to confront the dilemmas of combining work and motherhood that she had repressed in the past:

A: I was going to be in the foreign service. Then [in college] I was starting to think, "How does all that fit in with being married and having a family?" I don't think I was willing then to make any conscious choice between the two and somehow figured everything would work out, just ignore the fact that maybe there's a decision to make between the two. Occasionally I'd think about them, but I'd usually shunt them aside because at the time I wasn't really faced with deciding.

Of course, in the long run these issues must be faced—if not consciously and deliberately, then by default. For most women, resolving these ambiguities and dilemmas proved harder than formulating childhood hopes.

Ambivalence and Change

This chapter has examined the models, messages, contexts, and early aspirations of the respondents as children and adolescents. It has argued that early childhood experiences are *under*determining. Taken alone, they poorly predict and do not explain adult behavior or orientations.

First, parental models and messages tend to bear a weak relationship to children's later life choices. Mothers, fathers, and the wider familial and social environment had often offered mixed, ambiguous, and even contradictory messages to the respondents as children and adolescents. In addition, children selectively filtered these messages, perceiving and responding to them on their own terms. Over time, if events and circumstances promoted or allowed it, some respondents "distanced" themselves from their childhood, psychologically and socially, as well as temporally.

Second, even as children and adolescents, these women had experienced a wide variety of hopes, ambitions, and attitudes toward becoming mothers and workers. Some felt strong desires to bear children; others felt weak desires for or even a strong aversion to motherhood. Some were highly oriented toward work or career; others rarely gave work a thought. The richness of this variety alone flies in the face of most accounts of early female socialization, whether conservative or feminist in character, which argue that most little girls are successfully encouraged to focus on becoming wives, mothers, and homemakers to the exclusion of other adult pursuits. Yet the acquisition of domestic aspirations as children neither accurately describes this group as a whole nor satisfactorily explains its members' later life choices and goals.

Third, as these women matured, they dealt with the mixed messages of their childhoods in a variety of ways. Ambivalence, confusion, and the postponement of final decisions were among the more common responses. Thus, a childless, divorced teacher wondered at her childhood idealism, for she had assumed that she would have a career and, that if she had children, they would be cared for by a babysitter: "But," she stated, "I didn't understand what a career takes out of you."

This thirty-one-year-old physician, also single and childless, reviewed the contorted route she took toward and then away from work as she began to face the costs of a career:

A: The reality of not having gotten married [in my early twenties] brought up the fear of not ever getting married, and that was a threat. So, I dropped out. A career was too threatening. [I was feeling] that it would be too much of a demand, that I would have to suppress too much of my other interests and personal life. And I remember very vividly such a question in my mind: I don't know that I can be the kind of professional, the kind of wife and mother, and the kind of person that I want to be, and I didn't see the three as complementing. I saw them severely in conflict. And I was very depressed, very, very depressed.

Eventually, however, all women confront the conflict between work and family. Given a context that is rife with contradictory signals, understanding how and why they choose to affirm one model, message, or path over others becomes critical.

As Table 5 demonstrates, among those who reported domestic childhood aspirations, only 33 percent were oriented toward domesticity as adults. Among those reporting some form of nondomestic early aspirations and expectations, a full 63 percent became domestically oriented as adults. Remarkably, change was more common than stability, and this result is not an artifact of the college-educated sample: The proportion of changers to nonchangers is even higher among the high school–educated group.

Those with college degrees were slightly more likely to begin adulthood with a nondomestic orientation than were those who possessed only high school degrees. This is hardly surprising, given the link between going to college and expecting a good education to lead to occupational rewards. However, as the data in Table 5 demonstrate, at the time of the interview some ten to twenty years later, the proportion of the group with a domestic baseline who retained domestic orientations in adulthood was higher among those with college degrees than among those without them. Similarly, the proportion with a nondomestic baseline heading in a domestic direction was higher among the high school–educated group. Thus, overall, the proportion with domestic current orientations and future plans had evened out considerably across levels of education. In general, and of greatest significance, *both* educational groups show notable change over time in life goals and orientations—whether the movement was in a domestic or nondomestic direction. Respondents with similar baselines veered in different directions, and respondents with different baselines veered in similar directions. (Percentages in Table 5 and elsewhere are presented to show the general contours of change and stability and the

Table 5 *Percent Currently Domestic by Baseline Orientation and Educational Level*

	Domestic Baseline	Nondomestic Baseline	All Respondents
High school degree	25%	75%	46%
	(16)	(12)	(28)
College degree	41	56	49
	(17)	(18)	(35)
All respondents	33	63	48
	(33)	(30)	(63)

NOTE: The total N for each cell is in parentheses.

general direction in which change occurred. The sample is, of course, too small to interpret the actual numbers as representative or statistically significant or to infer their significance for larger groups.)

In light of these findings, the process of change and the factors that facilitate or hinder adult change become the proper focus of a study of women's choices. The respondents themselves often hinted at the importance of this process, although in most instances they were not consciously aware of it.

> A: You think, when you're young, that's the way life is going to be for me, because I'm female and I'm going to get married and have kids. You change.

This respondent is referring to change that led her away from motherhood and into the world of work and heightened work aspirations. Others found themselves moving in the opposite direction—away from the workplace and toward exclusive motherhood. The next two chapters examine the adult decision-making process and untangle the forces that led some women toward domesticity and others away from it. Their stories show why things did not turn out as planned for many and what distinguishes these women from those whose early expectations were realized. These stories also show that early life experiences may foreshadow adult tensions and conflicts but do not dictate how these conflicts will be dealt with later in life. This depends on the experience of adulthood itself.

4 | *Veering Away from Domesticity*

This chapter examines the events, experiences, and processes that led some respondents to veer away from childbearing, child rearing, and domesticity and toward strong work commitments in adulthood. The events that marked significant turning points in the lives of these women deserve attention for two reasons. They not only shed light on the process of change, but they also help explain why some lives were *not* marked by significant change. An analysis of change-inducing events highlights the often hidden and taken-for-granted factors that promote stability and inhibit change over the adult life courses of many women.

Although we will be examining both the causes and the processes of individual change, this analysis makes no assumptions about either the speed or the consciousness of change, both of which are variable. Some women may change gradually, so that the fact of change itself is imperceptible. Others may be subjected to experiences so compelling that rapid change is not only necessary, but also self-evident. Thus, both the speed and the awareness of change vary substantially among respondents. In addition, the act of reconstruction may encourage some to speed up in their own recollections what was actually a slower process. The turning points analyzed in this and the next chapter, then, do not necessarily refer to sudden, conscious changes in life direction. The speed of change may vary from gradual to rapid. Change may also occur without the conscious awareness of the individual undergoing change. In the long run, however, the fact of change matters more than its form.

Rising Work Aspirations and Family Ambivalence

Among those women who began their adult lives with traditional (if sometimes vague) notions of domesticity as their ultimate goal, two-thirds developed nondomestic orientations as their lives proceeded. Over time, these respondents developed strong ties to the workplace and usually high ambitions as well. As their attachment to the labor force rose, they were progressively less inclined to want to bear or care daily for children or to define themselves as homemakers. This group, above all others, exemplifies the processes and structural underpinnings of the subtle revolution now occurring in women's lives.

An unanticipated encounter with the structure of opportunities either at home or at work almost always triggered the change in these women's life direction. Such an experience tended to shake up their assumptions about the world, themselves, and their options; it prompted them to reevaluate past choices and plans and to reorient themselves toward a different future. In general, four kinds of events, either alone or together, triggered change in the nontraditional direction: instability in male-female relationships, perceived pressures on the family economy, dissatisfaction with domesticity, and expanded workplace opportunities. The first three pushed women from the home; the fourth pulled them away from it.

Fragility and Impermanence of Relationships

The experience of instability in marriage or in a heterosexual relationship was one of the most powerful and disorienting events initiating a process of reassessment and change away from domesticity.[1] Idealized notions of home and children tended to disappear quickly when male support for such options collapsed or failed to materialize. This childless secretary in her mid-thirties reported how more realistic

1. No respondents were openly homosexual, and none claimed or appeared to be "in the closet." It remains the task of future research to specify the ways in which sexual preference shapes women's fertility and work choices.

plans replaced her idealized vision of domesticity when a long-term relationship shattered:

A: I really got seriously involved, and I thought, "Well, in the future we'll settle down, and we'll have children." This went on for about three and a half years. The possibility of marriage had arisen, but the relationship didn't end very well. I guess it was a good experience in a way, because I suppose it showed me the typical thing of women when they suppress their own desires and let the man's desire be supreme. When I look back on it, I see that that situation wasn't right for me. It was probably good it did break up, even though, you know, those things are painful. But I think from that experience also I could see that this white knight on the dark charger was not going to come up and carry me away into the great, glorious sunset. I'm more realistic now.

The realization that a man would not always be there to care for them led respondents to conclude that self-reliance was the only reasonable alternative. When they were faced with the necessity of remaining or becoming independent for an indefinite period of time, work took on greater importance.

If the breakup of an extended relationship channeled heretofore diffused energies into work, then the breakup of a marriage tended to have an even stronger impact. Faced with the need for economic self-reliance, this respondent, during the process of divorcing, went from being a maid to running a small company:

A: I moved to Utah with my husband. We decided the time together was more important than my career. He was an airline pilot. I worked six hours a day, six days a week at a ski lodge. I was the head chambermaid; I cleaned toilets and made beds. Then we returned to California, which I considered my home. That's when we were separated, for two years, and were divorced three years ago. And that's when I really consider I started working for myself, with a career in mind, that I was going to support myself. This is the way it was, and I'd better get busy doing something that was meaningful, that had a future as well as an income.

When the marriage had been especially unpleasant, the desire not to repeat the experience prompted many divorced women to reassess the definition of work itself. Divorce led this mother of two to decide that working for meager pay as a clerk was no longer enough:

Q: When did those feelings of wanting a career start to develop?

A: When I decided that getting married wasn't what I wanted, which was after the divorce. Or if I did, it would have to be a super-special person. Before that it was just a job to keep us going.

Thus, divorce not only undermined respondents' faith in marriage, it also forced previously unambitious women to reexamine their commitment to paid work and to place better pay and a more satisfying job higher on their list of priorities.

For some, divorce triggered not only stronger ties to work but also an even larger reassessment of their life plan. When work came to be seen as a lifelong reality rather than as just a time killer before marriage and motherhood, a whole new outlook emerged for this divorced, childless administrative assistant who lacked a college degree:

Q: Why did you decide to pursue a career?

A: Oh, there are so many reasons. One was my divorce and suddenly being faced with being single again, and being more selective if I should get married. The fact that basically I *am* ambitious. I don't want to stay doing remedial jobs. I like to learn, basically, which I never realized until I became serious about my life.

In addition to sparking work ambitions and promoting the discovery of talents and interests that had been previously hidden or suppressed, the breakup of a relationship also altered feelings and plans about childbearing. For many who experienced such transitions, plans to bear children changed into plans to postpone or forgo children altogether. Because most defined marriage as a prerequisite to childbearing, the dissolution of a marital bond often entailed reassessing plans for childbearing as well as work. This childless ex-teacher recalled that the need for personal survival overrode her fears that divorce meant childlessness:

Q: During all the time you were married, did you ever consider having a child?

A: Yeah. I considered it. I remember they were passing out health insurance in a staff meeting at school, and you could get maternal coverage for X more dollars, and I sat there thinking, "Do I want to have a kid?" By that time I was twenty-six, and I thought, "Oh, what if I never had kids?" But at the same time, it just wasn't the time. Our marriage was rocky. I was also seeing that wives of biochemists made lousy mothers because they took out their neuroses on their kids, and I didn't want to do that to any kid; so I was

beginning to question whether indeed I would have
children. I was ambivalent. . . . It was a survival thing to get
out of that marriage. I would have gone nuts if I had stayed
there.

In the case of those whose childbearing strategy had been postponement, the process of deciding whether or not to have a child was
often so slow that a favorable decision simply came too late. By the
time this childless high school teacher concluded that she did indeed
want children, she no longer had the means to accomplish this goal:

A: When I was thirty-two or thirty-three, I didn't get pregnant
     I went to a gynecologist and finally found out, *here's* what
     you do to get pregnant. And that was about the same time
     my father died, and I started thinking about what my life
     was really all about and whether I was happy living it, and
     I became very dissatisfied. All this introspection made me
     very unhappy with my marriage. And about the time I
     discovered what I had to do to have a child, I discovered
     that perhaps this wasn't the right father for my child. At
     that time, I was thirty-five years old. And now it's just too
     late.

Wanting a child in the abstract is thus not enough. Most were willing
to become mothers only in partnership with someone they perceived
to be a potentially suitable father.[2]

Even short of divorce, a shaky marriage had a substantial effect on
decisions about children and work. The threat of a breakup also initiated a process of reassessment and led some away from motherhood
and toward a greater emphasis upon work as a career. A temporary
separation thus led this childless librarian to a critical juncture—where
she chose to begin a law career instead of having a baby:

Q: What went into your decision to go to law school?

A: It was a decision to change what I was doing at the time
     more than anything else. And there are a lot of things that
     went into the decision. Doug and I had not been getting
     along very well, and had split up for a couple of months,
     which I'm sure entered into it very strongly. I was thinking
     about the future, and I think I probably decided that it was
     time I set up my life the way I wanted it. I think the fact that

___

2. The varying definitions women offered for "suitable father" are presented and
analyzed in detail in Chapters Five, Six, and Seven. For the present discussion, suffice
it to say that these definitions varied with the different circumstances women faced and
the differing orientations to parenthood they developed.

we were on shaky ground had a lot to do with it. I thought
I'd be wise to go into this career that I had wanted to do;
it's a more independent thing than I was doing before.
Children are one of those things that I was thinking about
at the same time. Like maybe we'll just have some kids
instead, and that will sort of work things out.

Thus, in most cases, the decision to establish greater commitment
to work involved not one, but two related choices: the choice to take
work more seriously *and* the choice to forgo bearing a child, at least
for the present. A decision to postpone bearing children also usually
implied a decision to enter or become more closely tied to the workplace. Both decisions postponed domesticity, allowing time for other
experiences to occur and other options to develop that could potentially alter the long-term balance of incentives between home and work.

Economic Squeezes in the Household

Instability in marriage or sexual relationships is only one among a
number of factors that triggered shifts in women's choices and orientations. Even if a marriage was lasting and stable, other circumstances propelled some women away from domesticity.

A perceived squeeze on the income of the one-paycheck household
also could restructure women's choices, even among the stably married. This inability of the male income alone to support a family at
the level a couple had come to define as acceptable had a dual impact
on married women. First, whether or not they had young children, it
pushed married women into the work force and toward stronger work
ties. In addition, despite the presence of a spouse, it limited married
women's fertility options. Children became both expensive in their
own right and an added burden in a marriage where both partners
had to work.

Thus, although those who remained strongly motivated to have
children still planned to do so, the most common short-run response
to a felt economic squeeze was to delay an affirmative decision and to
reject the immediate inclination to have a child. This childless worker
rejected pregnancy in favor of a job she disliked because of financial
uncertainty and the need for her income:

A: We moved to a very, very small town that didn't have any
      [jobs]. . . . I worked for McDonald's and absolutely *hated* it.
      At that point, I didn't doubt that I was good at what I could
      do, that I was a responsible person; yet they made me feel
      very poor.

Q: Did you think about quitting and having kids instead?

A: Steve was getting out of the service at that point. We were very unsure of what would be happening to us later on, had no medical coverage, that type of thing.

A decision to resist pregnancy temporarily in order to work usually seemed small and inconsequential at the time, a mere postponement of an ultimate decision in favor of motherhood. The final result, however, was often the opposite of this early expectation, as this secretary approaching thirty explained:

A: There was a time when I wanted a child, yes. We thought it would be really neat to have one child. When I was about twenty-five, twenty-six, we talked about it, but it never materialized. At that time, we couldn't afford it, and time kept passing and passing. Now it's too late, and we still can't afford it now. It's just awful. I don't see how people do it.

A strategy of postponement, then, can start one down a path that may lead in an unanticipated direction. It allows time for new opportunities to arise and changes to occur. Thus, this respondent ultimately opted for permanent childlessness:

Q: If you could afford it now, would you want to have a child?

A: It's beyond that now. We wouldn't at this point. I want to work. I'm too old, I guess. I just don't have any urges to raise a baby now. I want to be able to just pick up and go when I want to, selfish reasons.

Childless women were not the only group susceptible to this kind of economic constraint. The addition of a child to a household may make it inconvenient for a woman to work, but it also increases a family's financial needs. Thus, some young mothers, too, often found that, contrary to their domestic expectations, they had to go to work permanently. This mother of two was surprised to find herself back at work soon after the birth of her first child:

Q: So you had a child and then decided to get a job at your husband's urging?

A: At that point, we realized that, in order to really live comfortably, I'd have to have some sort of a job.

Note here the phrase "live comfortably." What people perceive their financial needs to be may be distinguished from actual level of wealth or income. Middle-class families were as likely as working-class families to experience economic squeezes, especially when they faced a potential drop in their standard of living or a gap between their expected and real economic statuses. Economic factors that pushed women out of the home were thus not strictly related to class position or income level and members of each class experienced varying degrees of economic stress (see Table 7 in Chapter Five). Above a certain minimum level, actual income was less important in shaping long-run choices than was a woman's ability to find satisfying work as an alternative to domesticity. A woman's exposure (or lack of exposure) to genuine workplace opportunities strongly influenced her *perceptions* of economic need and her motivation to meet felt needs by working at a paid job.

Thus, although a return to work after the birth of a child or a postponement of childbearing in order to continue working may have been unwelcome at the time it occurred, whether it remained so in the long run depended on what happened in the workplace. If work proved stifling and unpleasant, the desire to return to domesticity tended to grow. If work turned out to be an unexpected pleasure, then an earlier constraint was transformed into an opportunity. As one working mother put it:

> A: The choices I made did not follow what my parents did,
> as I look back on it. I don't think that was necessarily good,
> what they did. It was mainly for financial reasons that I
> went back to do something, but my husband said off and on
> that I would not have been happy, or he would not have
> been happy with me, if I had not had something else
> to do. . . . I've learned a lot more by working.

In conclusion, perceived economic squeezes in the household economy of married couples had both direct and indirect effects on women's fertility and work choices. These squeezes did not affect women's childbearing activities as the result of some strictly economic cost-benefit accounting, as some economists argue.[3] Nor did such squeezes automatically tie women to the labor force permanently. Instead, they combined with other factors in a less immediate and obvious process. Felt economic squeezes encouraged the postponement of fertility decisions and provided an incentive to try new avenues, where, over time, exposure to unexpected experiences promoted personal change and the redirection of life goals.

Finally, economic squeezes are as rooted in perceptions and expectations as they are in actual economic circumstances. There appears

---

3. Becker's "human capital" approach to understanding marital and fertility behavior views children as economic commodities and fertility choices as the result of rational processes of economic decision making (1960, 1965, 1981). See Sawhill (1977) and Blake (1968) for overviews and critiques of this perspective; see Huber and Spitze (1980, 1983) for an example of a more sociological approach to Becker's work.

to be a rising imbalance across the class structure between families' economic aspirations and husbands' salaries. In addition, decisions about bearing and rearing children are usually made when most workers, both male and female, are still in the early stages of their earning careers. As a result, income tends to be low, but family costs (for example, housing and child-rearing expenses) tend to be high, creating a "life cycle squeeze" (see Oppenheimer, 1974, 1982; Wilensky, 1981). This clash between needs and resources accentuates the felt erosion of the purchasing power of the single, male paycheck and promotes strategies of postponement, limitations of family size, and even permanent childlessness.

Domestic Isolation and Devaluation

Ironically, the very act of becoming a housewife or mother also set in motion a process of change that led some women out of the home. Among those who had expected to find fulfillment in traditional pursuits, finally realizing these domestic goals was a revelation in itself. A life defined exclusively by housework (in the case of childless women who experienced periods when they were out of work) or motherhood (in the case of women who bore children) did not turn out to be all that some women with traditional baselines had expected. Disappointment with the reality of domesticity thus encouraged these respondents to change their orientations toward work and family.

Boredom, a sense of isolation and exclusion, and a lack of direction or purpose were common reactions to domesticity. However surprising such a discovery seemed, it often led to a new understanding and definition of the self. It also usually led to stronger work commitment. Witness, for example, the experiences of this childless woman in her late twenties:

A: At the time I got married (eighteen, real young), I didn't see [working] indefinitely. As it progressed, I saw it indefinitely, yes.

Q: When did your attitude change?

A: I don't know exactly when it did; probably at about twenty-one or so. I got more aware of, I don't know, more aware of myself and what I manage with my own self. I have had various times within my working career that I have not worked for a couple of months or so. During that time I never accomplished the things I always said I was going to accomplish. . . . Then I go back to work, and I see all those things I was going to do when I wasn't working. Somewhere

along the line, I realized that I'm that type of person. . . . I
can get bored very easily. . . . I like to go out and work.

The experience of working offered a comparative perspective from
which to view domesticity. When the work experience was pleasant
and nurturing, staying home felt like a demotion, a step backward
from the adult world. In this context, rather than being a source of
fulfillment, a baby came to be seen as the reason for confinement to
the home and thus the means for the diminishment, rather than the
enhancement, of self-worth. Motherhood threatened to impose not
only isolation, but also, and perhaps worse, personal denigration. This
perceived danger prompted some respondents to reject domesticity
and potentially motherhood as well, as this twenty-nine-year-old,
childless secretary reported:

A: I don't think [children] would improve what I think of
     myself. I would just probably be relegated to the drudgery
     of the house. I wouldn't be able to get out in offices and out
     in the world and keep abreast of everything that's going on
     in the business world, thinking all the time and stuff like
     that. Anybody can have a baby.

If temporary periods of confinement to the home tended to trigger
a process of insight and reassessment, then becoming a mother for
the first time had an even stronger impact on those who discovered
that the reality of motherhood differed markedly from their expectations. Rossi (1968) points out that, by insulating adults from children
and families from each other, the modern industrial system obscures
the realities of parenthood for those who have never reared children.
This unrealistic context leaves most new parents ill-prepared for the
arrival of a first child and the vast changes in their self-definitions and
daily activities this event requires. Thus when hopes for personal fulfillment did not materialize with the birth of a child, newly formed
career ambitions often emerged to offset the disappointment these
women found in mothering. In the following instance, having her first
child did not dampen this clerk's work goals, as she had anticipated;
rather, it led her to aim for a better job that commanded greater
respect and offered better future prospects:

A: I didn't realize until after Danny was born that I really liked
     working. I thought that after I had children I would stay
     home. But after working for so long, I couldn't get adjusted
     to cleaning house. It was really difficult. I needed to be
     around other people my age or in business, working. I went
     through a really hard time, didn't know who I was, what I
     wanted. I came to the conclusion that I liked to work. I don't

know why, my independence, I guess. I didn't want to stay
the same thing all the time. I wanted to go further. I knew
I wanted a family, I knew I wanted to be married, [but] I
wanted to be not just a clerk. If I was going back to work,
I was going to be the boss [laughter]. If I was going back
to work, it was going to be for something better than what
I had.

Thus, once a psychological switch is made from a temporary and
tenuous to a permanent and strong commitment to work, the willingness to settle for just "any" job diminishes. Among respondents who
made this switch, ambition grew when domesticity was experienced as
a dead-end street. Rising workplace aspirations were often accompanied by a newfound courage to stand up for oneself and make
demands at work, as this same respondent related:

A: When I came back from my maternity leave, I kind of stood
     up for myself and went in and told my new boss that,
     because of my experience, I thought I should be upgraded
     to the job that he had left. He upgraded me; it really kind of
     surprised me. So I came back.

The experience of isolation at home and disillusionment with the
reality of mothering led some not only back to the workplace and to
heightened career ambitions, but also out of marriage altogether. In
the context of her dissatisfaction with domesticity, this new mother
decided old constraints and ground rules were unacceptable. As she
confronted the frustration of full-time mothering, she rejected her
husband along with her plans for more children, and she traded these
domestic ties for rising work aspirations:

A: I hated staying home. I had a very small child that did
     nothing but eat, shit, and sleep. Excuse me, but that's what
     she did. It was boring. Little babies aren't what people tell
     you they will be. There isn't a whole hell of a lot you can
     do with a child four or five months old. They are not
     particularly responsive to anyone's needs except their own.
     It's a hell of an adjustment. Nobody ever tells you about
     all the work that is involved, the sleepless nights. They
     lie to you. My mother told me my prince would come
     [laughter]. . . . At the time, my husband wanted to have
     more children, and I started taking a good long look at
     myself, and what I really wanted, and decided that this
     wasn't what I wanted to do for the rest of my life. I tried
     staying home six months. I was ready for the looney farm.

I'm not a homebody. That's when the marriage really went bad. We were just totally unsuited to each other. [And] that's when the career started to become important.

Even the anticipation of domestic isolation and devaluation propelled some in the direction of work before they gave the domestic option a chance. A bank clerk, single and childless at thirty, pondered the negative consequences she feared homemaking would entail:

Q: Did you ever think about marrying somebody and having him work while you stay home with kids?

A: I thought about that [laughter]. But my mother says once you've worked as long as I've worked, you'd never be able to stay home, which is probably true because you get to the point where you enjoy getting out of the house. And I'm not one for staying home and doing nothing.

When women focused on the costs of domesticity, they often viewed marriage itself as a trap that foreclosed other, more desirable possibilities. These fears resemble the fears men have traditionally expressed concerning marriage as a trap (see Ehrenreich, 1983; Fiedler, 1966). Given Bernard's (1972) findings that married men fare better mentally and physically than single men, but married women fare worse than single women, women's fears may more accurately reflect marriage's dangers.

Whether it was experienced directly or viewed from afar, the isolation and devaluation of domestic life affected these women's choices in two ways: Their desire to bear and care for children diminished, while work ambitions became a new and increasingly powerful motivating force in their lives.

Expanded Work Opportunities

However powerful the forces that pushed domestically oriented women out of the home, a newly emerging nondomestic orientation was sustained in the long run only when these pushes were supported by strong pulls into the workplace. Otherwise, the desire to return to domestic pursuits grew with time. Access to work offering a sense of accomplishment, upward movement toward a goal, and significant material and emotional rewards critically influenced the process of developing strong ties to the workplace, heightened work aspirations, and a growing ambivalence toward domestic pursuits. How, then, did some women gain access to a job that, unlike traditional "women's work," contains both the rewards and the demands inherent in what

Table 6   *Occupation by Education*

	College Degree (N = 35)	High School Degree (N = 28)	Total (N = 63)
Female-dominated occupations			
Clerical, service, sales	17%	89%	49%
Teachers, nurses, librarians, and other "female" professions	37	—	21
Male-dominated occupations			
Business and administration	26	11	19
Law, medicine, and other "male" professions	20	—	11

NOTE: All nurses received a two-year college degree. Those respondents not currently employed are classified according to last job held.

is usually termed a career? (See Caplow, 1954, and Wilensky, 1960, for discussions of the empirical and theoretical differences between job and career.) And how did getting work of this sort influence a woman's motivations to work, to bear children, and to change her self-definition and orientation?

Mobility Routes and Class Position.   Over two-thirds of the women who expressed rising aspirations toward nontraditional pursuits experienced some form of upward mobility out of dead-end jobs, and especially out of job categories dominated by females. The routes they took, however, differed by class. Just as occupation is closely linked to educational level and general class position, so, too, are advancement routes out of "women's work."[4] As Table 6 demonstrates, college-educated respondents tended to be spread across a variety of occupations and professions, but high school–educated respondents were concentrated in the female labor ghettos of clerical, service, and sales occupations. Accordingly, how respondents who moved up at work were exposed to opportunities for advancement differed by educational group.

4. Although it is reasonable to define class position solely on the basis of occupational status, a definition based primarily upon educational level is more appropriate here because the sample was drawn according to this criterion. This sampling procedure yielded a number of college-educated respondents who presently or last held "working-class" jobs in the female-dominated clerical, service, and sales sectors of the labor market but who nevertheless do not clearly qualify as members of the working class by virtue of their educational background, their husbands' occupations, and their total family income (see Table 6). In any case, the label is less important than the social processes that affected both groups.

The college-educated women gained occupational mobility by changing their jobs or professions, typically from work in a female-dominated occupation to work in a male-dominated one. Those without college degrees were more likely to find their opportunities constrained by the structure and policies of the organizations for which they worked. For these respondents, expanding work opportunities resulted from promotion within the bureaucratic hierarchy that characterized their work setting. Thus, although college-educated respondents were able to advance through active choice and a conscious decision to change, those high school–educated respondents fortunate enough to move upward at work were typically dependent on the work organization itself.

Occupational advancement among the college-educated usually involved a decision to avoid or switch from a traditional female occupation in order to join a traditionally male one. This decision implied a critical change in the way these respondents viewed work; instead of aiming for "just a job," their occupational goals shifted to the pursuit of a career. Although the choice to turn away from fields dominated by women and seek careers in areas they had once defined as out of bounds was usually conscious and deliberate, it was by no means straightforward. Often these respondents concluded that they *wanted* careers only after a long process of trying out traditional female options, pondering the desirability of other alternatives, and discovering fortuitously that they could hold their own in male occupations.

Typically, these respondents started down a traditional female path and were diverted by some event or series of events. In the following case, a nursery school teacher who was biding her time before having children while her husband finished his education discovered almost by chance that she had skills and ambitions of which she had been unaware:

A: I worked for years as an elementary and a nursery school teacher. It was fun for a while, but I sure didn't want to spend my life as a nursery school teacher. It was a status thing, too, and the money was not enough. At the same time, I was county coordinator for a political campaign, coordinating four thousand volunteers. I discovered I had lots of skills and talents I didn't know I had. It was a tremendous amount of work, and I really got involved with it. I was supervising twenty-six people. I did a great job, and I was getting tons of strokes and feeling good about myself, and there was this whole new me I didn't know existed. And this was on top of teaching, and I wasn't too sure of myself anymore. So it was just like a whole new world, a whole new me. It was fantastic. It really kind of changed my life.

Many tried a traditional female occupation but found it unacceptable. The lack of status, challenge, or personal control on the job felt demeaning after years of schooling. Years as a secretary doing work few appreciated propelled this childless worker into a nontraditional field:

Q: What made you decide to go to medical school?

A: I had no future in terms of income, no future in terms of interesting work. What I was doing was boring. I was doing stat work for other people, and it was totally unchallenging. I knew I had more to offer something, someplace, someone than merely doing somebody else's work. I had a big sign on the wall that said, if you're doing what people regard as an insignificant, stupid job, people will think that you are insignificant and stupid. And that holds true. Everybody assumed I was a secretary-typist and that was my potential, my level. I hated it. I really resented it.

Still others found themselves in situations where they worked closely with male professionals. Once in a working environment with these men, they realized that they held exaggerated images of what it takes to be a professional in a male-dominated field. Given a basis for real comparison, they were surprised to find themselves equal or even superior to their male colleagues and easily capable of performing similar tasks. Armed with this new information, they reconsidered jobs that they had previously sifted out of the pool of possibilities. This ex-librarian took a circuitous route to law school:

A: After I went to library school, I got a job working at a law library. I did research and editing and things like that. They always hired law students for the summer, and I was supervising them. It dawned on me that I was just as smart as they were, and I liked what they were doing more than what I was doing. I'm sure I probably never would have gone to law school if I hadn't worked there. It was a real eye-opener.

These unanticipated experiences triggered the growth of ambitions and self-confidence that had been suppressed, as they often are for women. These discoveries led in turn to highly consequential actions. Because they were not already hampered by heavy family responsibilities and because their education and class resources provided the necessary skills and financial bases upon which to move into professional careers, these women were able to act on their new insights and emerging desires.

Circumstances, however, are often not so propitious. Without economic and educational supports, it is difficult to translate a newfound aspiration into an actual career choice. Those who lacked college degrees typically faced this more constrained situation. For working-class respondents, the range of job options was limited and the freedom to choose among them circumscribed. They were, therefore, far more dependent than their college-educated counterparts on the structure of the workplace itself for both the discovery of new insights and access to work that could nourish and support developing capacities.

For those who lacked college degrees, unanticipated promotion within a firm was more likely to heighten career aspirations and work commitment than were self-conscious attempts to better their occupational position. Although their experiences are far from the norm for working-class women, these respondents took jobs without the expectation of moving ahead, only later to find that upward movement was both possible and actually being offered to them. This bank loan officer began as a teller almost on a whim:

Q: How did you get into banking?

A: [I] didn't know what I was going to do, didn't know what I wanted to do. I went to an employment agency. I went on these totally ridiculous job interviews. Finally, someone said, "Gee, would you like to be a banker?" I thought, "That sounds pretty good." I went on an interview, and they tested me, and they hired me on the spot. I was a teller-trainee. I've been a teller off and on for the last ten years.

Q: How did you get promoted to assistant loan officer?

A: We went through a transition. We had one guy who was in charge, the big boss who was totally against women in any sort of managerial positions. He wouldn't have a woman loan officer. When he left, we had a guy who was totally different. We had a woman who was a full vice-president with an MBA, a woman loan officer, a woman operations officer. It changed for me, too. The chance was there to advance if you worked really hard. He would recognize your talents or abilities. Now I tell them, "Someday I'm going to be chairman of the board!"

These unanticipated opportunities were generated by the changing structure of work organizations, which have faced increasing social and legislative pressure to cease discriminating against female employees. The unsuspecting individual who fortuitously joined an organization with affirmative action employment policies saw these opportunities as chance or good fortune. Nontraditional aspirations developed, however, not from chance, but from structural arrangements at work. Without the experience of upward mobility, which was rooted in the structure of the work organization itself, high work ambitions and commitment would probably not have emerged.

Because these expanded opportunities seemed fortuitous, some women felt an urge to resist advancement. Change, no matter how good it may turn out to be, tends to shake up accustomed, comfortable assumptions and self-images. Thus, some viewed even positive change as unwelcome, threatening, and dangerous.[5] But with time, most overcame this initial resistance and chose to take advantage of the opportunity for change, almost invariably with positive consequences. An ex-clerk overcame initial fear as she gradually assumed managerial responsibilities:

> A: [When they] started developing me for management, I
> didn't have any confidence in myself. When I first was told I
> was going to be covering for my supervisor, it frightened me
> so much I thought I was going to be sick for two days,
> because I just didn't know if I could do it. Finally, in the
> end, I just decided that I was going to do it because it was
> the only way I'd get over the fear. Now it's a snap. [If they
> told me I couldn't go higher], then I'd leave.

Expanded work opportunities fueled the ambitions and work commitment of the college-educated and high school–educated alike. They took different roads, but these roads led in the same direction toward similar ends. However they happened upon it, these respondents found unexpected success in their lives as workers. This success became inviting and seductive.

These women did not behave according to Horner's "motive to avoid success" syndrome (Horner, 1972). Most greeted their newfound and unexpected success enthusiastically. Among those who did fear the changes that advancement at work imposed, this emotion neither exhausted their range of motivations nor prevented them from succeeding. To the contrary, most who initially resisted expanding opportunities overcame their fear or moved ahead in spite of it. Those

---

5. Marris (1974) describes how the process of change, even when it is positive, can be extremely painful and difficult to negotiate. He argues that it tends to provoke a "conservative impulse" to hold onto the past. Under the right circumstances, however, an individual will work through a process that involves grieving, letting go of the past, and ultimately adjusting to the new situation.

who ultimately declined advancement opportunities had powerful incentives to do so, as the next chapter shows.[6]

Consequences of Expanding Work Opportunities.   Whatever the route taken, expanded work opportunities changed most who were exposed to them. Work opportunity altered not only the motive to work, but feelings and decisions about children and marriage and personal assessments of ability as well.

Psychologically, work was transformed from a time killer and means of survival into a source of challenge and reward. Work accomplishment became a primary life goal, and tenuous work ties grew strong. As this process occurred, both ambition and self-confidence grew. This ex–office manager thus developed a new sense of worth along with a new career:

A: I got my present job very fortuitously, and I've made the transition from a semiprofessional administrative assistant into a very professional vice-presidential executive. And now I feel I can go just about anyplace in the U.S. and get a job as a middle management executive, even though I've no formal training.

Building a career also had ramifications that extended far beyond the work sphere. Investing greater time, energy, and self-definition in a job inevitably upset the earlier balance at home as well. As new resources were discovered at work, for example, some decided that male domination at home, which they had once accepted without question, was no longer tolerable. An independent base at work provided both a source of power and an avenue of escape, enabling some to redefine their marriages or sexual partnerships as unacceptably oppressive. Thus, expanding workplace opportunities not only nourished ambition; they also broke apart the established order at home— especially when this order had been built upon a woman's acceptance of male dominance. Support at work gave this upwardly mobile phone company employee the courage to demand equality at home and leave when she could not attain it:

A: When I first got married, I was very passive and very withdrawn. . . . But one day I said, "Hey, wait a minute. I am

6. Subsequent studies have cast serious doubt on the validity of Horner's findings (see, for example, Kaufman and Richardson, 1982; Miller and Garrison, 1982; Weitzman, 1979; Zuckerman and Wheeler, 1975). These studies show that fear of success applies to both sexes, is not consistently present in either sex, tends to be elicited only in situations where people expect negative consequences, and, when present, is not consistently related to either academic achievement or career choice.

a person. I have ideas. I have my own thoughts, my own mind." And when I stopped taking orders, trouble started. . . . One particular supervisor was developing me on the job because she recognized certain potentials and made me realize them in myself. Because my husband had made me feel so inferior, I was at a point where I felt I was stupid, wasn't capable of doing things.

Encouragement at work thus fed an undernourished self-image. A new sense of self-confidence, in turn, reverberated into the private sphere and undermined home influences that had held some respondents back. The ultimate result in these cases was a power struggle that often ended in divorce and abruptly altered fertility plans.

When divorce occurred, the effects on fertility were obvious: A postponed child never resulted from that marriage. But when the marriage remained intact, increased work opportunities still influenced fertility decisions. At critical points when dissatisfaction with work made the prospect of bearing children an attractive alternative, a well-timed promotion tended to reinforce the choice for a career even among the stably married. This twenty-nine-year-old, childless computer programmer chose a promotion over a child even though she was committed to her marriage:

A: I've been with my job seven years. I started out as a keypunch operator–secretary, and I moved up to supervisor, and then programmer trainee. There was a point when I thought I wanted to quit because I had started to tire of the whole business. Right about that time I thought, "I'll work a little bit more and then start having children.". . . I kind of felt like I wanted to quit work and see what other things in life were like.

Q: Why did you stay?

A: Because my boss asked me if I wanted to be a programmer trainee. . . . And I've really liked my job ever since, as a programmer and now as a programmer analyst.

Upward mobility at work thus supported the postponement of childbearing and often left ultimate decisions in question. Another computer programmer concluded:

A: I'm not sure how convinced I was when I was younger that I was really going to work. It was a fluke I got this job at all because I had no training. I could have ended up being a salesgirl. But then I was sure I wanted a career because they trained me. Why train that long if you're not going to use it?

> [Then] there comes a point where you stop thinking about
> whether you're going to become a wife and mother because
> it's easier than trying to deal with it, in terms of what you're
> doing right then.

For such respondents, expanding opportunities gave work at least a
temporary victory over motherhood.

As opportunity at work promoted metamorphoses in personality,
increased self-confidence fed the development of new capacities. An
unexpected promotion at a utilities company helped this ex-clerk shed
her earlier timidity:

> A: At the time I was promoted, it was very big for me. I got to
> be an expert at working with field crews and engineers. It's
> very frustrating but very rewarding, too. I had always just
> wanted to be a clerk, but I decided I would like to be a boss.

Psychological changes nourished and were nourished by developing abilities. These changes appeared even more dramatic when an
emerging self-image was compared with the former one. A fortuitous
job change transformed an office worker's sense of self as well as her
work commitment:

> A: During my first marriage, I worked, but I worked for
> money strictly. Now I work for job satisfaction. At that time,
> I didn't really *plan* anything for myself. I was very passive.
> I didn't care what I did. I had no initiative. I just worked
> and came home. I was a nobody.
>
> Q: What has brought about the change?
>
> A: My first job was too strict. We couldn't talk. It was like being
> in prison. It really got boring after a while. . . . No one
> looked at *my* performance. It was very unsatisfying. There
> was no advancement there. . . . The company I work for
> now is very, very great. They're the ones who've given me all
> the initiative. . . . Here I started at order desk and then
> office manager. I do a lot of problem solving, a lot of
> thinking, organizing, planning. I love it. I wouldn't go back.
> Next I want to be branch manager, which my boss
> encourages. . . . [Now] work makes me feel like a whole
> person. This is the first time in my life that I've felt so good.
> I feel really good that I'm twenty-seven and don't have any
> children. My views are so different now than they were
> before. . . on everything.

Upward mobility was thus usually linked to other improvements in
the work structure. Greater personal discretion and autonomy, greater

challenge in the nature of the work itself, and increased deference from colleagues, subordinates, and supervisors commonly accompanied the move upward. The experiences of these women are supported by the findings of other studies. Miller et al. (1979) report that the structure of work situations powerfully affects the capacity for self-direction, flexibility, and intellectual functioning. They argue that these capacities emerge from the specific structure of the workplace itself and are not mere artifacts of preadult socialization. They also report that these workplace structures have similar effects on men and women. Kanter (1976, 1977) makes a similar argument in her case study of a large corporation. In addition, she isolates the hierarchical structure of work organizations as the critical variable influencing the work behavior, self-image, and motivation of both men and women.

A work-related improvement in self-image tended to undermine old assumptions about the assignment of responsibility for past failures as well. Later work success allowed earlier problems to be redefined in terms of the unfair structure of the situation, rather than inherent personal inadequacies. As this process of shifting blame away from the self and onto the old work situation gained momentum, newfound anger replaced old feelings of inferiority. An assured and resolute, rather than self-effacing and self-denigrating, person began to emerge. An upwardly mobile, high school–educated accountant remarked:

> A: I get very bitter now when I think of when I worked at ____.
> I didn't think [advancement] was important, mostly because
> I didn't think I could do the job. I was afraid. I did apply
> for a couple of jobs that were a little over what I was doing,
> a better job, and was told I wasn't qualified. I had the brains,
> but I didn't have the background to go with it, just high
> school. When I see what I'm doing now and how they felt I
> wasn't qualified, it just angers me. I guess I want to go back
> and say, "Look at me. Look what I'm doing."

Conclusion

A number of factors sent some initially traditional women veering away from domesticity. Unstable marriages or relationships with men, perceived economic squeezes in the household economy, expanded opportunities for work or career advancement, and disillusionment sparked by the isolation and devaluation of homemaking and mothering—all these factors, either alone or in combination, pushed these women out of the home and pulled them into the world of work despite their childhood experiences and expectations. These forces triggered adult change. They promoted the development of new priorities, life choices, self-images, and personal abilities. The development of new aspirations and talents in turn created increasing ambivalence toward bearing and rearing children.

For some, a nondomestic path became not only the most sensible, but also the only possible route. When a number of factors converged, their combination reinforced the impact of each and foreclosed the domestic alternative. The combined effect of divorce and job advancement, for example, made the rejection of domesticity not only the path of least resistance, but the only viable alternative for this childless secretary in her mid-thirties:

Q: What made you decide that you were better off taking work more seriously than quitting to become a mother?

A: Several things happened to me when I was a file clerk. The supervisor started developing me, and I went through my divorce in that job, and I got promoted as a result of my work on that job.

However triggered, only real opportunities could sustain emergent nontraditional goals. Without structural avenues for fulfilling these goals, nondomestic ambitions would ultimately lose their attraction. For this group, however, opportunities to advance did arise to sustain emergent ambitions. Because this outcome was rarely anticipated, it was often greeted with surprise by the unsuspecting respondent. An upwardly mobile, childless businesswoman in her mid-thirties exclaimed, "I certainly thank my lucky stars for what did happen to me. It was totally accidental, incredibly good luck."

At the individual level, exposure to nondomestic opportunities was, to some extent at least, a matter of "luck" or chance. At the group level, however, individual luck resulted from a shifting structural context of opportunities and constraints. However difficult the transition and however many sacrifices it required, moreover, most who traveled this path found it worth the sometimes heavy price that was paid. Divorced and childless at thirty, an upwardly mobile naval office worker missed the family she did not have but valued the autonomy and self-respect she had gained in exchange:

Q: How do you feel about moving from a clerk to a supervisor?

A: I love it. I'm always learning. At the same time, I'm always surprised at myself, with what I've already learned by being able to answer a problem. When I come up against a problem and I know the answer, I feel pretty good. You have to have a certain independence when you work and have been single as many years as I have. I'd have to be neurotic if I didn't feel good about taking care of myself. [Had I stayed in my marriage], I don't think I would feel this good about me. I think I would have felt somewhat overshadowed.

This childless office manager now rejoiced that her impotent ex-husband thwarted her earlier plans for motherhood:

Q: Before your divorce, did you consider having children?

A: I think, if my husband could have made love to me, I would have. For sure. I guess I wanted children because it would have made my life seem whole. There was definitely something missing, but I didn't know what it was. I know now that the best thing that ever happened to me was that I got a divorce and didn't have any children. I'm completely, completely different now than I was then.

These respondents found themselves leading far different adult lives than the ones they had imagined as children. Although they had expected and planned for motherhood and domesticity, social circumstances intervened to push these women off a traditional path. Some experienced this unexpected change as the opening up of new and exciting possibilities; some experienced it more acutely as the cutting off of old ones. Whatever her reaction and evaluation, each found her adult life marked by unanticipated change, and each greeted this change with surprise. Although no change is purchased without some cost, the types of costs and benefits depend on the type of change. Let us now turn to a group that also experienced significant adult change, but change in a different direction.

5 | *Veering Toward Domesticity*

Like the lives we have just examined, the lives of the women analyzed in the first part of this chapter underwent significant change in adulthood. These women, however, moved in the opposite direction: Over time, they traded their earlier work ambitions and aversions to domesticity for motherhood and domestic orientations. They began adulthood with high aspirations and a strong ambivalence toward domestic pursuits, but adult events and experiences intervened to challenge their assumptions and redirect their lives. In contrast to their nontraditional counterparts, these women were exposed to forces in the home and on the job that loosened their psychological and actual ties to work and replaced them with children and domestic aspirations.

The backgrounds of this group's members were not substantially different from those of the other respondents. Indeed, taking socialization factors and starting points alone into account, these women were, if anything, more predisposed to seek out a nondomestic life pattern. Over 60 percent of those whose early life orientations were nondomestic veered in a domestic direction (refer back to Table 5). This chapter explains why this group veered toward domesticity and what distinguishes it from those who did not. It also analyzes a third group of women—those who did *not* experience change in life direction. As adults, members of this third group were able to fulfill their early life goals, whether domestic or nondomestic. By comparing this group with their counterparts who did change, this chapter locates the social factors and processes that either promote or inhibit change over the course of women's lives.

Declining Work Aspirations and the Home as a Haven

Like nontraditional women, women who veered toward domesticity experienced events that pushed them off their expected tracks. This group, however, was propelled down a different road. Unlike nontraditional women, they were subjected to the traditional package of incentives and constraints that have historically made domesticity attractive and other options difficult and costly for women to choose. Members of this group were more likely than those who veered toward nontraditional pursuits to become committed to traditional marriages that undermined efforts at career building, insulated them from economic squeezes, and allowed them to implement domestic choices. They were also more likely to encounter blocked work opportunities, which enhanced the pull of motherhood and domesticity. They were thus drawn toward domestic commitments despite the structural changes leading other women to eschew such choices. In this sense, their lives underscore the continuing force of traditional arrangements, which have persisted even as new alternatives have gained growing numbers of adherents.

The Precedence of Personal Relationships

For those who veered toward domesticity, stable marriages and committed relationships with men provided the conditions that made the bearing and rearing of children possible. Committed heterosexual partnerships also promoted the development of the desire to do so.

Most in this group struck a traditional bargain with male partners. Through a negotiated process, they exchanged allegiance to their partner's career for emotional and financial support. This bargain exacted a sometimes subtle, sometimes obvious cost at the workplace because the male partner's job took precedence over the respondent's own. Long-term commitment to a heterosexual relationship thus gradually undermined these women's work commitments and directed them toward mothering and domesticity.

Developing Commitment to Marriage over Work.   Women who traded work accomplishments for committed relationships confronted an intractable conflict between their public and private commitments. Either directly or circuitously, these women had to *choose between* a valued relationship and the promise of satisfying work. When a relationship was an accomplished fact and a career a risky possibility, the option of family was more compelling than the option of work. This married woman in her late twenties thus relinquished a promising job in a male-dominated occupation in order to preserve a relationship she valued more:

Q: If you were so happy being a customs inspector, why didn't you stay with it?

A: The customs thing was interesting, exciting to me, but at that point I got married and *that* became very important to me. So it was to keep that relationship. It was more desirable to live with Don than to be a customs inspector.

For women faced with a conflict between commitment to work and commitment to an intimate partner, a number of factors promoted the choice of love over work. First, these traditional partnerships were based, at least in part, on a mutual, if often unspoken, assumption that the male partner's work mattered more. Because women in this situation generally perceived that they benefited from their partners' success, they became enlisted in the process of male career building. When conflicts arose between two careers, as they often did, it was the woman who sacrificed job opportunities.

For example, career building often required geographic mobility. When the male partner's career took precedence, women in these relationships were forced to go along with their partners' work demands at the expense of their own. (Papanek, 1973, and Kanter, 1977a, 1977b, discuss how middle-class male careers have historically required the efforts of two persons—a man at the office and a woman at home.) This need to follow where the male career led made it difficult to establish a solid base at the workplace or to take advantage of advancement opportunities when they arose. This homemaker and mother of two declined a promotion so that she could follow her spouse during the early years of their marriage:

A: I did take a job with the telephone company and left when I had my first child and was offered a management position. I know a lot of people at the phone company now, women who are making exorbitant salaries, and then I think, "Gee,

that would have been me if I had stuck with it." [But] we
were doing a lot of moving. . . . I couldn't really make a
commitment to anyone, because Jeff was in a training
program, and every time he got a promotion, we moved.
I go with my husband wherever he goes; that was always a
very clear thing.

The threat of losing a valued relationship also posed a powerful
obstacle to female career development. When success could be purchased only at the expense of a relationship, women in traditional
relationships chose to forgo longstanding dreams as well as real opportunities. This respondent chose to avoid competing with her spouse,
for she feared a win at work would entail a greater loss at home:

Q: Why didn't you pursue your interest in retail
merchandising?

A: I explored the field when we were first married, but it was a
strange situation. We laugh about it now. My husband was at
_____. I had interviewed with _____, and I thought, "Well,
gee, what if I get to be a buyer and he doesn't? That could
really blow a relationship." So I guess you would say I
deferred a little.

Some women translated the fear of losing a relationship into a fear
that they lacked the ability to handle a more demanding position. It
is difficult to distinguish between fear of success and fear of failure in
these instances. Despite this twenty-eight-year-old, childless secretary's
elaborate efforts to convince herself that she really did not want a
promotion, she acknowledged that her partner wanted it less than she
did. She thus perceived that a career could be purchased only at the
expense of love, security, and motherhood. Faced with such potentially
high costs, she declined to take advantage of advancement opportunities that arose:

A: I had a couple of opportunities to get into sales, and I
passed them up. I don't know if that was wise, but anyway. . .

Q: Why did you pass them up?

A: I know the business and everything, but now I'm living with
Bill. He's not a businessman; he's a country boy, and he likes
me to spend my time with him. I think my main reason for
turning it down was I was scared of it, too, you know. Bill
expressed his opinion, although he would never say to me,

"Don't do it." But I think deep down inside the idea scared me.

Q: Why did the idea scare you?

A: Bill wanted me to be a secretary. And I thought, why should I take on more responsibility and travel and entertain and get involved? So I just decided no. But I think deep down inside it just sounds like such a big challenge for me, and I think I'm scared about it. . . . I'm getting older, the family image. I really want to become a mother someday, and that's really on my mind, I think. And I guess I keep thinking, if I get into sales, that's going to get further and further away [from having a family]. . . . I'm really kind of split right down the middle, because you could eventually make a lot of money being in sales, and I like that part of it. But, like I say, my personal life means so much more to me. I'm really happy with Bill, and that means more to me than my job.

Although it may appear that these women behaved according to Matina Horner's "motive to avoid success" syndrome (1972), their actions did not result from a psychological handicap peculiar to the female sex. Their choices were rooted in structural circumstances that forced them to choose between love and work and threatened to exact a great price if they chose work over love. In short, these women *did* have something to lose by succeeding. To the extent that they perceived their options correctly, they made sensible choices in an effort to preserve personal happiness. They did not respond in peculiarly "feminine" and irrational ways.

We must look, therefore, to the decision-making context as a whole to understand when fear of success is experienced and why such fear is acted on rather than overcome or ignored. A psychological process may set up a tension, but it does not predetermine how an actor will resolve it, especially when she experiences a variety of conflicting emotions. Fear is only one of a number of potentially motivating emotions, and not necessarily the most influential on behavior. We may fear the very goals we are motivated to seek, but fear will not in itself prevent us from seeking them.

Actual choices, as distinct from fears or hopes, thus depend on social circumstances and on how the social context sets up a balance of gains and losses. Because women face different sets of costs and benefits, they vary in the extent to which success at work threatens other valued life pursuits. They also vary in the degree to which they "fear" success rather than embrace it unambivalently and in the degree to which such fear actually impedes their work mobility. For women in traditional partnerships, who were faced with a choice between love and work, the high cost of work success was simply not deemed worth the price.[1]

If subtler inducements failed to dampen their enthusiasm for work commitment, women sometimes faced more overt opposition from traditional husbands. In these instances, a male partner intervened directly to thwart a woman's work plans so that he might preserve some valued aspect of his life. Patriarchal authority prevailed when this mother of two sought to enter police work:

Q: What happened to your plans to become a policewoman?

A: I got married, and my husband said no. He didn't feel that was a position for his wife and the mother of his kids to be in. It's not an eight-to-five job, and sometimes it's an eighteen-hour job; so he didn't go for that.

Q: Were your plans for becoming a policewoman serious at that time?

A: They were at the point when I realized I had to make a choice, and they became less. I didn't particularly *like* it, but I didn't have much choice.

Men also intervened less directly to dampen women's chances for success at work. In some instances, simply caring for a man led to the loss of workplace opportunities. This homemaker's first husband required as much attention as a child, eventually reducing her career aspirations to the hope of mere economic survival:

A: [In my] early twenties I was very work-oriented. I did get married when I was twenty, a previous marriage, and that sort of sidetracked it. Where before I think I'd been more

1. Gilligan (1982) argues that women tend to stress a morality of intimacy and interconnectedness over a morality of autonomy, objectivity, and independent accomplishment. This female morality, she suggests, contrasts with a male morality that affirms independence, rationality, and personal success at the expense of connectedness. She concludes that the male stress on accomplishment at the expense of intimacy is as skewed as, or even more skewed than, the female stress on interpersonal connection at the expense of individual autonomy.

A morality that excludes connectedness is surely as suspect as a morality that excludes autonomy. Gilligan thus provides an important corrective to prevailing and one-sided theories of moral development. However, her characterization of the first perspective as distinctively male and the second as distinctively female is questionable. There is nothing inherently masculine or feminine about stressing independence versus interdependence. Many women place success before interpersonal commitment. Moreover, some women's concern with interpersonal relationships and some men's concern with success reflect and emerge from the structural constraints each group faces. The fundamental problem for both sexes stems from structural arrangements that force people to choose between the equally important pursuits of love and work.

career-oriented, marrying left it as "work" rather than career.

Q: What happened?

A: It wasn't a decision. It happened that the man I married was more of a babysitting job; so to maintain the marriage was as much as I could handle. Work became just something I had to do to feed us without really having the energy to put myself into it, to consider it a career. In fact, at the time, I worked at a bank, and they had an opening. But because my personal life was so fouled up, it sort of shot down my possibilities of getting that, which was a bad move on my part.

Thus, through a variety of mechanisms, commitment to a traditional relationship directly and indirectly undermines a woman's work ties. Although the proportion of marriages (or heterosexual partnerships) that operate according to these traditional rules is on the decline, arrangements that grant precedence to the male's career and penalize a woman for having one persist and continue to provide powerful incentives for women's domestic orientations. When a husband has strong incentives to see his wife succeed at work—as in the case of the economically squeezed family—the advantages he gains through her success may offset the marginal power he loses at home. Supportive spouses are not unknown in many modern marriages, and a supportive partner feeds nontraditional aspirations just as surely as a nonsupportive one undermines them. Recent studies show, however, that although husbands support a certain measure of success on the part of their wives, they tend to get uncomfortable when that success, especially as measured by income, equals or surpasses their own. (See, for example, Blumstein and Schwartz, 1983; Huber and Spitze, 1983.) Patriarchal marriage patterns persist, however, not simply because men continue to benefit from them. Many women, too, continue to uphold patriarchal marriage because they have interests of their own to protect. Income inequality between the sexes, for example, reinforces a traditional sexual division of labor and supports the priority of the male career on practical grounds.[2]

2. Despite a dramatic rise in the ratio of employed women to employed men, large earnings differentials persist according to sex. According to Masnick and Bane (1980:100), "The mean earnings of female workers stand at about 56 percent of those of males, a rate that has been surprisingly constant over time. In 1955, the median earnings of year-round, full-time female workers were about 64 percent of males, 60 percent in 1965, and 59 percent in 1975. The ratio of female to male earnings has, if anything, declined slightly over time." This earnings gap persists even when age, educational level, prior work experience, and number of hours worked are controlled (Barrett, 1979). I analyze these trends and their larger significance in Chapter Nine.

The financial and emotional benefits of traditional partnerships led respondents with declining work aspirations to overlook or minimize the price they were paying. Indeed, this gradual decrease in work commitment was not typically experienced as a cost. Rather, respondents in traditional marriages felt fortunate to retain a domestic foothold in the face of so much change around them. They did not experience "patriarchy" as domination, but rather greeted it as their good fortune in securing spouses willing to care for them and support their preferences for domesticity. This ex-secretary regarded her dependence on her husband's paycheck not as domination, but as liberation:

A: There's this mystique about the charismatic man, who's not a decent and dependable sort of man. They're movie types. . . . [My husband] goes to work at eight and comes home at five, and [people] say, "Isn't that boring?" And I say, "No, not at all," because it gives me time to [do what I want]. I'm not always struggling down at the bottom of the ladder. Once you get that and taste it, you never want to let that go.

A part-time nurse felt privileged to have an option her husband did not share:

A: [My husband] thinks I'm getting my cake and eating it, too. I get to stay home and am enjoying it. And he has an ulcer.

Commitment to a traditional relationship thus tended to exact gradual, often imperceptible costs at the workplace. Whether or not these costs were perceived as costs, women in this situation faced a choice between a satisfying personal life and satisfying work. This set of options made their choices not a matter of whether they lost, but rather what they chose to lose. For those with declining work aspirations, forgone work opportunities were easier to bear than the loss of emotional ties and a secure family life.

Consequences of Marital Commitment.   However it was evaluated, the sequence of events that led these women to choose commitment to a man over commitment to work had two interdependent consequences. First, pressures to maintain a valued relationship diminished the chances of securing satisfying work and ultimately made domesticity more attractive. This mother of two chose homemaking after the search for challenging work proved futile:

A: Becoming a teacher was sort of a little dream I had. When I did meet my husband, right after graduation, we just hit it off so perfect, I didn't want to jeopardize any relationship

we might have by running off to go to school. [So] I went
to the business school instead. [But] I didn't like typing and
taking shorthand that well, so I ended up as a keypunch
operator. I really didn't like that either, but I didn't know
what I wanted to do. I just finished that, and I went to work
as a keypunch operator for an insurance company. If I work
again, I want it to be something I really like.

Second, decisions that built a committed relationship with a man
also created a context in which childbearing became feasible and desirable. When the experience of intimacy was coupled with declining
work opportunities, it sparked a new attitude toward children and
motherhood. Work aspirations lessened, and children came to be seen
as a natural expression of the relationship. Newly awakened desires
for parenthood emerged to replace work goals, and old ambivalences
toward childbearing subsided. A deepening commitment to her spouse
nurtured a new desire for a child as this pregnant ex-saleswoman
wearied of work at thirty-three:

Q: Have there ever been times when you seriously considered
     having children before now?

A: I think I'd make a good mother, but I've never yearned for
     motherhood per se. The only time I ever *really* felt a desire
     to have a baby was with my husband before we were
     married.

Q: So it's very tied up with the man?

A: With the loving. And the way it's going, because if it hadn't
     been going right and if it hadn't been unfolding as it is, we
     wouldn't have had children. There was a time when I felt I
     would never have children. Around five or six years ago I
     felt that way.

The desire for a child did not result from an abstract, generalized
"mothering need." It arose in the context of a specific relationship and
from the commitment, goals, and desires this relationship fostered.
In this context, having a child became an expression of commitment
and a means for establishing a permanent home, as this thirty-six-
year-old ex-nurse and mother of two explained:

Q: Thinking back to when you first got pregnant, what were
     your main reasons for having a child at this time?

A: Because I wanted one [laughter]. I don't know. I guess after
     you live together so long, you just want more, and a baby
     really does fill it. It doesn't make your house a place where
     you stop in to sleep. It kind of brings you closer.

Although the stereotype that women leap hungrily into motherhood, dragging their reluctant husbands along, persists in theory as well as in popular culture, many mothers reported a reverse process. This thirty-four-year-old mother of three acquiesced to her husband's strong desire for children:

A: Jim was the person of primary importance, and he wanted kids. If I had married a man who didn't want children, fine. I would have gone along with that, too. I didn't think much about it. Motherhood was no big thing to me. I took it very casually. I had no great emotional interest in it. I didn't fight it or anything. [But I did it] to please my husband.

Indeed, some planned for or bore children despite their own reluctance. These reluctant mothers (most of whom are members of the nondomestic group) viewed childbearing not as an end in itself, but as a means of pleasing a valued partner and cementing a relationship that might not otherwise endure. This motivation also prevented some from pursuing more autonomous goals. Remarriage to a child-oriented man thus prompted this thirty-three-year-old, childless teacher to suppress her ambivalence toward motherhood and trade her emerging independence for the security of home and family:

A: After my divorce, I first became fully aware of the choices that I had. I liked not being responsible to anyone, just being in charge of myself. I realized the limits that a marriage places on that, that you can't always do what you want; you have to reach a compromise. But Peter is very understanding and willing to listen and willing to sacrifice in my behalf. So I'll probably have children. I don't know if freedom is worth the loneliness. You have to give up something to get something. I don't want to lose Peter, and children are very important to him. He has definitely made the difference in my decision.

Finally, for some, marriage itself was a package deal. The decision to marry automatically implied the decision to have children. For this part-time saleswoman and mother of two, the choice to bear children did not involve a conscious process:

Q: Why did you decide to have children?

A: I was very naive. You get married; you get pregnant. We were only married a month, and I got pregnant. I guess I wouldn't have thought of getting married and *not* having children; put it that way. For me, the way my family grew was natural for us. It just was not a conscious decision-making thing.

The packaging of marriage and children had a greater impact on work aspirations than did marriage alone. The early arrival of children in a marriage placed immediate pressures on the new wife to withdraw from school or work. This robbed her of the time postponers had to be exposed to alternative options and opportunities. Thus, the decision to marry, itself, was a critical turning point when this thirty-five-year-old mother of two chose family over career:

A: I was twenty-one when I got married. I was not planning on marrying at that age. I was sort of starstruck. He was a hero from Vietnam, a green beret. He was also trying to decide if he was going to . . . go back to Vietnam. He was set for another tour then. I guess it was a big decision: Am I getting married, or am I going ahead with my career? We decided on marriage instead. At that time, I was very unsure about wanting to get married. My husband had strong feelings about having his own family. And I was at that point beginning to think I could financially put myself through school. There were a lot of mixed emotions at that time.

Q: Why did you get pregnant right away?

A: My husband wanted children because he was adopted. As he put it, either we get married and we start our family, or we just end our courtship and he goes back into the service. . . . That was a very strong factor [in having a child]. Like I said, I was starstruck at the time.

The packaging of marriage and childbearing thus led some previously ambitious women to forgo strong work commitments.

The structure of traditional (or patriarchal) marriage and the maintenance of a committed relationship within such a marriage promoted the choice of family over committed work. Over time, women in traditional relationships watched opportunities outside the home slip by and workplace aspirations erode. As this happened, mothering took on greater importance in their lives.

Even in the absence of marital pressure, however, the relatively flat mobility structure of "women's work" promoted domesticity and the defusing of ambition. Blocked opportunities at the workplace not only reduced women's motivation to work; limited job mobility also changed their orientations toward mothering, childbearing, and homemaking.

The push *out* of the workplace was thus as important as the attraction of a traditional marriage in encouraging initially ambitious women to veer toward domesticity.

Blocked Mobility and the Lure of Domesticity

In contrast to those whose exposure to expanded opportunities sparked increased commitment to work, blocked mobility promoted disaffection from work among those who experienced declining aspirations. Unlike their counterparts who veered away from domesticity, this group did not gain access to the widening job opportunities for women in male-dominated occupations that opened to some during the 1970s. Instead, they remained ghettoized in female-dominated, pink-collar occupations with limited chance for advancement (Howe, 1977), often despite their fondest wishes and best efforts.[3]

Consigned to occupations that failed to provide significant upward mobility over their work careers, these respondents experienced declining work aspirations. Although their jobs often appeared promising at the outset, this initial glow tended toward monotony and frustration as blocks to upward movement were encountered. The resulting demoralization at the workplace dampened their initial enthusiasm for paid work, eased their ambivalence toward motherhood, and turned them toward the home in spite of their earlier aversion to domesticity.

Routes to Blocked Mobility. Most who experienced declining aspirations entered the work force with high hopes, only to find that the opportunities available to them did not measure up to their expectations. A thirty-three-year-old, full-time mother of two took a secretarial position that seemed to promise initiative, responsibility, and eventual status, only to find that it rapidly degenerated into busywork:

A: In my early twenties, I knew I would get a job, and I knew what I needed. By this time, yes, I was thinking career. I was

---

3. Although unprecedented job opportunities in male-dominated occupations opened to women during the 1970s, most women workers remain in overwhelmingly female occupations with relatively blocked advancement ladders (Howe, 1977). Clerical, service, and private household jobs account for almost 55 percent of all women workers (see Chapter Nine). These female-dominated occupations are rarely structured to provide significant upward mobility over a work career. Moreover, whether an occupation is male-dominated or female-dominated, men tend to occupy a disproportionate share of the positions at the top. In sum, although growing, the percentage of female clerical workers, secretaries, bank tellers, saleswomen, nurses, and the like able to rise into the ranks of management or into the better rewarded occupations still dominated by men remains small.

on my own. I wanted a job that had responsibilities and no slack time. When I interviewed, I'd rather be adamant than get the wrong job.

Q: Why did you take the job as a secretary at _____?

A: In the beginning, it was terrific. It was a brand-new plant; they had to hire two hundred people. I had the responsibility for setting up all the filing; the job of figuring out how to set up a lot of record-keeping systems was mine. They sent me back to Virginia to a seminar to pick up on that. The fact that they would send *me* to fly back instead of sending my boss—I thought that really showed promise. Then everybody *got* hired and all my systems were set up and worked very well, worked too well. I would finish my work on Tuesday morning and have to sit there until Friday afternoon. And that for me, personally, was as much agony as anyone could impose on me.

Others entered dead-end "careers" not as the result of initial enthusiasm, but because they possessed no better alternative. These respondents were unable to break out of traditionally female occupations despite their own desire to do so. This thirty-three-year-old homemaker and mother of two found that even a college education did not open the door to occupational opportunities. Economic necessity and lack of parental and social support forced her to relinquish the hope of joining a male-dominated profession in favor of work in a female-dominated one—work she ultimately grew to detest:

Q: What did you do after college?

A: I was sort of ambitious at that point. I was thinking of law or business. It was pretty much put down by the family, who felt that was ridiculous; it was better to get the teaching credential, which was *their* thinking. It was a woman's work, blah, blah, blah. I did *not* want to go into teaching. I was forced into that because I needed to get a job. So I went to get the credential to get a higher paying job than the secretarial shit. I wanted to get out of the house; I wanted independence. There were no other options for me at that point. I was desperately angry. I saw my brother get offered his job right from the placement center and then they hired me to type.

Q: What happened after you got your credential?

A: Then the series of nightmares began. I can only think of teaching in terms of nightmares, I'm sorry to say. They gave me a permanent job teaching art. It was just gruesome. I

made money, but it was awful. There was no way out. You
can't go up in a job like that. You can't change it in any way.
It's a war zone teaching in the public school system. I really
didn't like it.

Thus, among both the high school and the college educated, the
route to blocked mobility involved a process of channeling women
with initially high work aspirations into female-dominated occupations. Some entered these occupations enthusiastically; others were
forced to opt for work they had hoped to avoid. Whatever their initial
feelings and motives, however, the structure of opportunity they
encountered was the same. Nurses, librarians, primary school teachers, and other female professionals generally faced the same low pay,
circumscribed discretion, and limited advancement opportunities that
their clerical counterparts confronted. Whether clerical or professional, these workers encountered poor working conditions and blocked
mobility. In addition, female-dominated professions tend to cluster
among those "helping professions" where the gap between clients'
needs and the limited resources available to help them leads to high
rates of "burnout" among workers (whom Lipsky, 1980, calls "street-
level bureaucrats"). Low status and an erratic work schedule left this
ex-nurse disillusioned:

A: I liked working, but I just couldn't stand working at nights
    or on weekends. Things were getting worse and worse, and
    I couldn't stand being put down.

The route to blocked mobility began with the choice of a traditional
female occupation. This choice, whether forced under protest or
embraced enthusiastically, held unforeseen and unintentional consequences for both working-class and middle-class women with initially high work aspirations. Unlike their peers who experienced rising
work aspirations, these women encountered blocked advancement and
a host of attendant frustrations. Limited movement upward combined
with low pay, low status, circumscribed control, and a lack of challenge
to encourage a downward spiral of work commitment among this
group of initially aspiring women.

The choice of a female occupation, however, does not inevitably
lead to this conclusion. Among those who veered away from domesticity, some were given unanticipated chances to advance and others
were able to switch occupations rather than forsake work commitment.
Whatever the route, women who veered away from domesticity were
generally able to break out of the female labor ghetto. In the process,
they improved their position at the workplace as well as the conditions
of their work.

Unlike their more fortunate peers, however, women with declining aspirations did not meet unanticipated opportunities at work and were unable to break out of traditional female jobs. What distinguishes these women from those whose disenchantment with their jobs sparked an occupational change rather than a rejection of work altogether?

Just as the time was not "right" among members of the first group to opt for domesticity when workplace dissatisfaction mounted, the time was never quite "right" for those with declining aspirations to make an occupational change that would have improved their work situation. Both groups were constrained, but in different ways. The first group lacked the means to opt for domesticity (for example, a willing partner); the second lacked the means, and especially the economic means, to escape from unrewarding work to pursue a new occupation. Even though events triggered the desire for change, the means were not available. At such critical points, women with declining aspirations were forced to stay in a bad situation that ultimately led to work disaffection.

Constraints other than commitment to a heterosexual relationship, especially economic constraints, also served as powerful inhibitors to career development. Financial pressures prevented this discouraged primary school teacher from pursuing a profession that promised greater social and personal reward:

A: I was separated in 1974. That was kind of a turning point because teaching just wasn't very gratifying. I felt I really needed something more for myself. I signed up for the LSAT and went through all the red tape, but I never took it.

Q: Why?

A: I seem to be unable to leave what I'm doing, because of the financial risk of losing the income and taking a chance on that, maybe not finding something else. I have felt trapped. I didn't feel that I had a choice to stop and quit and find another job because I've always had financial obligations. So here I am eleven years later, doing something I don't like doing. I feel overall my life has been wasted.

Thus, financial need kept some in jobs they disliked, which led to waning self-confidence as well as work disaffection. Because there is usually a delicate balance between economic need and how much a woman is motivated to work, job commitment persisted only for those who found satisfying employment that fed their egos as well as their bank accounts. When this search proved futile, a woman's outlook turned toward other pursuits, as in the case of this disillusioned government bureaucrat approaching thirty:

Q: Has working affected your feelings about yourself in any way?

A: It has in terms of I'm really disappointed that I haven't changed before now, that it's taken me so long to get my rear end in motion and jolly well take the risk of change.

Q: Why do you think you haven't changed jobs?

A: Probably because it has been so economically unfeasible. But now I know the house will somehow get paid for. The relationship will go on; somehow we'll make it if I don't earn this many dollars. So if I don't like it, I'm really an unpleasant lady to live with, and I ought to be doing something else.

Q: So you think you'd prefer staying home and having children?

A: I think it would be better because the gratification I'm *not* getting from the job hopefully I would get from being a parent. I would get a lot more instant feedback and more control over the situation. My change in behavior, attitude, activity, whatever, would have a direct effect, which I really don't feel now. The only reason I say that is that I have not achieved any goal in work.

As their hopes for work accomplishment dwindled in the face of blocked opportunities, these women veered toward the home. They looked to motherhood to provide the fulfillment work had failed to offer.

Consequences of Blocked Work Opportunities. The consequences of blocked work opportunities reached beyond the confines of the workplace itself into the most private spheres of these women's lives. As their work expectations turned to disappointment and disaffection, women with declining aspirations began to look elsewhere for meaningful "work."

Two additional changes in outlook accompanied declining work aspirations. Previous ambivalences toward motherhood subsided, and domesticity became more attractive than it had earlier appeared. These changes were closely related, and one enhanced the pull of the other.

First, the decision to have a child typically coincided with mounting frustration at work. This thirty-three-year-old, full-time mother of two decided to have her first child at twenty-seven, when her secretarial job hit a dead end:

Q: Was secretary as high as you could go?

A: Apparently. The company was good about using young men; they had a lot of young male executives. I didn't see any young female executives.

Q: What happened next?

A: By this time I had married Jim, and we were talking about having a family; so it became a case of waiting it out. I wanted to have a baby. So the last six months was an extremely frustrating waiting period until I got pregnant. The career went down the drain, and it was extreme boredom.

As the experience of working soured, motherhood provided an enticing alternative, and doubts about childbearing turned to curiosity and enthusiasm.

The experience of blocked work mobility, although not the only factor, was a major contributing factor in this group's decision to become mothers. It promoted declining work aspirations, which in turn lessened old ambivalences toward motherhood, gave childbearing a more fulfilling aura, and halted the strategy of postponement. Although those who encountered unanticipated work opportunities found the childbearing decision increasingly problematic, those who faced blocked mobility found motherhood an increasingly attractive option.

A second consequence of blocked work mobility and the declining aspirations it fostered is that the decision to bear a child became linked to and reinforced by the decision to withdraw from the paid work force to rear a child. In the context of dissatisfaction with work, the meaning of motherhood changed: Bearing a child became not simply an end in itself; it also furnished an alternative occupation. In other words, motherhood provided an avenue—in most cases, the only avenue—toward domesticity.

The linking of childbearing with domesticity, which made childbearing problematic for women with rising aspirations, had the reverse impact on those with declining aspirations. These women came to define motherhood as full-time mothering. This disillusioned teacher, for example, let go of earlier aversions and embraced motherhood as the only acceptable escape from work conditions she defined as oppressive:

Q: What changed your feelings about having children?

A: To be honest, what changed is that I reached a point in the job where I was just hating it daily, plus we were also moving into a new house. It's almost as stupid as saying, "What color do I paint the room? Yellow. We'll have a baby in there. Let's get pregnant." We went and got pregnant. The time seemed right. It was a relief not working, the relief of not having that pressure. I was doing something I wanted to do.

This ex-teacher's aide wanted more than a child; she wanted the chance to stay at home as well:

Q: What were the main reasons you got pregnant when you did?

A: I'll tell you the truth. I wanted an excuse to stay home. I wanted an excuse to do my own thing—not to be a housewife, but to do my own thing. I loved having my own time. Being a woman is the neatest role. You can choose what you do with your time, whereas men still have that pressure. I was glad I quit [work]; I hated the nine-to-five drag.

A would-be mother did not typically see the link between the development of disaffection from the workplace and the decision to have a child, but this process was all the more powerful because it was hidden. The birth of a child seemed natural and unforced in these cases. As this ex-clerk who could "hardly wait to stop" working explained:

Q: Why did you decide to have a baby?

A: We really loved each other, and we wanted to share in creating one. . . . We decided the time was right.

This ex-secretary, for whom work was becoming "terrible," agreed:

Q: Why do you think you decided to have a child at that time?

A: I don't know. I never really enjoyed children. I don't know what it is you feel. You just want one.

The "right" time to have a child was consistently linked to job dissatisfaction. This ex-teacher came to view childbearing as a natural, inevitable choice, despite her earlier doubts:

A: I think there's a very ambivalent period, before you're married or just after when you *don't* have any children, and you look around and you see your friends and they are tied down and you say, "Well, I'll put this off for a while." And more and more of your friends do have children, and you sort of join the crowd and have a couple, and that's what happened. I don't think *anybody* is *desperate* to have children.

Maybe there are cases, but I wasn't that desperate. I just did it one day.

Although not apparent to the person making the choice, the movement toward motherhood was rooted in the structure and experience of work itself. Blocked mobility triggered a downward spiral of aspirations and gave childbearing a liberating aura by comparison. In this context, the choice to bear a child—and the choice to withdraw from the workplace to rear it—felt natural. In important respects, women's work is organized to promote this turn toward a home-centered life. The structure of blocked work opportunities thus encouraged a set of related responses in this group of initially aspiring women—the choice to bear a child, the choice of becoming a full-time mother, and the perception that both these choices were "natural." In some cases, blocked mobility and frustrating work were even judged to be good fortune. An ex-teacher and recent mother exclaimed:

A: If my career had really taken off, it's conceivable to me that I could have come to a decision not to have children. But I don't think that would have been a good idea. I think I was meant to have children.

Domesticity as a Way of Life

For women veering in a traditional direction, the decision to bear a child involved two closely linked and mutually reinforcing choices. Becoming a mother and becoming a homemaker came to be defined as the same act. Unlike those who veered away from domesticity, respondents with declining work aspirations found this "package" of choices all the more inviting because these two acts were united: Each aspect of the choice enhanced the pull of the other. An ex-nurse favorably compared her position as a homemaker to the alternative she would face if child rearing did not consume her daytime hours:

A: [If I didn't have children,] I'd probably still be working at the health department, and I would feel just awful. I don't know whether the tension [I felt at work] was because of the health department. I shouldn't say that the children make me *not* tense. Just being home is much more relaxing.

Q: And you wouldn't be home if you didn't have children?

A: I don't think so. I would probably want to be, but with society the way it is, everybody thinks you should be working if you don't have children. I don't know if I'd be strong enough to buck it.

Thus, even when a return to work had been planned, unpleasant work experiences and blocked mobility sent these new mothers into the home. One day back on the job convinced this ex-secretary that mothering was far more rewarding and challenging than the work she was paid to do:

Q: How did you feel about the idea of quitting work to care for your child?

A: I loved it. I hated my job. I didn't quit right away. I took a leave and then went back after he was born and worked one day and quit. I had people tell me, "After you're off for a few months, you're going to get so bored; you're going to want to come back to work." What they didn't realize was that there was no way I could be as bored. [I wouldn't go back] unless somebody wants to make me the boss, but I have doubts that that's ever going to happen.

The realization that staying home was preferable to working came as a surprise to those who saw themselves as committed workers. They made the decision to mother full-time only after the birth of the first child, when they were finally in a position to make a comparative assessment between the job of child rearing and paid work. An ex-clerk discovered unexpected pleasure in full-time mothering:

A: I thought I could work and have a child, too. I was totally prepared [to return to work], and the only thing I hadn't prepared myself for was how I was going to feel the day she was born about going back to work. I thought it would be easy; I thought I'd be able to do it. Then I realized that I couldn't stand being away from her. [And I was] frustrated on the job because I really didn't have the job I wanted. The best alternative seemed to be quit and stay home.

After a history of ill-rewarded jobs and thwarted aspirations, these women chose domesticity as the better alternative, even though they could have pursued other avenues. They concluded that motherhood was the only occupation that did not threaten to disappoint. This ex-secretary decided to have a second child rather than return to work:

Q: What about the decision to have your second child?

A: I had intended to quit work when I got pregnant with Jenny, to wait until Jenny was in school, and then go back to work. But when I went back, I wanted to go back as other than a secretary. I thought, would I like to be an electrician, a fireman? What is there in the world that I want to spend the rest of my life at? Then it came to me that I really enjoy what I'm doing now more than anything else I've done or anything that I could think of doing. So I decided to have another baby. For a year I had been going back and forth. Yes, no, yes, no. Once I had eliminated the other [a career] and only that was left [a child], it sort of solved itself and then became a strong desire.

For these women, mothering became their "career." They concluded that domesticity offered them many of the things they had sought in the paid work force and failed to find: self-control, self-expression, self-direction. An ex-clerical worker explained:

Q: And now you like staying home?

A: I don't have to have anybody bossing me around! I like being with my children most of the time. Sometimes I don't, but . . . I like taking care of my own house and being in charge of what goes on in my own household.

This choice of domesticity was not without its costs. The hardest cost to bear was the lurking fear that, by giving up earlier work aspirations, these women had disappointed themselves and others. Because many of their female friends and neighbors *did* work, they faced either overt or covert social disapproval as well as personal doubts. This ex-secretary absorbed the disapproval of her peers, but nevertheless contested its validity:

A: [Sometimes I think] "What's wrong with you? You want to be home." But I really don't have any need [to work] at this point in our lives.

For those whose work experiences were deflating and discouraging and whose future prospects at work promised more of the same, domesticity offered freedom from market work and its attendant ills. Motherhood provided the route out of the workplace and into a more fulfilling job. Like their nontraditional counterparts, these respondents did not greet the accompanying devaluation of homemaking with enthusiasm. Given their other alternatives, however, they saw these drawbacks as a necessary and acceptable price to pay for the chance to engage in the more personally rewarding (if less socially rewarded) work of caring for children.

The Traditional Sexual Division of Labor

Implementing a domestic choice required more than motivation; it also required structural support. Domesticity depended on the presence of a breadwinner who was willing and able to provide the economic means for his partner's withdrawal from paid work.[4] Those who veered away from domesticity often lacked this structural support. In contrast, those who veered toward domesticity could do so only because their spouses' economic support allowed it to happen. This enabling circumstance was a necessary, if not sufficient, condition for domesticity. It was, however, a circumstance that many took for granted. This salesman's wife, for example, mentioned her spouse's financial support almost as an afterthought:

Q: Why did you decide not to return to work after your children were born?

A: It really wasn't a conscious decision to work or not to work. It was just my life-style. I never had any doubts about my husband's ability to support us; so I didn't look for work outside the home for financial reasons. We always had a place to live, and we enjoyed the way we lived; so there was no burning need to go out and work.

Remember, however, that assessment of need is a subjective process. It involves agreement between *both* spouses that the emotional benefits of female domesticity outweigh the economic costs. This homemaker, for example, looked to her husband, a trucker, for "permission" to stay home:

Q: Did you consider working after your children were born?

A: I just knew when my babies were little that I wanted to be the one to take care of them, and I know my husband thought that was just fine. His mother worked a lot when he was growing up, but he didn't feel I had to work because he never depended on my income. We didn't have any money worries at all. My husband's job was adequate. He never made super big money, but we didn't have any bills.

This reliance on the male paycheck had important repercussions on the sexual division of labor within the home. Those who opted for domesticity "earned" their economic security by performing the least

4. Despite the rise of the dual-income family, a significant number of women retain the social and psychological option of economic dependency. In contrast, men who feel trapped at the workplace are rarely able to muster similar material, social, and emotional support for *not* earning a wage—for themselves and their families. Even among the nontraditional respondents in this sample, who placed great importance on their own economic self-sufficiency, few expressed a willingness to provide full economic support for their partners or to indulge male partners who might prefer total domesticity to paid work (see Chapter Seven).

desirable tasks associated with caring for a child. This homemaker took total responsibility for all-night vigils in order to avoid paid work:

Q: How did you make a decision about not working?

A: When Gail was born, it was sort of a joke. Charlie said, "The first time I have to get up and change diapers in the middle of the night, you go back to work," because he was working and I wasn't. If he had to get up in the middle of the night, there was something wrong with the arrangement. So I made sure I got up in the middle of the night.

The inequality in the income commanded by each partner reinforced this traditional exchange and made role reversal an option in name only. Trading places with her husband, a businessman, was unthinkable to this ex-nurse:

Q: Did you ever consider working and having your husband stay home to look after the baby?

A: That would have to be an economic question. Work is not a hobby. You work primarily to make money. It becomes a trade-off. If I could make more money than him, that's another thing.

In this context, it became difficult to distinguish preferences from real options. When a respondent realized that she would have to add paid employment to the work performed at home, her motivation to work outside the home decreased. Faced with the complications of combining home and market work, this ex-secretary concluded it was easier to stay home:

A: Our understanding was, if I wanted to work, I could work— as long as I made adequate provisions for the children. Well, the pieces didn't fit. It was a very strung-out kind of puzzle thing; it just didn't all fit right.

In the face of mounting duties at home, work for pay became increasingly less attractive, and the pride of earning a paycheck was replaced by the pride of caring for others in less strictly economic ways. This eased the acceptance of economic dependency, even among ex-workers, such as this thirty-three-year-old ex-secretary who had been accustomed to supporting herself for many years:

Q: Was it difficult for you to adjust to not earning money?

A: No. I liked it. My husband gives me money. It's not hard for me.

Once committed to domesticity, moreover, these women perceived events forcing others into the workplace as threats to a preferred way of life. Having relinquished occupational aspirations, this twenty-seven-year-old ex-clerk feared the loss, especially through divorce, of her construction worker husband's earnings and the way of life it permitted her to have:

Q: Has having a child changed your feelings about yourself in any way?

A: It made me very dependent, which is just the reverse of what I used to be. . . . I think [my husband] was attracted to me because I was very independent, and now I'm very dependent. I don't know what I would do if things didn't work out between him and me and we had to separate and I had to go to work to support my child. . . . I just don't know if I could handle that, taking her to some lady's house and saying, "Here. Take care of my child while I'm at work." It's scary to me.

In opting for motherhood, women with declining work aspirations traded what they had come to define as a bad job for what, in comparison, came to be seen as a good one. Disenchantment with work created the context that made mothering attractive; it also reinforced a traditional structure of marriage and parenting. This process involved gradual changes in orientation that were generally not experienced on a conscious level. Because breadwinning is a historic male responsibility and not working for pay a historic female "right," the balance of male economic responsibility and female economic dependency was rarely noticed unless it was threatened or upset. For this group, disruptions in the traditional sexual division of labor did not occur. Rather, a set of interrelated and reinforcing circumstances made traditional arrangements the preferred alternative.

Comparing Domestic and Nondomestic Groups

Women who veered toward domesticity, like those who veered away from it, experienced unanticipated turning points in their adult lives. If we compare the triggering events that marked change in the lives of these traditional women with those of the nontraditional group, we can see why each group's choices made sense in their own context and why each moved in a different direction. Women who veered away from domesticity experienced a high degree of instability in their relationships with men, but women who veered toward domesticity established stable commitments in which male careers took precedence. The nontraditional group also tended to find expanded opportunities in the workplace, but the traditional group found blocked mobility and frustration at work instead. Members of the first group were more likely to be exposed to economic crises within the household that forced them into the labor force, but members of the second group were relatively insulated from the erosion of the male "living wage." Members of the traditional group, moreover, were less inclined to see themselves or their families as experiencing economic stress.

Finally, members of the first group found participation in the labor force a welcome alternative to the comparative isolation and devaluation of homemaking and mothering. In contrast, members of the second found the relative freedom and self-control of homemaking and mothering a relief from the comparatively stifling conditions they had experienced at work. As members of the same cohort, each group faced a common set of dilemmas and choices, but each was exposed to different sets of constraints and opportunities. These differences in exposure and experience affected perceptions as well as actions and led each group to different assessments of the relative costs and benefits of mothering, homemaking, and committed work. The forces that triggered change, moreover, were interrelated and reinforcing: once the process of change was set in motion, it became increasingly difficult to halt or reverse it.

If we take each respondent's personal understanding of her actions at face value, we might conclude that her choices and emerging orientations were isolated, individual reactions that resulted from either preordained developmental processes or from mere "accidents of fate." We can see that, taken as a whole and approached comparatively, these choices were not unique, accidental, or inevitable. They emerged from a structural, historical context that shaped women's options and their motivation to choose one option over another.

Although a variety of events triggered change in the lives of these respondents, no event taken alone fully explains their behavior or orientation. Rather, through a negotiated process, these women responded to triggering events and struggled to define their alternatives and construct their lives. This negotiated process best explains both their decisions and their emerging orientations. These triggering events stand out as especially important, however, precisely because they served as disruptive forces in the respondents' lives, shattering past assumptions, expectations, and behavioral patterns and forcing them to reassess and redirect their life paths. Let us look briefly at those who were sheltered from this process of change.

Stability and Change in Adulthood

The two groups thus far examined differ in the kind of events they encountered, the kind of choices they made, and the direction of change they experienced, but they are united in the fact of change itself. Both groups stand in contrast to those who did *not* undergo substantial change in life direction or psychological orientation. Whether traditional or nontraditional, these stable groups developed along expected paths as their adult lives proceeded.

Because the lives of those who did *not* veer significantly in a new direction were not marked by discernible turning points, their decisions are more easily understood by contrasting them with the decisions of those with similar baseline orientations who *did* experience change (refer back to Figure 2). Indeed, were it not for comparisons with the "changers," it would appear that the life choices of the "nonchangers" resulted from the inevitable unfolding of psychological predispositions instilled in childhood. In comparison with those who *did* change, however, the lives of those who did not become equally problematic. From this comparative perspective, stability is no more given than change. It, too, is a construct only as strong as the social arrangements that support it.

Tables 7 and 8 compare the frequency of exposure to triggering events among those with similar baseline orientations who veered in different directions over the course of their early adult lives. Those who remained on track, whether in a domestic or nondomestic direction, were relatively sheltered from the conditions that caused those who veered away from early baselines to redirect their original goals and plans. In every category, the stable groups were comparatively underexposed to the triggering events that promoted new choices and life directions among the changers.

Among those who began adulthood with domestic aspirations, those who actually sustained domestic choices and orientations disproportionately entered early, enduring marriages with men who were economically able to support the household. They also typically chose female-dominated occupations that they were subsequently either not motivated or not able to leave. They neither changed occupations nor encountered expanding opportunities within their chosen fields. Consequently, their early preferences for motherhood, domesticity, and loose, secondary work ties were never seriously challenged. They were insulated from the changes in family structure and work organization that induced or forced their exposed counterparts to reject the domestic alternative and seek new paths outside the home.

Similarly, among those with early work ambitions or an early aversion to motherhood, those who retained this nondomestic posture

Table 7 *Adult Pathway by Frequency of Triggering Events for Initially Domestic Respondents*

Type of Event	Domestic Baseline Becoming Nondomestic (N = 22) (College + High School = Total)	Stably Domestic (N = 11) (College + High School = Total)
Instability with men and marriage	6 + 9 = 15	0 + 0 = 0
Divorce	3 + 6 = 9	
Separation	1 + 0 = 1	
Never married	2 + 3 = 5	
Expanded workplace opportunities	8 + 7 = 15	0 + 1 = 1
Promotion	2 + 6 = 8	
Job change	6 + 1 = 7	
Economic squeeze in household	3 + 4 = 7	0 + 2 = 2
Experienced domesticity, mothering, or loose work ties as relatively isolating and devalued	5 + 5 = 10	1 + 1 = 2
Isolation	0 + 3 = 3	
Devaluation	5 + 2 = 7	

NOTE: The total number of events surpasses the total number of respondents in each group because respondents typically cited more than one triggering event.

were disproportionately exposed to avenues that enabled them to implement their initial aspirations. Members of this group did not find their nontraditional path blocked by obstacles that might have reduced their chances for success or dampened their determination. Such obstacles, however, did block the path of those who veered away from work and turned toward mothering and domesticity.

Those who maintained high aspirations, strong ties to the workplace, and deep ambivalence toward the bearing and rearing of children tended disproportionately to reject traditional marriage and relationships with partners who would require unconditional loyalty to the male career. Instead, they found partners who supported their aspirations (in deed and not just in principle), or they rejected marriage altogether. Moreover, they found real opportunities for upward mobility, primarily in traditionally male occupational preserves. In important respects, the historical times were right for these women. Surely fewer of them would have been afforded either the structural supports or the general atmosphere of acceptance for their non-domestic choices in an earlier period. However, because the expansion of new opportunities is still confined to a minority, albeit a growing

Table 8 *Adult Pathway by Frequency of Triggering Events for Initially Nondomestic Respondents*

Type of Event	Nondomestic Baseline Becoming Domestic (N = 19) (College + High School = Total)	Stably Nondomestic (N = 11) (College + High School = Total)
Stable marriage	9 + 9 = 18	4 + 2 = 6
Geographic mobility and precedence of male career	6 + 2 = 8	
Spouse nixes career	0 + 3 = 3	
Spouse pushes for children	2 + 1 = 3	
Blocked workplace opportunities	9 + 7 = 16	1 + 1 = 2
Unable to advance at work	4 + 3 = 7	
Unable to change jobs	5 + 4 = 9	
Absence of economic squeeze in household	7 + 7 = 14	2 + 0 = 2
Experienced domesticity or loose work ties as relatively satisfying	7 + 8 = 15	0 + 0 = 0

NOTE: The total number of events surpasses the total number of respondents in each group because respondents typically cited more than one triggering event.

minority, many of those with originally high ambitions were unable to attain their early goals and ultimately replaced them with domestic orientations.

In sum, stability over the life course is unremarkable in many respects. Events that shake up basic assumptions and lead to personal change are easier to isolate than are the ongoing mechanisms that reinforce and reproduce what is already espoused. This stable context makes individual life patterns appear preordained and reinforces the belief that childhood socialization explains adult choices. This is especially the case for respondents with stable developmental paths who neither experienced change nor were positioned to compare their experience with others. Despite a frustrating job and a husband eager to become a father, this ex-nurse attributed her mothering orientation to childhood socialization alone:

Q: When you found out you couldn't have children, did you think about work as an alternative to adopting?

A: I was ready to have a family, and it must have just been something that had been programmed from early on. I was going to get married, and I was going to have a family. I *could* go to work, but I wanted to have a family and try to get back on the right track if possible. I knew motherhood was not all a bed of roses, [after] my experience in public health. . . . So I can't say I was sitting there thinking, "Oh, wonderful job." I don't know; it must have been a sort of instinctive thing. And it must have been instilled from early on that I'd have a family. My husband wanted a family very much.

Because a substantial proportion of those with similarly traditional childhood orientations did not make domestic choices as adults, neither childhood experiences nor a maternal instinct can explain the paths taken by stably traditional women. The lack of change in these women's lives, however, muted the perception of structural forces and promoted a belief in psychological explanations. They tended to attribute the cause of their actions, as well as their outlooks, to personal, individual sources rooted in notions of a "feminine personality" and early childhood socialization.[5]

A more comparative perspective, however, illuminated for some stably traditional women both the structural underpinnings of action and the delicate interaction between structural constraints and psychological motivation. Those in a position to compare their own paths with others who took a different route were thus more sensitive to the fragility of their own biographies. They sensed, somewhat uneasily, that, were it not for favorable (or unfavorable, depending on how the outcome is judged) circumstances, they too might not have moved so directly toward their original goals. This ex-nurse and new mother, for example, felt relieved to have been insulated from forces pushing other women out of the home:

A: I guess I'm lucky in a way because I don't feel a strong desire to have a profession. I feel kind of sorry for them because it's an important thing if you want to have a career and if you have a strong motherhood drive also. They are drives that really are hard to combine. I don't feel I've given up anything. Maybe in the future I'll be frustrated, but right now I feel lucky. I guess I'm lucky, too, 'cause I have the supports around me that don't expect that of me. . . . I know that today a lot more people have pressures to be more than

---

5. Gerth and Mills (1953) make the important distinction between "vocabularies of motive" and actual causes of behavior. They analyze the problematic nature of individual attempts to locate the sources of personal actions and motives.

just a mom. And I just feel that I don't have that pressure right now—not from my husband or my family or anywhere.

Others experienced this awareness of how a changing social context is restructuring women's choices not as a feeling of relief and good fortune, but as a nagging sense of lost possibilities and roads not taken. This ex-teacher and full-time mother of two wondered whether the smooth road she had traveled to domesticity was a blessing or a misfortune:

Q: Did you ever consider changing jobs instead of having a child?

A: Never. But it does play in; friends of mine went on and didn't get married when they thought they would. I think there's a time, there was for my friends, when they realized certain things weren't jiving according to the game plan, and then they really started to look at their career on a serious level. That didn't happen to me.

Q: Everything did go according to the game plan and therefore you didn't think about doing something else?

A: I think they went through some very difficult times where they were puttering around with a job or something, and they'd say, "Hey, I may be doing this for ninety years." It makes you grow up. Maybe it retards you, what I'm doing. I'm not sure yet.

Whether they judged their ultimate destinations favorably or unfavorably, those who traveled stable developmental paths, like those who did not, were responding to deeply anchored structural forces of which they were usually only dimly aware.

Conclusion

Chapter Four demonstrated how and why some women with domestic childhood orientations moved toward nondomestic life choices as adults. This chapter has shown how and why other women experienced the reverse movement from nondomestic childhood orientations to domestic adult choices and has contrasted each of these groups of changers with nonchangers who did not veer from their baseline goals and expectations. This comparative analysis has shown how and why respondents with similar points of departure moved away from one another in adulthood while others with different points of departure moved toward the same ends. Many routes were taken, and the roads traversed were often winding and blocked. The point of departure did not and could not explain the path that was chosen.

The lives of these women suggest that the adult life course is neither a predetermined outcome of childhood experiences nor a series of predictable, orderly steps from one stage to the next. In contrast to classical theoretical schema that stress a single set of hierarchical stages of development across the life span (for example, Erikson, 1963), these women took a variety of routes through adulthood. Their lives show that adulthood is neither a stable period of continuity with the past nor a single progression of movement from stage to stage leading ultimately to an identifiable end point. Rather, under current social conditions, adulthood, like childhood, is a tumultuous period when new life tasks are confronted in the context of old choices and conflicts. To some extent, both sociological and psychological outcomes remain open over the adult life span.[6]

There is currently no one typical or correct developmental path for women. There are, instead, many paths women can take, some of which lead toward domesticity and some of which lead away from it.[7] Moreover, neither society nor the psyche is tightly organized and stable enough to ensure the smooth development of the self or to guarantee the resolution of developmental conflicts. Instead, the possibility for change, if not the fact of it, remains in adulthood. Whether the direction of passage is toward domesticity or away from it, each destination contains inherent dilemmas and contradictions and poses a specific set of problems.

6. Recent research corroborates these findings on change in adulthood (see, especially, Rossi, 1980; Rubin, 1979; Smelser and Erikson, 1980). For popular versions of this emerging perspective, see Sheehy (1974) and Scarf (1980). For a discussion of classical perspectives of adult development and overviews of the field, see Brim (1968), Simmons and Mortimer (1978), Smelser and Smelser (1963). Wilensky and Edwards (1959) and Chinoy (1955) present empirical studies that document the process of adult change for male workers whose early expectations were thwarted by blocked work opportunities.

7. Gilligan (1982) argues that the classical stages of moral development are actually stages of *male* moral development. To complete this picture, she proposes to add a perspective that includes female development processes. The perspective and balance she adds to moral development theory are long overdue. There are, however, many avenues women can take as they respond to developmental conflicts and tasks. Surely this variety holds true for men as well. Her approach thus needs to be extended to allow for a variety of developmental paths and moral values for both women and men.

6 | *Homemaking Versus Childlessness*

Whether respondents developed a new orientation or sustained an old one, adult events and experiences shaped the way they all built their life paths. Whatever pattern they chose, however, structural cross-pressures made it difficult for them to implement and sustain their decisions and preferences. Women who chose to place family and children before other life commitments confronted the dilemmas of how to overcome the isolation that homemaking can impose and how to defend their choices against the growing social devaluation of domestic pursuits. In contrast, women who established committed ties to the workplace faced dilemmas about whether and how to integrate children into their lives. Although each group faced a different set of obstacles and central concerns, both confronted dilemmas that lacked established, institutionalized solutions. Both faced different forms of "structural ambiguity" in which they were forced to choose between mutually exclusive but equally problematic alternatives. As Oakley (1974b:81) puts it, domestic and nondomestic women alike confronted

> a contradiction between alternatives [that] are mutually exclusive, because the achievement of both calls for more time, energy, and commitment than one person can reasonably supply, and because . . . "the full realization of one role threatens defeat in the other."

Oakley terms this situation "structural ambivalence" and argues that it is a defining feature of women's position in modern societies. She builds on the analyses of Komarovsky (1946) and Epstein (1970: 65), who defines ambivalence as "the social state in which a person . . . faces contradictory normative expectations of attitudes, beliefs, and behavior" (see also Coser, 1974, and Merton and Barber, 1963).

I use the term "structural ambiguity" to distinguish between the ambiguity of structural arrangements and the psychological ambivalence this ambiguity produces in individuals. Structural ambiguity should not be confused with the functionalist concept of "role strain." Role strain (or role conflict) presumes a conflictual but static structural arrangement to which individuals must adjust. Structural ambiguity assumes a dynamic process in which new social patterns can potentially emerge as social actors develop creative responses to the dilemmas and contradictions they face.

Structural ambiguity, as used here, thus refers to the uncertainties within and contradictions between the various work and family structures women confront, and not to the functions these structures might serve. These contradictions and uncertainties promote not only psychological ambivalence within individuals and social conflict between opposing social groups, but also creative individual and social responses. As Giddens (1979:131) points out, "don't look for the functions social practices fulfill, look for the contradictions they embody."

The structural ambiguity faced by the women studied here took different forms and provoked different reactions, depending on the particular orientation a woman developed. Whatever her orientation, however, structural ambiguity produced more than psychological ambivalence. It necessitated strategies of adjustment—strategies that tended either to reproduce traditional patterns of gender relations or to act as a force for change. As respondents reacted to the particular form of structural ambiguity they faced, they participated in either creating new social arrangements or reproducing old ones. Because they all faced historically unprecedented conditions, however, none could avoid the active struggle either to invent new responses or to preserve old ones.

Figure 3 shows how each group developed two possible responses to the dilemmas posed by the structural ambiguity of their respective situations. Among those with domestic orientations, some had both the resources and the desire to make full-time homemaking a career. Others, more frustrated at home or without the financial resources to stay home full-time, were either currently in or planning to join the paid labor force part-time. Among those with nondomestic orientations, some concluded that they would never have children; others

Figure 3 *Alternative Adult Pathways and Future Plans*

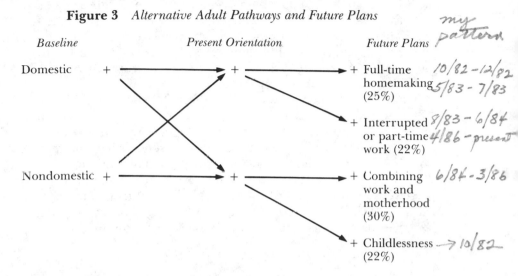

NOTE: The total sums to 99 percent due to rounding down. For a breakdown by educational level, see Appendix C, Table C.22.

were either preparing to or currently attempting to combine full-time employment and parenthood.

These variable responses and the strategies they entailed do not all have the same implications for social change. Even when traditionally oriented women sought part-time or intermittent work to supplement a strained family income or to ease the frustrations of homemaking, their actions did not promote far-reaching changes in either the organization of their domestic activities or the structure of male-dominated work institutions. At home, domestically oriented women lacked both the incentive and the leverage to rearrange the sexual division of parenting, housework, or economic responsibilities. At work, their limited commitment left them without the incentive or leverage to push for sexual equality in pay, position, or job structure. Their dependence on traditional marriage gave them little reason to upset traditional arrangements. Rather, it motivated them to reproduce gender relations based on a clear sexual division of parenting versus economic responsibilities.

In contrast, whether they opted for childlessness or attempted to combine work and motherhood, women committed to nondomestic paths made choices that promote social change far beyond the scope of their private lives. Those who decided to forgo childbearing altogether represent more than a challenge to the essential rationale for the traditional family and women's traditional place in the social order, although this in itself would be enough. Their choice for career over motherhood also contributes to the growing pressure to achieve sexual equality at the workplace.

Those who planned to combine motherhood with career also promote the forces of social change. To make this option viable, they pushed for structural and ideological changes both in the workplace and at home that would ease their parenting responsibilities and reduce work penalties that motherhood threatened to entail. They thus joined their childless counterparts in forging new, if fragile and only dimly perceived, pathways for adult women. As long as the social forces that led these women away from domesticity persist, this group will also persist in its efforts to remove the obstacles that continue to block nontraditional paths.

Nondomestic women, whether childless or combining work and motherhood, represent important alternatives to the domestic pattern. Their choices have played and will continue to play a significant role in instituting and defining the contours of social change. Their strategies can be understood, however, only in comparison with the strategies adopted by domestically oriented women.

This chapter and the next examine the choices, plans, and strategies adopted by respondents in the face of structural ambiguity. These chapters compare and contrast the roles of ideology, men, and material and social resources among three groups: domestically oriented women, nondomestic women who opted for childlessness, and nondomestic women attempting to combine career and parenthood.

This chapter contrasts the domestic group with the childless group and shows that, starting with the shared assumption that the demands of career and child rearing are irreconcilable, they reached opposite conclusions about how to direct their lives.[1] Chapter Seven contrasts

---

1. Most respondents, whether they were full-time homemakers, part-time workers, or full-time workers, distinguished between working and having a career. The term "career" implied not mere labor force participation, but rather long-term, full-time attachment to paid work with the expectation, or at least the hope, of advancement over time. In other words, respondents defined "career" as both the psychological and behavioral state of being committed to work over the long run.

The commitment to a career does not, however, necessarily imply the attainment of a professional job; rather, it implies a strong emotional attachment to paid work and a coherent pattern of work participation. This point is important because full-time, closely supervised, working-class jobs located at the lower rungs of bureaucratic hierarchies can be even more exacting of one's time and thus even more in conflict with family commitments than more prestigious professional and managerial jobs, which offer greater personal control and discretion (Daniels, 1983).

both domestic and childless women with "reluctant mothers" who challenged the assumption that career and motherhood are irrevocably incompatible. These women underwent a process of ideological change as they struggled to resolve the contradictions they confronted.[2] Faced with cross-pressures to have a child *and* a career, they developed coping strategies that challenged the foundations of gender inequality at home and at work and that redefined inherited assumptions about what is possible for women in the modern world.

The Persistence of Domestic Patterns

In spite of the forces promoting change, many respondents decided their best chance for a secure, satisfying life remained centered in the home and depended on a traditional, "patriarchal" family structure. These women retained a vested interest in maintaining arrangements that support and justify female domesticity. The attractions of a traditional sexual division of labor when compared to the experience of paid work led them not only to reproduce traditional patterns in their own lives but also to fear and oppose emerging alternatives to these patterns. The persistence of domestic incentives influenced both behavior and ideology.

There were two behavioral consequences of the incentives for domestically oriented women to reproduce traditional patterns. First, although work remained an option for domestically oriented women, careers—in the sense of full-time, continuous, committed labor-force attachment with advancement as a goal—did not. Thus, 53 percent of this group were committed to full-time homemaking, and the remaining 47 percent had erratic work histories and planned to work outside the home either part-time or intermittently for the foreseeable future. The part-time, intermittent, and generally limited nature of their labor force participation meant, however, that their ties to the workplace did not compete with their family responsibilities or their male partners' positions as primary breadwinners.

2. As used here, the term "ideology" refers to a set of beliefs and theories people construct to make sense of the world and guide their actions in it. Although some of the ideologies I discuss have been used by dominant groups to control the behavior of subordinate groups, the analysis that follows does not employ the term "ideology" in order to distinguish between true and false consciousness. Rather, it considers how and why various social contexts, dilemmas, and contradictions promote different meaning systems among women. (For the classic analysis of ideology as beliefs promoted by ruling elites in order to maintain and perpetuate their position of dominance, see Mannheim, 1936.)

Part-time, intermittent workers have historically accounted for a large proportion of the female labor force, although the size of this group has declined over the last decade. The percentage of women workers who worked year-round, full-time rose from 36.9 percent in 1960 to 43.7 percent in 1980 (U.S. Department of Labor, 1980:19). Masnick and Bane (1980:61–63) argue, nevertheless, that there is a wide gulf between the precipitous rise in women's labor force participation and the less rapid rise in women's labor force attachment:

> Participants in the labor force are a diverse group. They range from women who spend trifling amounts of time and energy at work to those pursuing full-time careers. . . . The revolution in labor force participation has not extended to attachment or to contribution. From our reading of the data, we believe that a second revolution is underway in attachment, particularly among the women in the younger generation born after 1940 who also are revolutionizing family structure.

Thus, although almost half the domestically oriented women chose to work in order to relieve the tedium of homemaking and ease the strain on the family income, work commitments were carefully subordinated to family commitments. By defining work as a secondary commitment—and distinguishing it from career as a primary one—this mother and part-time worker avoided a perceived conflict between work and family:

A: I wouldn't have gone into a career, not with [my children] little. That's what I liked about the work. The hours were flexible. I didn't feel guilty quitting whenever I wanted to. A career, to me anyway, means full-time work and maybe work at home even. I don't want work to have to come home. I really didn't want to get all that involved; I felt like a career *would* get overinvolving.

This clerk concluded that part-time work was the ideal compromise between her needs for social contact, recognition, and autonomy and her primary commitment to her two young children:

Q: What are the main reasons you're working?

A: Because I want to. I enjoy being with people; I enjoy being my own person; I have my own identity; I have my own friends; and I have to admit, the money's nice.

Q: Why do you prefer working part-time?

A: Because I could quit tomorrow. I would never want to get us in a situation where I would have to work, because then I would really hate it. I don't work to have a career. If ever I set my goal on a career, I'm cocky enough to know I could have one. Without a career, I can quit a job whenever I want. To have a career, you have to stick with it, and it takes a lot. I'm not willing to give that much of myself. A job, I don't have to give up anything. In order to have a career, I'd have to give up a lot of things my kids need, and it's not worth it to me.

The simple fact of working thus does not by itself entail significant social change. Women who maintain tentative, vague work commitments represent neither a significant departure from past patterns nor a significant force for change in the future. Instead, they remain committed to a traditional family structure and dependent on a male breadwinner who leaves them responsible for child rearing and housekeeping. Commenting on the tendency for many women and few men to opt for part-time work, Vickery (1979:119) points out how little such options are likely to upset the balance of power between the sexes:

> If a shorter work week evolves only for women, the outcome will be a new variety of sex-typed work roles. A part-time female worker who has important home responsibilities outside of her market job cannot compete in either time or devotion with a full-time male worker who has a wife providing a supportive home life. . . . Women would be coupling their homemaking duties with part-time labor market jobs that do not compete directly with men . . . this outcome is a far cry from the goal of sexual equality, and it would perpetuate the subordinate position of women in our society.

Whether or not a domestically oriented woman worked, a traditional sexual division of labor was reinforced in the home. The female partner not only participated in but actively supported these arrangements because she had little to gain by upsetting the marital balance of exchanges. This homemaker explained:

Q: On the whole, do you prefer raising your children to working outside the home?

A: Oh, yes. I never plan to go back. I'm too spoiled now. I'm my own boss. I have independence; I have control; I have freedom, as much freedom as anyone is going to have in our society. No job can offer me those things.

No one in the traditionally oriented group expressed either the desire or the expectation that her spouse should or would participate equally in child care. More specifically, none of these women wished to trade her responsibilities for those of the male breadwinner. After their generally sour work experiences, all agreed with this part-time nurse that, whatever its costs, domesticity compared favorably with the task of economically supporting a family:

Q: How would you feel about working while your husband stayed home to care for the children?

A: There might be a little bit of jealousy in there—his being able to be home and my having to go off to work.

Given the limited opportunities these women encountered in the paid labor force, such a stance is hardly surprising. Men generally do not enjoy the domestic option that these women are afraid of losing. Although many men (especially if they are white and middle class) enjoy an advantaged position in the labor market, others (especially poorly educated whites and nonwhites) face job opportunities as constricted as those of many traditional women. As more women with poor job prospects face losing the domestic alternative, they understandably fear coming to resemble the alienated male worker who is afforded no means of escape from the frustrations of ill-rewarded paid work. (For portraits of frustrated male workers, see Chinoy, 1955, and Rubin, 1976.)

This preference for a traditional sexual division of labor did not mean that homemaking held no frustrations or drawbacks. Traditional women accepted the costs of domesticity as the price they had to pay for an otherwise preferred alternative. Many of the full-time home-makers thus expressed some dissatisfaction with their position, and almost all the part-time workers looked unfavorably at the prospect of staying home full-time. In terms of their behavior, however, none saw full-time work or career as the solution to these problems. The costs of domesticity were not great enough to override the benefits of motherhood or the costs of trying to combine career and parenting.

Because alternative paths looked even bleaker, traditional women engaged in a process of "discounting," or minimizing the importance of, the costs associated with the domestic option. Perceived costs such as social isolation and devaluation diminished in the eyes of this ex-secretary as she compared them with the perceived costs of returning to work:

Q: Is there anything you dislike about staying home?

A: Yes. There are times when it gets lonely, because most women work. There are times when it's boring, but that's true of any job. Sometimes I think, "I have to clean the house again because it's Monday," and that upsets me. But I think, if I were working, I'd be doing such and such number report every Monday; so it really doesn't matter what you do. And . . . I suppose there are times when I have some trouble with *my* identity; *that* has to do with being a mother. Because of society, sometimes the recognition or lack of it bothers me.

Although an ex-clerk lamented the lack of respect she received as a full-time mother, she concluded that a return to paid work would entail greater frustrations:

Q: Has not working affected your feelings about yourself in any way?

A: Sometimes I think I miss it, but I really do know better. But people put no value on a housewife. If you have a job, you're interesting. If you don't, you're really not very interesting, and sometimes I think people turn you off.

Finally, traditional women were also motivated to reproduce the ideology that supports traditional family patterns. This set of beliefs meshed conveniently with the structure of alternatives they faced. Because these beliefs represented continuity with the past, they appeared obvious and were easily accepted as fact. This group thus continued to espouse two principles that have historically served to reinforce the domestic choice—that a child (and therefore its mother as well) suffers from an absentee mother and that, as a consequence, a woman can have children or a career, but not both. When asked, for example, how they felt about a woman with young children working outside the home, even if her family did not need the money, only 47 percent of the traditional group answered that it was "generally okay"—compared to 76 percent of the nontraditional group. When asked how they felt about husbands and wives splitting the housework, only 33 percent replied that "each should do about half," compared to 70 percent for the nontraditional group. Even when help with child rearing was readily available, these women were reluctant to trade mothering for committed work. This clerk, who was trying to get pregnant, spoke for the group when she expressed her determination to be her child's primary caretaker:

Q: What about getting regular babysitting help?

A: It's important to us that we raise our children the way *we* want to, not as our neighbors or someone else could do it. Both my sisters-in-law have said, if the situation were to arise and if I wanted to continue working, they would be more than happy to take care of the baby. It would be fine, maybe a couple of hours a day, something like that. But for me to go back full-time knowing that someone else was raising my child, I'm not too keen on the idea, and I can't really say why.

Whether homemakers or part-time workers, domestically oriented women faced an opportunity structure that motivated them to reproduce both a traditional sexual division of labor and an ideology to justify that arrangement. In addition, as they watched friends and neighbors depart for the workplace, those remaining at home had to struggle in a greatly altered context to preserve social legitimacy for their choices. Domestically oriented respondents perceived that new alternatives threatened their interests, and many expressed their resentment toward the growing social pressure to eschew domesticity. An ex-nurse lamented:

> A: I have been feeling lately a lot of pressure . . . there's a lot of pressure on women now that you should feel like you want to work. Sometimes it's hard to know what you feel, because I really don't feel like I want to [work] but I think I *should* feel like I want to.

The development of nondomestic pathways posed a dilemma for domestically oriented respondents. Threatened with the erosion of the structural and ideological supports for domesticity, they struggled to justify choices they could have taken for granted only a short time ago. Most responded to this challenge by holding tightly to a set of beliefs that has historically served the cause of female domesticity while some simultaneously made limited, tentative movements toward part-time work.

In contrast, nondomestic respondents felt threatened by traditional beliefs and domestic behavioral patterns. Their coping strategies were reactions not only to structural dilemmas, but also to traditional patterns that they opposed. In the process of creating new strategies, nondomestic women had to respond to traditional notions of good mothering and decide whether to accept them or change them. Their decisions held important implications for their own commitments and for social change.

Nondomestic Responses

Those who rejected domesticity, whether by preference or necessity, faced a "motherhood dilemma." This dilemma hinged on a simple yet intractable aspect of the alternatives facing nondomestic women. On the one hand, neither their social environment nor the prevailing ideology provided institutionalized supports for combining committed work with child rearing. On the other, most had difficulty embracing the historically unpopular option of forgoing children altogether. Given a choice between two unattractive alternatives, they struggled with the questions of whether and how to integrate children into lives already defined by established commitments to work.

The considerable costs that children threatened to exact often overshadowed the potential rewards of parenthood for nondomestic women. Caught between the perceived costs of parenthood and the perceived costs of childlessness, these respondents reacted with ambivalence. At thirty, this childless executive felt contradictory pressures to bear a child and to hold on to the comparative freedom of childlessness:

> A: Like I say, I really *want* to want children. It kind of bothers me that I can't just settle down and want children, because I'd very much like to *want* a family. But I'm having too much fun doing what I'm doing right now, and I see a child more than anything else as a big veering in the life pattern.

She felt paralyzed by the negative consequences of *both* options:

> A: I'm hung up on the negative things, on the responsibility and the problems and the loss of freedom and everything else. But I keep hoping that, when the time comes for me to have a family, I'll just automatically get ready. I think it would be nice if I were looking forward to it. I really hope that I will be a happy mother someday. I would like to have it work out that way because it's so much of a hassle to make a decision *not* to have the family . . . in terms of pressure and psychological feelings of having failed or not fulfilled myself that I anticipate I would feel later in life.

The structural contradictions between career and motherhood produced ambivalence toward childbearing. Most upwardly mobile women could not decide whether children would be more a benefit or a detriment. This ambivalence was often so deep that some, such as this twenty-nine-year-old, upwardly mobile, childless office manager, openly expressed contradictory stances toward the motherhood dilemma:

> Q: How do you think you'd feel if you had children right now?
>
> A: Extremely unhappy. It's taken everything I have to get to where I am now—to help myself. I couldn't imagine having someone depend on me. If [a child] said, "I need you," it would make me go bananas.
>
> Q: Then what are the main reasons you want a child?
>
> A: This sort of contradicts what I said before, but having someone who needs you. I eventually want someone

who needs me and whom I can help, but not right now.
But if I could have one at fifty, I'd probably wait till I'm fifty.
I hope I'll be ready for it when it's time.

Ambivalence toward motherhood was expressed in contradictory and conflicted behavior as well. Because nondomestic women perceived children as both rewarding *and* costly, approach *and* avoidance marked their decision-making processes. Their fertility behavior in particular was hesitant and uncertain, leading to the selection of different options at different times. Ambivalence led to an abortion in one instance, but to pregnancy in another. Although she had aborted two previous pregnancies, this thirty-seven-year-old executive still planned to have a child:

Q: You said you had two therapeutic abortions. What was going on at the time?

A: It was *very* emotional. I was absolutely freaked out. Consciously, I was thinking how our life would have to change. We'd never be able to have a house like this, never be able to travel together again. Just the impact of having a small child around, the nuisance, and the bother—that's what I consciously thought. I was so upset. I'm sure there was a lot more going on in my head.

Q: What do you think has changed so that now you think you will have a child?

A: I think probably ever since I've been married to Dick, the idea has been in the back of my mind. It's just taken a lot of getting used to. I can say that now, but I was ready to get an abortion the instant I got pregnant; so I don't know.

In contrast, a thirty-one-year-old hospital administrator became and remained pregnant despite her fears and inability to decide consciously:

A: It's difficult for me to see children in my image of myself and my life. I so clearly see myself in my work role. And with the demands it puts on me, it's difficult to imagine myself as a mother, and having the kind of responsibilities a child imposes. I'm afraid I will lose control over my life and my time.

Q: What made you finally decide to get pregnant?

A: I didn't really decide. I just decided to play Russian roulette. When I realized I was pregnant, I considered having an abortion. [But] I hate to miss any of life's experiences.

Unfortunately, this one lasts longer than most of the others I've tried. Also, my ambivalence. You know, my thinking that I might regret it if I don't, because I also faced the issue that, if we were going to have kids, we had to have them pretty soon. Just because I'm getting old. It's the early thirties crisis!

With or without the ambivalence, these women had to decide about childbearing, if only by default. With their prime childbearing years slipping by, decision-making deadlines were nearing. What factors led some to resolve their ambivalence in favor of motherhood and others to decide against it? What structural and ideological consequences followed from the responses these women developed to resolve the contradictory and ambiguous alternatives they faced?

Among those who had developed nondomestic orientations, 24 percent had already borne at least one child and another 33 percent expected to do so in the near future. The remaining 42 percent, however, did not expect ever to bear a child. (The total sums to 99 percent due to rounding down.) Although most nontraditional women either planned to combine work with childbearing or had already begun to do so, a substantial minority thus planned to remain permanently childless. Furthermore, most "combiners" remained ambivalent about their plans; few had successfully resolved the tension between establishing a family and maintaining their hard-won right to a life outside the home. Why, then, did some plan to remain childless while others joined or planned to join that growing group of women attempting to combine parenthood with committed work?

For those not oriented toward domesticity, the process of deciding for or against motherhood involved assessing the potential costs of having a child and of not having a child and weighing these alternative costs against each other. For most, this process was largely unconscious, and for some, it was far from conclusive. Those who concluded that parenthood had substantially higher costs than childlessness decided to reject motherhood. In contrast, those who perceived the denial of parenthood as more costly than parenthood itself did not enthusiastically embrace motherhood, but they were less inclined to reject childbearing altogether. They began, instead, to move slowly and reluctantly toward motherhood, simultaneously struggling to minimize the costs of children. The degree of pressure they felt to bear a child and the strategies available to reduce the potentially negative consequences thus strongly influenced nondomestic women's responses to the motherhood dilemma.

Although a perspective that views children as "costs" may seem one-sided, such an analysis presumes that there are intrinsic "benefits" to parenting as well. If children were not in some sense desirable and desired, the question of whether or not to have them would not be problematic. The difficulty arises precisely because children appeared both rewarding *and* costly to nontraditional women. Because domestically oriented women did not attach the same costs to parenthood, they were able to choose more easily in accordance with motherhood's perceived rewards. (Daniels and Weingarten, 1978, distinguish between motherhood as a job and as an identity.) As this childless lawyer pointed out, what might be central to a domestically oriented woman was only one of several desired ends for a nondomestic woman:

Q: How would you feel if you never had children?

A: I would prefer to have them, but it wouldn't be the end of the world because it's really going to be difficult. I don't need it to give myself something to do. That just isn't a guiding force in me. Children, clearly you love them and give them a lot of your attention, but for it to be your fulfillment in life and your only function—I don't agree with that.

What factors, then, determined how nondomestic women perceived the costs of parenthood? What responses emerged as they struggled to resolve the ambiguities of their situations? Workplace arrangements were not decisive because they were not a variable factor. For this group, pulling back from the workplace to any significant degree was not an acceptable alternative. Such a strategy would have jeopardized their advancement possibilities, their financial solvency, or both. This computer analyst was acutely aware that, were she to devote less time to work, her employer could easily replace her with a childless woman or a man with few parenting responsibilities:

Q: If you have children, do you think you'll be able to change your schedule at work or cut back on your hours?

A: I don't think so. They figure that I'm to have my career, and what I do at home is my own business, but it better not interrupt the job. I think if I were working part-time, they'd stop pushing me to advance. I'm sure they would, because you can't supervise people if you're not there. I've been pushed as far forward as I have because I was a maniac and I never went home.

Like their domestically oriented counterparts, these nondomestic women also distinguished between work and career. Preserving the chance to accomplish what in most cases were very high work goals effectively excluded part-time work from the range of strategies available to work-committed women. As this administrator explained:

Q: So you plan to work full-time?

A: Yes. It's really not the kind of job . . . it's either full-time or not at all. And if I stick with this organization, I don't rule out being president.

Given this intransigence at the workplace, factors affecting arrangements at home became critical in influencing women's responses to the motherhood dilemma. Although their work situations were similar, their home situations varied. Work-oriented women faced diverse domestic pressures and possessed diverse domestic resources. These factors were decisive in shaping their fertility decisions.

First, men played a major role in shaping both the pressures nondomestic women faced and the resources they could muster for bearing and rearing children. For most, marriage was a precondition to motherhood, and some concluded that marriage itself was not a viable alternative. Among those committed to marriage, spouses played a critical role. Male partners directly and substantially affected the perceived costs of motherhood versus childlessness by providing a major source of pressure either for or against childbearing and by lightening or refusing to lighten the burden of child rearing.

Nondomestic women also approached the motherhood dilemma with a set of beliefs concerning the proper role of mothers in child rearing. Almost all inherited a traditional child-rearing ideology that argues that full-time mothering is the only "good mothering" and that children will suffer if their mothers work full-time. This belief implied an "all or nothing" approach to women's place: A woman can have either a career or children, but not both. Given their commitment to work, nontraditional respondents were left to choose between not bearing children and revising the beliefs they had inherited. Depending upon the structure of their alternatives, and especially the pressures and resources provided by men, some remained trapped in this ideological double bind that pits the mother's interests against the child's, but others proceeded to alter their previously unquestioned assumptions about the incompatibility of working and mothering.

Thus, the combination of ideological conditions and objective resources and pressures shaped the perceived consequences—to career, potential offspring, and personal well-being—of having versus not having children. These two factors interacted and changed over time, ultimately shaping work-committed women's responses to the motherhood dilemma. Some concluded that children threatened to exact too high a price and opted for childlessness; others concluded that they could keep the costs of motherhood within acceptable limits and that, in contrast, the costs of childlessness were intolerable. These "reluctant mothers" began moving slowly toward motherhood. As their decisions unfolded, nonmothers and reluctant mothers alike engaged in a process of "discounting." Childless women discounted the potentially negative consequences of never having children; reluctant mothers discounted the potentially negative consequences of having children and also developed coping strategies to keep the costs of motherhood down.

Choosing to Stay Childless

Those who decided against motherhood concluded over time that children would entail greater costs than rewards. (Veevers, 1980, makes a similar argument in her study of voluntarily childless couples.) For some, these costs were intrinsic to mothering itself. Most, however, decided that they could not create a situation suitable for childbearing or that the responsibilities of parenthood would have disastrous consequences on other valued aspects of their lives. All ultimately agreed that the potential costs of motherhood were not worth the risk.

The decision to bear the first child must always be made without full knowledge of what the actual experience of motherhood will be. These childless women thus had to assess the perceived or possible costs and benefits of parenting, not the actual ones. However "natural" motherhood may seem to the larger society, those deciding whether or not to have a child for the first time saw it as a "risky choice."[3] As one young manager put it:

> A: Maybe all these reasons are smoke. I think I'm just afraid of having a kid because I don't know what it is. I don't know how to hold a baby. It's a strange little animal, and I don't know what to do with it, and really it comes down to learning to deal with being a mother, because if I really wanted a baby, I would find the solution to any other problem.

3. Luker (1975) analyzes contraceptive behavior as risk taking. The women in my study showed considerable sophistication about reproductive control. Only 8 percent reported that their first child was unplanned. Another 9.2 percent had chosen to have an abortion at some point in their adult lives. The remaining women had used birth control successfully and had either chosen to remain childless or had borne children that were defined as planned.

In the context of perceived risk, structural and ideological conditions combined to make the price of motherhood appear unacceptably high. Men and marriage provided important structural conditions that interacted with beliefs about proper child-rearing practices and their perceived consequences for career, personal well-being, and the child.

Men and Marriage

Men raised the cost of motherhood to intolerable levels for nontraditional women in three ways. First, in most cases, a male partner represented a precondition for an affirmative decision. Second, men's own parenting motivations set up pressures to which their partners had to respond. Third, male partners offered the best hope for lightening the load of motherhood. When a stable marriage (or relationship) was not an attainable or acceptable option, when male partners were either opposed to or uninterested in parenting, or when they were unwilling to share the domestic responsibilities that accompany the arrival of a child, the perceived costs of motherhood rose to offset whatever personal desires for children these respondents may have formed. Any or all of these circumstances held for the woman committed to childlessness.

Impermanence and Commitment.   The respondents unanimously agreed that the most fundamental precondition for parenthood was a partner. After all, they argued, men and women become—or fail to become—parents together, and every time a woman creates a child, so does a man.

Like this thirty-year-old divorced clerk, they all rejected the option of childbearing outside of either marriage or a committed heterosexual partnership:[4]

4. Anthropological evidence suggests that societies in which a substantial proportion of the population opts for childbearing outside of committed heterosexual partnership are rare. (See Malinowski, 1930, for the classic analysis of the social importance and near universality of the "principle of legitimacy.") Although the United States has shown a rise in the rate of illegitimacy over the last thirty years, most of this upturn has been confined to teenagers and very poor women from minority populations, where, for a myriad of reasons, legal marriage has not been as widespread as in the general population. Ladner (1971), Liebow (1967), and Stack (1974) document the economic, social, and psychological "rationality" of illegitimacy among poor minority groups in the United States.

Among nonpoor, nonteenage, white women, however, there is little indication that childbearing outside of either marriage or a committed heterosexual partnership has become a popular choice. (See, for example, Bane, 1976.) Although illegitimacy rates

Q: So you wouldn't have a child out of wedlock?

A: I would never have a child to have a child—for a lot of reasons. I would prefer, like I'm sure any woman would, maybe some would not, to be in love and have children and raise a family. But I would not have a child if I weren't married and loved the man. First it's love and marriage; then it's children. As much as I would like to have children, I *still* will not unless there is someone.

This reluctance to bear a child without a partner was not simply a fear of social reprisal or a moral conviction that such an act was wrong. Rather, all agreed that deciding to bear a child alone was both impractical and dangerous. Even in the context of a stable partnership, childbearing threatened to pose almost insurmountable obstacles; in the absence of the emotional and economic supports a partner could provide, the consequences of childbearing to mother and child alike appeared disastrous. Without a partner, these women reasoned, they could not muster the time, money, or emotional and physical energy to bear and rear a child successfully. (Ironically, however, many others have or will unwittingly become single mothers as the result of divorce.) This thirty-one-year-old divorced bookkeeper explained:

A: I have been tempted to have children, even without a father, but then I think it would tie me down, plus it would be very expensive. I was pregnant once and I had an abortion and that was because I wasn't in love with the father. I could have had the baby, but it would have caused complications. I think it probably just isn't meant for me to have my own kids, for some reason. I kind of believe in fate.

Because marriage was considered a prerequisite for childbearing, those who over time could not or would not commit to a long-term relationship concluded that the precondition for having a child was beyond reach. When the institution of marriage seemed fragile and

---

among this group have risen notably in recent years, children born to white women in the later stages of reproductive lives are much more likely to grow up in one-parent families because of divorce than because they were born into them. Thus, although a small proportion of this generation may choose to become parents alone or in the context of a lesbian partnership, the aversion these respondents expressed to childbearing outside of either marriage or committed heterosexual partnership probably fairly reflects larger social trends and relationships. (For a discussion of the constraints of "compulsory heterosexuality," see Rich, 1980, and Snitow et al., 1983. However compulsory heterosexuality may be, it remains the dominant institution in which most childbearing decisions are made.)

impermanent or when distrust and skepticism characterized relationships with men, motherhood became a remote and costly possibility. At thirty-two, this divorced executive concluded that the kind of relationship that makes rearing children a reasonable option was not possible anymore:

Q: If you were to predict the next ten years, would you expect to have children or not?

A: Probably not. If I were to take an educated guess, the answer is no. I just don't foresee the situation developing, to be perfectly honest. Men, marriage, whatever. . . . It's strictly a question of the man. And I would not consider having a child out of wedlock. I sometimes do wonder about the whole family structure, because I really do feel marriage is obsolete. In a society like ours, I think the notion of a happily-ever-after marriage with a happy wife and mother is obsolete. It's charming, like a Victorian dress. With marriage, there is still this sense of being trapped, giving up my independence. And having a child doesn't feel like that to me. But it's the having to get married in order to have a child.

These women were attracted to the idea of childbearing but were averse to the necessary preconditions for parenthood. Difficult and unhappy experiences with men had convinced them that marriage was too hazardous and too costly to risk and that motherhood was thus out of reach. Most especially, those who struggled to break free of a suffocating marriage or relationship did not welcome a return to such a state—even if the ultimate consequence was permanent childlessness. They greeted this choice unenthusiastically, but saw it as the least of a number of bad alternatives. At thirty-two, a divorced, upwardly mobile secretary concluded:

A: If things keep going the way they are, I probably won't [ever have children]. I don't believe in having children if you're not married, and if you don't have a good foundation, you know, for a home, then I just don't believe in bringing children into it. I used to be terribly upset that I was going to be alone, and I was terribly irresponsible when I first got my divorce, because I went directly from my family's home to my husband's home, where he took care of everything for me. When I got out of that, I was more or less *forced* into doing things for myself. I am right now what circumstances have made me. Sometimes you wonder, when you look back on things, if you blew it. As much as I hate thinking about being alone when I get older, I'd rather be alone than be miserable for the rest of my life.

This rejection of marriage was not simply a fear of commitment. Rather, it was a fear of impermanence. Experience had convinced these women that a long-term commitment sufficient to rear a child to maturity was simply not possible. In the context of such interpersonal fragility, childbearing entailed unacceptable risks not only to the child, but also to the ultimate well-being of its mother. Divorced and approaching thirty-five, an administrator decided that marriage and motherhood would undo her newfound success at work—success that was more important because marriage could not provide a safe haven from failure:

> Q: How do you think having children would affect your career plans?
>
> A: In the long term, it probably would set back my career . . . it would probably irretrievably set it back. . . . The real thing that fits in here is my skepticism about men and marriage, because if I had real faith that the marriage would go on, and that this would be a family unit, and that we would have two incomes and be providing for these children, being set back in my career wouldn't be that big a deal. But I have a tremendous skepticism about men and the permanency of relationships, which makes me want to say, "Don't give anything up, because you're going to lose something that you're going to need later on, because they won't be there."

Choosing parenthood thus seemed a shortsighted and irrational act that promised to backfire eventually for these women. Childbearing was an immediate temptation they could resist. Indeed, even an ongoing relationship did not consistently erase the fear of impermanence among those who believed that heterosexual commitment was a fragile and easily broken bond. This childless bookkeeper, for example, mourned the children she never had even before her marriage ended in divorce:

> Q: Why didn't you have a child in your earlier marriage?
>
> A: I wanted to have a family, but I was not going to have a family and have Michael be the father. That's why I'm thirty-one years old and don't have a family. If I had not been so worried about my marriage not working out and had gone ahead and had a family when I was young, I would at least have that.

Even in the context of a steady relationship that spanned twelve years, this thirty-three-year-old interior designer doubted that she could establish the kind of commitment necessary to support the added weight of child rearing:

Q: What are the chances you'll change your mind and decide to have a child?

A: I suppose running into some unknown, different man might change my mind. I haven't really ever had any permanent feeling happen to me. Everything feels very temporary.

Q: Even though you've been seeing a man for the last twelve years?

A: We've spent a lot of time together, but I don't know how you can ever say you're committed to someone. It doesn't work when people get married; how can it work when you don't?

Some women found that, as they became increasingly independent, the range of potential mates narrowed. In the process of establishing autonomy, they raised the standards they applied to potential partners and learned to live happily without one. Waiting for the right man became self-imposed, if unintentional, childlessness. This divorced, upwardly mobile high school graduate in her thirties concluded that, although motherhood was attractive in the abstract, no acceptable candidate for fatherhood was likely to be found:

A: I think you can be in love with someone, but when you start thinking about being with that person for the rest of your life, it's hard. If somebody were to say to me, which would you rather be, single like you are now, going on the way you are, or married and have a child, two children, I would have to say it depends. I'm not going to go into a marriage with some guy making $5,000 a year and I'm making however much more than he is and have him tell me that he doesn't want me working and we'll live on $5,000 a year instead of what I'm used to living on. I'd rather not. It sounds terrible, but if I can't get what I have now or more, why do it? If [the alternative's] not the same or better, forget it. I'm not going to step back down.

The decision to reject marriage and thus motherhood as well was often experienced as a sentence imposed from without and even as a punishment for hard-won independence. At thirty-one, this receptionist reviewed the sequence of events that led to childlessness with bewilderment, sadness, and even guilt:

A: Sometimes I feel like I was gypped, even though I wasn't

gypped. It was my own choice, but I feel, why did I choose this? What made me choose to not have children when I really in my heart want to have children? I think back ten years ago. I was twenty-one and I was going to be a mother, and I think, "Gee, all this time has gone by and look where I'm at today, and how did this happen?" Maybe I'm being punished for having an abortion. It's not like I planned it this way.

The decision these women made to forgo childbearing was nevertheless a choice, albeit a constrained one embedded in a series of other choices. Because it was often only the best of a number of bad alternatives, it was for many a painful decision.

Men's Parenting Motivations.   Confidence in a committed partnership was a necessary but not sufficient condition for choosing to bear a child. Even faith in the permanence of a relationship did not ensure that children would follow. Instead, the partner's stance toward child rearing became part of the context in which the respondent made her choice. When a nondomestic woman's partner expressed cool to lukewarm feelings about parenting, motherhood appeared almost as difficult and dangerous as if the partner were not present at all. In these cases, concern that children would undermine not only one's career, but an established relationship as well effectively discouraged childbearing. A thirty-year-old librarian concluded:

Q: What are the main reasons you don't plan to have children?

A: I decided not to have them, and I stuck to that decision. Ned, of course, is 100 percent with me. He doesn't like children, but it's mostly that he doesn't like the responsibility and also the noise. I can see some redeeming values in children, and he won't admit any. I don't think I'd want to have children against his wishes. That would probably be very unpleasant. I'm not even sure we'd stay married. I just know we would argue about how to raise the kid in such a way that it would totally undermine our relationship.

Partners who were less strongly and vociferously opposed to parenthood were also effective. Most nondomestic women were ambivalent toward childbearing; so a merely uninterested partner tipped the scales against motherhood because he provided no offsetting pressure favorable to motherhood. Instead, he reinforced the perception that chilbearing would be a costly choice and eased the way to rejecting motherhood altogether. As circumstances converged to make child rearing difficult, this working-class couple mutually agreed to reject parenthood:

Q: How definite are your plans not to have children?

A: Fairly definite. We don't want any. Things have changed. I'm too old, number one. If I was to have a child, I'd have to quit my job, and we could not make it without my salary. Plus the added expense of the baby would make it near impossible right there. I don't really feel I want any kids at this point.

Q. How does your husband feel about children?

A: I think he would want a child if the situation were different. If we could afford one, yes, he'd want one. But I think not having one is not a great disaster for either one of us. It's just the way things are.

Childless women in close-knit relationships had difficulty distinguishing between their own and their spouse's opposition to bearing children. When parenting threatened to undermine the relationship as well as the career, it was easier to see the decision to forgo children as the result of mutual desires than to hold one's partner responsible. This married woman acknowledged, however, that a change in her partner's preferences might spark a change in her own:

Q: Do you think you might feel differently if John felt differently?

A: Well, sure. I think we're together, in the same boat. I think if he decided that he was going to flirt with the idea of having children, I would flirt with the idea, too.

Some respondents became involved with men who had already fathered and reared children. These women were especially likely to encounter either a lack of enthusiasm for or a strenuous opposition to sharing the responsibilities of parenthood. As relationships become more fluid and the incidence of divorce and serial monogamy rises, the chances increase that at least one member of new partnerships will have already had children and moved beyond the child-rearing stage of life. This development also increases the number of people, both male and female, who face mounting disincentives to bear their own children. This thirty-six-year-old high school teacher, for example, was committed to a man well past the family-building stage of his life:

Q: What are the main reasons you don't plan to have children?

A: Circumstantial. If I could have found a man I wanted to father my children, I would have had them. Even now, if I met a man who really wanted some children at this age, I might have them. But I'm happy with the man I have now. I guess I've never been driven by the children part. . . . [My present partner] was married very young and raised his children already. I *know* he doesn't want more children.

Of course, women who did not want children were probably inclined to select partners who shared their convictions. Surely a process of self-selection provides some of the explanation. Explaining "object choice" (as psychoanalysts call it) is a highly complicated problem beyond the scope of this study. But people choose a partner for a number of reasons, many of which have no relation to the parenting question. Once chosen, however, one must contend with the whole package this person presents. Just as men set limits on and condition women's orientations and actions, so women respond by attempting to change—and under the right conditions, succeeding in changing—men's orientations and actions as well. Given their own ambivalence, however, this group was not motivated to try to change their partners.

Like their counterparts who bore children, women committed to childlessness developed orientations toward parenthood that were closely tied to their partner's feelings and preferences. The decision to reject parenthood was not made alone. Rather, becoming a mother was judged inappropriate and dangerous in the context of male partners who were opposed or indifferent to childbearing. These partners shifted the largest share of the responsibility for deciding to have a child onto the woman. They also shifted responsibility for the care this child would require. Having a child thus not only threatened to unravel the relationship, but it also left the female partner facing the uninviting prospect of raising any child she bore largely alone. By withholding the promise of needed assistance in child rearing, these men provided a third reason for some nondomestic women to reject motherhood.

The Sexual Division of Parenting Responsibilities. Most male partners, even among those men who wanted to become fathers, resisted equal participation in parenting. When men were averse or unenthusiastic toward childbearing, however, their female partners lacked the leverage to bring them into the parenting process. Bereft of male support, these women faced a double load of work and parenting, unabetted by the contributions of a willing partner. This was often deemed one load too many for nondomestic women with careers at risk. This childless worker in her mid-thirties decided to forgo parenthood:

Q: How definite are your plans to never have children?

A: About seventy to thirty against. It would have to be a really extraordinary relationship with an extraordinary person who I felt could make that extra responsibility a real joy, as opposed to a burden. . . . I would *never* curtail my career goals for a partner. . . . I would not subjugate my career any more than a man would subjugate his career.

Q: What do you think are the chances of finding a partner who would share equally?

A: About seventy to thirty against. . . . I don't know anybody who says he wants an egalitarian relationship. Among the married ones with children, everybody says, "Sure, we'll share with children equally." But nobody does.

Those who decided to remain childless did not find, or were unable to induce their partners to become, that "extraordinary person" who could help relieve the double burden of caretaking and career building. Instead, they confronted partners reluctant to share in the "dirty work" of parenthood:

Q: If you did have a child, do you think you could depend on Bob for help?

A: Very limited help. I'm sure we'd fight all the time. He's told me over and over again, if I had a child, it would be my responsibility; that's one of his threats.

In the context of male recalcitrance, childlessness became the least dangerous alternative and the path of least resistance. When nontraditional women lacked partners who expressed enthusiasm for having a child or taking care of it, they also lacked the means to relieve the heavy costs parenthood threatened to exact. Because none of these respondents actually had children, it is, of course, impossible to assess the accuracy of their predictions regarding their partners' participation in child rearing. This is of little consequence, however, because their perceptions shaped their ultimate decisions. Bereft of both pressures and supports for childbearing, they clung to a traditional ideology that women must choose between committed work and motherhood. This reinforced their conviction that childbearing would entail intolerably negative consequences. They thus decided to reject motherhood and to bear the attendant social and psychological costs of childlessness.

Child-Rearing Ideologies and Childbearing Consequences

Nondomestic women who lacked a willing partner held a set of beliefs that resembled in important respects those of domestically oriented women. Despite their contrasting orientations toward work, they agreed that to attempt to have children *and* a career was to invite disaster. This traditional viewpoint reinforced nondomestic women's decisions to remain childless. They concluded that children would endanger their careers, that work would endanger their would-be children, and that both would endanger their own well-being. A traditional ideology led them to reject motherhood, not committed work.

Perceived Consequences for Career. Childless respondents believed, above all, that children would threaten their chances for success at work. Although they sensed the situation was unfair, they were convinced that motherhood would hinder their progress in a way that fatherhood did not hinder men's. Like her more domestic peers, a childless designer did not question the conflicts between work and motherhood:

Q: Why don't you plan to have any children?

A: I'd rather work, and I think you do either one or the other. . . . I could see that you could get very established and you could have children and work, but you would also be working on a certain level, wouldn't really be a very senior sort of involved person. Although men can be presidents of companies and have children, women can't.

When the struggle to advance at work had been hard fought, as it usually was, motherhood threatened to undo all earlier efforts in one critical step. Childbearing seemed at odds with the logic of previous adult development. Bearing a child became too dangerous for this thirty-two-year-old divorced administrator:

Q: Why do you think you won't have children?

A: It's getting into whether I'm willing to sacrifice where I've gotten in my career, which I've done really well for my age and training. That would be quite a sacrifice, I think. I'm not sure I'm willing to do that at this stage. . . . I feel real badly as I hear myself say that. But if I had a kid, I don't know what I'd do. Somewhere along the line, I would make a decision that family or job mattered more. And since I wouldn't want to be a goofy mother, I guess I would decide okay, I decided to have the child and that's *my* responsibility to do the best I can. If it means only going to level "A" instead of level "C", then that's where I am.

The decision to remain childless was never made easily and was often made with regret. This same respondent noted, however, that choosing motherhood over career would entail even greater regret:

Q: How would you feel about not moving to level "C" in order to have a child?

A: I think I'd be really upset. It's like here I had a chance to fly, and I'm not going to . . . but I really want to see what I'm capable of. I don't want to look back with regrets. I don't want to feel that I educated myself for a career and was started and suspended it, and then never quite got back on the ladder. That would be really hard.

These respondents concluded that child rearing entailed unacceptably high risks. As work investments, rewards, and demands grew, so did the perceived costs of children.

Perceived Consequences for Children. The possibility of raising a damaged child loomed as a second, and equally discouraging, fear to work-committed women. They reasoned that, just as children would undermine success at work, so work would undermine success in child rearing. Because they felt they would face the challenge of child rearing alone, they assumed they would be almost totally responsible for the kind of people their potential offspring turned out to be. Witness, for example, this reaction from a thirty-three-year-old executive committed to childlessness:

Q: What are the main reasons you plan not to have children?

A: Fear. To be perfectly honest, it scares me to death. I've never been interested in children. I'm really scared of kids, scared of the responsibility, scared of what I could do to their minds, to their lives, the responsibility of being a mother. I feel a tremendous burden about that. It's a fear of what I could do to them. Would I be a good enough mother, or would I put trips on them, or would I mess up their lives? Basically, [would I] be responsible for having developed a crippled individual in some way?

The specter of raising a crippled child served as a powerful brake on childbearing motivations. Respondents feared not simply that the child would suffer, but also that this result would rebound on the mother in terrible ways. This childless physician concluded that the conflict between her needs as a worker and her child's needs would negatively affect both:

A: As a mother, I tend to worry about becoming a harsh disciplinarian, impatient, frazzled, uninterested, uninteresting. . . . And I think women who do both don't end up doing either one well or doing only one well.

Q: And you'd rather not have a child than do a bad job of it?

A: Right. There's no undoing it. . . . At least in my career, I have a lot more confidence, a lot more experience. And I'd feel awful if I had three kids who all turned out to be rotters. To say, "Well, I *never* should have had children" is the most defeating thing that can ever happen to a parent.

Thus, unlike psychological theories that stress women's special mothering needs and abilities, both middle-class and working-class childless women viewed the huge and lonely responsibility of child rearing as a formula for failure. This thirty-year-old secretary, like her better educated counterparts, also feared failing, not at work, but at mothering:

Q: Do you think having children would affect your feelings about yourself in any way?

A: I think I'd feel like an inadequate mother, first of all: feeling I didn't get along with them and they don't like me and later on seeing they were really a pain, took a lot of work, and were noisy and troublesome. . . . It would ruin my self-image. What if you had a child that was perfectly normal and you caused it to be a juvenile delinquent? I may be missing something, but I just figure I couldn't do it. Maybe there are some women who never thought of doing anything else but having children. But I never had the slightest clue about that.

These fears did not result from a casual attitude toward child rearing. To the contrary, these women adhered to high standards in all they did, including their approach to mothering. Aspiring workers from both educational groups expressed a belief that children would require the same attention, care, and energy that they gave to their jobs. These high standards were in fact their undoing, for they could find no way to do both tasks well. These women decided to remain childless rather than alter their standards at home or at work:

A: The stepmother of a friend in college was perpetually baking cookies, making projects—super mom. Her existence was her children, and she never gave any evidence of wanting to do anything else. . . . I couldn't do that. I see myself conflicted by other demands and not fulfilling the role as I see it.

Although their college-educated counterparts provided somewhat more elaborate explanations, high school–educated respondents' definitions of good mothering included the same high level of commitment of time and energy:

Q: What are your main reasons for not having children?

A: I just think that they're a responsibility and you have to be willing to devote all your time to them. If you can't do that, I don't think you should have them. I know that's really old-fashioned, but I tend to believe it.

With so much emphasis in established psychological theory and public debate placed on mothers (to the exclusion of fathers) for the psychological health of the child, it is not surprising that these women perceived their own needs for personal development to be at odds with the child's best interests. The fear of raising crippled offspring persists despite the fact that decades of research have produced virtually no compelling evidence that mothers who work outside the home for pay provide a poorer environment for child development than do mothers who do not.[5] Yet, this concern that working would harm their

5. Years of research on the topic of working mothers has produced the general, if still contested, consensus that the effects on their children vary greatly and depend on other, qualifying factors in both the mother's and the child's environment. A mother's feelings about working seem to be more important than the *fact* of her working. Women who enjoy their jobs and are satisfied with the arrangements they have made for their children appear to provide at least as good and in some cases a better environment for child development than do nonworking mothers. Indeed, mothers who are frustrated at home but continue to avoid paid work because of a sense of duty to their children may unwittingly do their offspring a disfavor. (See Heyns, 1982; Hoffman, 1974; Nye and Hoffman, 1963. For an alternative perspective, see Milne et al., 1983.)

In light of these findings, it is remarkable that clinicians, researchers, and policymakers continue to focus on the "problem of the absentee mother" and to neglect the more pervasive, but ill-researched "problem of the absentee father." Critics of working mothers also tend to erroneously equate responsible caretaking with biological mothering (see, for example, Bowlby, 1969). Responsible child rearing can be accomplished by a wide range of people, including fathers and paid caretakers as well as mothers (see, for example, Pruett, 1983). Indeed, the burgeoning literature on child abuse suggests that many children would be better off if their biological mothers were not their primary caretakers. There is, moreover, no necessary logical connection and virtually no evidence linking working mothers with child neglect. Public debate, social policy, and academic research would thus be better served if attention finally shifted from the historical preoccupation with mother absence to the more fundamental question of how to provide high quality caretaking for children now that a large proportion of American mothers are in the labor force to stay.

children did not produce the once predictable response of forsaking work in favor of motherhood. Rather, it led these work-committed women to reject motherhood.

Perceived Consequences for Identity and Personal Well-Being.　Women committed to childlessness also saw children as a threat to their identity. Some even concluded that rearing a child in the context of their work commitments would undermine their sanity and their physical health. Because committed work was not a negotiable choice, childlessness seemed the only way to avoid personal breakdown. This childless secretary explained:

Q:　Is work a factor in your decision not to have a child, the fact that you don't think you could do both at the same time?

A:　I *could* do both at the same time, but I wouldn't want to. It would drive me nuts to come home to a baby to take care of. When I come home, I want to sit down; I want it to be quiet. So I guess work is a factor, but it sounds awful.

Those with declining aspirations focused on the liberating, nurturing, and fulfilling aspects of mothering, but these upwardly mobile women stressed instead its potentially negative consequences. At thirty-four, this childless, single professional equated child rearing not with growth but with physical and mental decline:

Q:　Do you think having children would affect your feelings about yourself in any way?

A:　Yes, I'm sure I probably do see it as a negative. I see on the one hand the mothering role, the creative, nurturing side, imparting love of learning, skills, self-worth, all those good things; but I tend to see myself more on the other side— as a person, seeing my physical deterioration, emotional deterioration. Seeing the children as being a drain—a physical drain, an emotional drain, and stifling creativity, stifling intellectualism. The women I see who never have children stay young longer. It may be narcissism, but they tend to be better groomed, be much more concerned about their own physical and emotional well-being, more active, more social.

Unlike a number of functional theories that argue that mothering and working require different and indeed antagonistic emotional skills (see, especially, Parsons and Bales, 1955), respondents did not view these two activities as psychologically incompatible. For them, the problem was not mutually exclusive psychological capacities, but rather the time required to do both jobs well. Because these childless women had no actual experience with mothering, their predictions about the consequences of rearing children were purely hypothetical. In this context of uncertainty, they chose to discount the relational pleasures parenthood might bring and focus on its discontents. This eased the decision to reject motherhood.

Coping with Childlessness

Nondomestic respondents who opted for childlessness concluded that, despite its potential pleasures, childbearing threatened to be too costly. The structure of their alternatives made this a reasonable conclusion. Faced with a lack of male support and a demanding job, they viewed children and work as an "either-or" proposition; they decided that it was impossible to integrate the two and do well at both. In contrast to their domestically oriented counterparts who held the same view, however, these nondomestic women affirmed their work commitments at the expense of motherhood. Although many had been unable to imagine remaining permanently childless at an earlier point in their lives, they gradually accepted this option as part of a wider set of choices. This professional concluded:

Q: Over the next five to ten years do you plan to work, have children, or combine working with having a family?

A: Realistically, from past experience, devoting myself to work. I don't see a family as a real viable alternative.

Q: Why?

A: I don't foresee meeting someone. I also foresee my career having its peak demands within the next five to ten years. If I were to start a family, I would abort my career or at least attenuate it. Ten years ago I wouldn't have even touched that line; but today, realistically, the possibility and probability of never marrying and never having children looms real.

Yet these women did not find it easy to opt for childlessness. The social and psychological importance placed on childbearing remains enormous. Opting for such an unpopular choice meant weathering social disapproval and personal doubt. These women did so by developing coping strategies that provided social and emotional insulation from the worst consequences of childlessness.

First, childless women mustered network support for their choice. One single professional in her mid-thirties described her efforts to sustain her decision for childlessness amid the pressures to procreate:

> A: Consciously or unconsciously, I surround myself with single women. I have very few married female friends, and I have almost no female friends with children. So my coterie of women confidantes are either childless or single, and we're a big support group. To some degree, we're all a bit frustrated about finding appropriate partners.

Childless women thus had each other. In an earlier historical period, they would have faced far greater difficulty finding peers to reinforce their personal rejection of motherhood. Thirty years ago, many women in a similar situation probably became frustrated mothers. Today, however, growing numbers of similarly situated women provide the means for voluntarily childless women to insulate themselves from the wider social expectation that any woman past thirty should have a child. Indeed, traditional women face increasing difficulty finding social support for having and caring for children.

Women committed to childlessness also minimized in their own minds the severity of the potentially negative consequences of never having children. In particular, they rejected the common belief that children serve as an effective insurance policy against the horrors of abandonment in old age.[6] This divorced secretary feared being old and alone, but did not view children as a guarantee against such a fate:

> Q: Is there anything about never having children that bothers or worries you?
>
> A: I think about myself when I'm at retirement age and have four walls to come home to. It's about the only thing that bothers me, whether it be children or a husband. If I thought about it long enough, it would bother me terribly, because even though I'm basically a loner anyhow, I've always got to know that there's someone around—not just friends, either. Someone that you're close to who you know accepts you the way you are.

---

6. A number of research findings suggest that these respondents' perceptions are not unfounded. Glenn and McLanahan (1980) found little evidence to support the generally accepted belief that children are a major source of psychological reward in the later stages of life. Studies of help patterns in American families typically show that the flow of economic, social, and emotional support moves in primarily one direction: from parent to child.

Q: Does this fear of being alone tempt you to have children?

A: No, because children are going to end up going off from you, having their own lives too, so no. I adjust when I have to adjust to something. I'll just make the best of my life the way it is. I'm going to be thirty-three next week, and I don't want to start having a family now. It's a little late as far as I'm concerned.

Rather than acting on the fear of future regret, childless women thus struggled to bring their feelings closer into line with what they could realistically create out of their lives, a process that somewhat resembles Hochschild's (1980) "emotion work." They discounted the potential benefits of parenting they feared they might be denying themselves.

To accept childlessness, most respondents grieved for what would never be and let go of old hopes and expectations. They also struggled to defend and justify their choice against others' expectations and their own self-doubts. An upwardly mobile secretary committed to childlessness explained:

A: When you get into your late twenties, people start questioning what you're doing and what your plans are, why you're not getting married. I give people a stock answer that I'm still waiting for somebody to wash dishes. It is an outright lie, but it shuts people up. That's what a man says, somebody to take care of him. I'm looking for somebody to take care of me. It took me a long time to get to that point.

Similarly, they rejected the argument that their identities, as women or human beings, would be jeopardized by childlessness or that they were denying themselves the possibility of meaningful human relationships. They emphasized, instead, their pride in their own independence.

Q: Is there anything about never having children that bothers or worries you?

A: No. I don't think I'm less of a woman, of a human being, or have not done my part for society or anything. No. I don't have any bad feelings about not having children, no fears about my old age. And I think that is just a rotten reason to have children, and put that on them. I will take care of myself until I die. I'll die with a checkbook in my hand!

With few supports to ease the integration of work and parenthood, these respondents concluded that the demands and rewards of work, personal accomplishment, and autonomy superseded whatever relational pleasures child rearing might bring. For this childless secretary, the costs of motherhood promised to outweigh the benefits:

Q: What are your main reasons for not having children?

A: I don't think I really wanted the responsibility for them because you have to devote your whole time to them. I know that sounds terribly selfish, doesn't it? I suppose it's like this: I can go enjoy my friends' children, go to their birthday parties and give them gifts, and watch their faces light up. And, sure, I get that feeling when I hold an infant in my arms. But on the other side of it, you've got to take what comes along with that, all the responsibility, all that part of your time. So it is nice, I think, to see human beings develop and know you've had some influence on them. But I just think one outweighs the other. And if it does, then you shouldn't have them. I don't plan to have children.

For this upwardly mobile professional, mothering did not promise to be rewarding and rewarded enough to compensate for lost work opportunities:

A: Children on a competitive scale with my work, comparing the two and running a race between the offering and rewards, children have really taken a backseat. It's not even a close race.

For these respondents, childlessness was judged to be not only the best of a number of bad alternatives, but indeed the only responsible choice available. They took solace in their conviction that they were making the right decision, whatever its pitfalls. This divorced administrator explained:

Q: How do you feel about the idea of never having children?

A: I think it's the kind of thing that, if I'm forty and the circumstances have been that it just never quite seemed the thing to do, I would work to let go. I would have regrets here and there, just like whether or not you should have entered your marriage. But it's something eventually that you weigh out and see that that was really the best decision, that I was really responsible in my decision, that I chose not to have children because I couldn't be the kind of mother I wanted to be, and that that was good.

Finally, in their search for reasons to explain what was experienced as an intensely private and individual decision, they tended to personalize the choice. Many assumed they lacked some special psychological quality possessed by others who were better able to combine work and childbearing. This childless secretary lamented:

Q: You don't feel you could combine work with raising children?

A: No. For women working and wanting children, I think it takes an extraordinary effort. Women do it, and it's to be commended, I think. I don't have the energy that I see some of my friends have. . . . I guess I don't want it that much.

Lacking structural support, respondents presumed that only superhuman effort and exceptional women could successfully combine work and motherhood. Of course, the process of combining work and child rearing does not require extraordinary abilities, only extraordinary human and situational supports. The difficult effort must be expended mustering this support. The next chapter demonstrates how extraordinary circumstances led some women to choose to add children to their already crowded work-committed lives.

7 | Combining Work and Motherhood

This chapter turns to a third group of women—those who chose to combine committed work with parenthood. This group differs from both groups discussed in Chapter Six, albeit in contrasting ways. Unlike domestically oriented women, these women were committed workers who viewed children as potentially costly to their work careers. Unlike permanently childless women, however, they decided over time that childlessness held greater costs than motherhood. These women thus neither wholeheartedly embraced motherhood nor rejected it completely. Rather, they approached parenthood reluctantly, aware of the problems it posed, yet fearful that a different course would hold even greater dangers. This chapter analyzes the process by which this group of work-committed women became, or planned to become, "reluctant mothers."

The reluctant mother's approach to childbearing was one of deep ambivalence, which is well illustrated by this thirty-year-old married worker's struggle to develop enthusiasm for childbearing amid fears that motherhood would upset the delicate balance of her professional and personal life:

Q: Over the next five to ten years, do you plan to work, raise a family, or do both?

A: I think I plan to combine working with raising a family. And the reason I say I *think* is that, if I want to have a family, I'm sure I'll want to combine working with a family. I'm having a little trouble wanting a family. I'm not quite sure where that's coming from.

Q: Where do you think it's coming from?

A: I'm not sure that I like children. It's more than that. I'm stretched so many ways now, in terms of demands on my time. And I feel that a baby, if I commit myself to a baby, I can't let it go for a week like I can the garden. I'm a little afraid of that extra commitment. That's just going to be a little more than I can take. I'm not sure yet what has to give where. I'm afraid of having kids, and yet that's hard because I know I'm going to hate myself when I'm sixty if I don't have any kids. It's a real up-in-the-air situation in terms of what I really want to do.

In contrast to those whose ambivalence about children led them toward childlessness, however, these women planned to add, or had already added, children to their lives.

Reluctant Motherhood

Reluctant mothers confronted different constraints and brought different resources to bear on the decision to have a child than did their childless counterparts. They were more likely to find themselves in relationships that would be seriously jeopardized by childlessness. They were also in a better position to minimize the negative impact children threatened to have on their lives. This group thus faced cross-pressures that lowered the perceived costs of childbearing and raised the costs of childlessness above a tolerable level. Childlessness became harder to choose and less attractive, leading these women to add children to their already established commitments at the workplace.

These features of their situation also made reluctant mothers less inclined to discount and more inclined to focus on the potentially dire long-term consequences of childlessness. They then developed coping strategies to reduce the perceived costs of motherhood and discounted instead the costs of combining work and family. In contrast to their childless counterparts, they came to believe that they could integrate mothering into their lives without significant sacrifice to themselves, their work, or their children. This upwardly mobile office manager concluded, for example, that bearing a child would pose no major obstacle to achieving her rapidly rising work aspirations:

Q: Why do you plan to have children and work at the same time?

A: I don't want to have to give up anything to have children. I don't want to have to change my life-style at all. I look at it as an addition to my life. I'm not planning on changing anything.

Several factors led these women to decide that they could successfully combine work and motherhood without "giving up anything." First, as in the cases of childless women, men played a critical role in shaping these women's responses to the motherhood dilemma. Unlike the pressures men exerted on childless women, however, the pressures exerted on reluctant mothers by their male partners pushed them toward motherhood rather than away from it. Second, given the social and emotional pressures they faced, reluctant mothers were less able than childless women to discount the costs of childlessness. They were also better positioned to develop contextual supports for combining work and motherhood.

Men's Parenting Motivations

The women who chose childlessness lacked a committed relationship or, paradoxically, had a valued relationship that children threatened to undermine. Reluctant mothers generally faced the contrasting situation: Forgoing children threatened to undermine a relationship more than did having them.

Reluctant mothers typically had partners who, directly or indirectly, encouraged and pressured them to bear children. In contrast to the stereotype of the manipulative and overanxious wife coaxing her reluctant husband into parenthood, these respondents found themselves being pushed toward childbearing by husbands impatient to become fathers. This computer programmer explained:

Q: So you're feeling a lot of pressure at this point to have a child?

A: Mostly it's from my husband. Not because he's deliberately doing it, but because I know he wants to make babies, and he has been very serious about talking about it. When are we going to do it, this and that, until finally I said, "Please back off because I'm not ready for this yet."

Q: Do you think it would affect your marriage if you decided to never have children?

A: Yes, because if I decide I won't have children, my husband has to decide if he wants to keep me. . . . Because he wants a family, and I think that's really important to him. I would prefer not to do that, having a baby just because the husband wants it, simply to please him. If I'm to go through being pregnant, I prefer to be deliriously happy about it.

The male desire to have children and the prospect of losing a spouse or partner if one opposed this desire were often decisive in opting for motherhood. In the context of personal ambivalence, pressure from her spouse pushed this secretary to decide in favor of parenthood:

Q: What are your plans regarding children?

A: Doug and I are really at odds over it. He has always said he wants children. I never really see children in the future, but I don't see them *not* in the future either. The few times we have really talked about it, he's said they are very important to him; so I don't know. If I were to get pregnant now, I would be, I'm sure, unhappy about the situation when I first found out, but I would deal with it and make the best of things.

Q: So you feel that your husband is a major factor?

A: He could be maybe a *deciding* factor. If I'm getting closer to it, he might bring me over nearer the edge. I think if I were with a man who did not want them, it would be definitely no. But the more we have talked about it, and it has been recurring more often, Doug has said he really *does* want children; so I think that would be a major factor in our relationship. For me, I don't really foresee it. It boils down to how much he really wants to push me. I don't really have that much of a desire.

Such male pressures did not apply solely to those who planned to become parents. Reluctant motherhood was often a fait accompli because a spouse had already succeeded in his circuitous, but effective, efforts to gain his wife's acquiescence. Although unable to consciously decide to get pregnant, this thirty-one-year-old office worker abandoned contraception in the face of her husband's pressure:

Q: Was this child planned?

A: Not exactly. As you probably gathered, I have difficulty making some of these decisions. My husband wanted to have

> kids. I was unwilling to make a conscious decision to have
> one, but between all the scary things they say about being on
> the pill, I was willing to take chances. My number came up
> much sooner than I ever expected. I made a decision only to
> the extent that I wasn't absolutely going to prevent it from
> happening.

Q: So your husband was important in the decision to "take
chances?"

A: Well, if he wasn't really all that interested in having a kid, I
probably would have had less ambivalence about *not* having
one. You know, my ambivalence, my thinking that I might
regret it if I don't.

Pressure from a spouse also operated in more subtle ways. Just as
an uninterested partner pushed some women away from motherhood,
mild forms of support pushed others toward it. Male support became
especially powerful when it led a woman to equate a committed relationship with children. In this context, children implied costs and
problems, but they also expressed the value of the relationship itself.
Thus, at twenty-seven, this lawyer viewed child rearing not as a form
of individual fulfillment, but rather as a biological and emotional
extension of her commitment to a man:

Q: What would you say are your main motivations for having a
child?

A: I see it closely as an identification with my husband. He
wants them. He's *very* family-oriented. It's never been
discussed, but it would bother him if he didn't think he was
going to have them. But if I found I was biologically unable
to have them, I don't think I would adopt. Having kids will
really be a hassle and complicate life. It's going to be very
inconvenient, and I think a strong reason I want children is
to have a child with my husband rather than to have
children per se.

Finally, even though reluctant mothers did not define children as
the fulfillment of their identity or nurturing needs, they often viewed
them as a way of fulfilling their spouses' needs. Depriving their partners of children meant depriving themselves of the pleasure of giving
something important to the person they valued most. Her spouse's
enthusiasm for parenthood assuaged this secretary's ambivalence:

Q: Is there anything about not having children right now that
bothers you?

A: I miss parts. Children can really be a job, but I miss [it during] the times Steve is with other children, and I watch him. He's really good with them, and that makes me feel sad or whatever that he does not have a child of his own. I think he would be very, very good, and that part does bother me at times. That would be a major thing for me. I would feel a lot of satisfaction for him to have satisfaction in that type of relationship.

Just as an uninterested or openly hostile spouse dampened the desire for children, so an encouraging or assertive one led other non-domestic women to overcome or at least act against their ambivalence toward childbearing. These accounts suggest, furthermore, that theories that picture men as universally uninterested in children and uniformly underdeveloped in their nurturing needs, capacities, and desires oversimplify both men's orientations toward parenting and women's experiences with men. These male partners' parenting motivations went beyond the desire to reproduce offspring merely to prove manhood or to perpetuate the family name and genetic structure. At least in the eyes of their female partners, these men possessed a genuine desire and ability to nurture children. (Recent research by Pruett, 1983, on a sample of primary caretaking fathers supports this conclusion.) Were these parents or would-be parents not of the male gender, one might be tempted to label their motives as a need or desire to "mother." Similarly, reluctant mothers' reasons for wanting babies resemble those commonly attributed to men for wanting to father children.

As the strength and legitimacy of the nondomestic path for women have grown, men have faced added pressure to acknowledge their parenting motives and to push for children in their marriages. Because men do not typically view their options as a choice *between* work and family, they are less likely to focus on the negative consequences children might exact from their work careers than are their nondomestic female partners.

If we credit these reluctant mothers' perceptions, we must conclude that both men and women vary significantly in their desires to bear children and in their reasons for doing so. We must also conclude that men's and women's parenting motivations are related and interactive. Reluctant mothers appear to have responded as much to their partners' desires to procreate and nurture as to their own. Despite their own ambivalence, reluctant mothers were propelled by their partners slowly and haltingly toward motherhood. These accounts challenge the tenacious view held by social theorists, psychoanalysts, and ordinary people alike that women uniformly become mothers primarily to fulfill strongly felt needs to nurture and men typically seek parenthood grudgingly.

Perceived Consequences of Childlessness

Because these respondents experienced strong contextual pressures favoring motherhood, they were less able to insulate themselves from their fears of what childlessness implied in the long run. They therefore tended to focus on the negative consequences of childlessness rather than discounting them.

As pressures mounted, reluctant mothers were increasingly haunted by the costs of permanent childlessness: social disapproval, consignment to a lonely and desolate old age, and the loss of a major life experience with intrinsic value beyond its social measure. The fear of these costs had powerful psychological ramifications for childless women facing pressures to parent. An upwardly mobile worker facing pressure from her spouse worried:

Q: How do you think you'd feel if you never had children?

A: Guilty, guilty. I really think that my approach toward having children at this point in my life is more based on what is expected of me than what I expect of myself. I think the only reason I'm considering having children right now is because it's heresy not to consider having children. The strongest thing will be the guilt and putting up with the disapproval. I don't think there's ever an end to the push. You get the pressure all your life from one place or another. It's just incredible.

Although childlessness had been the path of least resistance in early adulthood, fears of the negative consequences of never having children took on greater significance as respondents entered their thirties. At thirty, this same respondent conceded:

Q: But the negative consequences of *not* having a child also bother you?

A: That's right. I'm going to hate myself when I'm sixty. I won't have any grandchildren, nobody to take care of me in my old age, all that kind of stuff.

Thus, although children were not welcomed in the present, the long-term consequences of childlessness grew increasingly more ominous for these reluctant mothers. They gradually came to see parenthood as their best chance for establishing intimate, enduring interpersonal bonds. Some even concluded that rejecting motherhood would foreclose the possibility of meaningful human relationships altogether.

A lawyer, for example, viewed children as her only protection against an otherwise impersonal world:

Q: What are your main reasons for wanting children?

A: I think it would be really sad to be forty or fifty years old and not have a family. I think families are extremely important. Our society is getting so splintered as it is that I think it's really nice to have this close group of people, besides just your spouse.

Despite parenthood's drawbacks, reluctant mothers began to switch their focus from its costs to its intrinsic benefits. These included not only the continuation of the family unit but also the experience of creating a human being and adding balance, fullness, and renewed purpose to a life skewed too heavily in favor of work. Although strongly committed to work, this accountant came to view child rearing as the ultimate challenge:

A: When you go into life and everything, you're living day to day. You can have one job or another job, you can do something, but whatever you do is not an influence as much as raising a family. So I think it's really important. It's the most challenging thing that anybody can do.

And this lawyer rejected the traditional imperative that would deny her the right to build a life structured around both work and family:

Q: What are your main reasons for wanting children?

A: It's more of a family unit, a continuation of life. I don't think it's fair that professional women can't have kids. They make things fuller, more complete. I think it rounds out your life better.

In conclusion, reluctant mothers responded to social and personal cross-pressures by focusing on the costs of childlessness rather than discounting them. Torn between fears of the disruption that children would cause and offsetting desires to please their spouses and affirm their interpersonal commitments through children, these women mustered a variety of reasons, some positive and some negative, to bolster their halting commitment to motherhood.

Consciously and unconsciously, they developed coping strategies designed to lower the costs of children and ease the way toward child-bearing. Some strategies rebounded on male partners who exerted pressures in favor of parenthood. Because their partners desired children, reluctant mothers could bring more leverage than their childless counterparts to the process of negotiation with their partners about how to rear their shared offspring. Spouses and male partners thus found themselves pulled more fully into the parenting process and pushed to redefine both their beliefs about proper child-rearing practices and the actual sexual division of labor within the home. Reluctant mothers acted back upon the dilemma they faced, using whatever material and ideological leverage they could muster to control and limit the costs of motherhood.

Coping Strategies

Reluctant mothers rejected childlessness and were unable or unwilling to loosen their work commitments, so only one viable response remained: lower the costs of children. This group developed three strategies to accomplish this task. They decided to limit the number of children they bore; they struggled to bring their male partners into the parenting process; and they redefined their traditional notions about how to rear children. Each of these strategies represented some form of change—in how they organized their lives, in how they dealt with the people around them, or in how they theorized about mothering.

Limiting Family Size.   A common strategy for holding down the costs of children was to hold down the number. Historically, this response has led to the rise of the so-called typical family of 2.5 children, with a concomitant decline in the percentage of larger families (Masnick and Bane, 1980). Reluctant mothers joined this trend despite their earlier hopes of having larger families. Some stopped at two children even though they had originally planned for more:

> A: Two is a manageable number. My husband would have liked a larger family, but at that point, for financial reasons, I would have not been able to work. And I would not have felt right having three of them.

Despite the historical decline in family size, until recently, a pervasive aversion to families with fewer than two offspring has prevailed. Many following a nondomestic path, however, found themselves settling not just for smaller families but for one-child families. Fifty-three percent of those who planned to combine work and family also planned to limit their family size to one child. This decision was reached by a number of routes, but it was usually made for the same reason: One child became a convenient compromise between a reluctant mother's determination to avoid a life defined primarily by domestic responsibilities and the pressure she felt to bear a child. This alternative became especially attractive when motherhood appeared foreboding, but childlessness looked even worse. Many reluctant mothers agreed with this thirty-three-year-old academic that one child would round out their lives, but more than one would overcrowd them:

Q: How do you respond to a woman who has decided to never have children?

A: When I look at *them*, I feel like they've missed something. I don't know if it's necessary to have a child to have a fulfilled life, but somehow I see that they could have another dimension in their life they didn't have.

Q: So you don't want to never have children any more than you want to be a full-time homemaker?

A: I don't think so. Actually, when it comes down to it, I probably want to have one, just so I can have that experience, too. In a way, it seems more attractive to me than having two because there are fewer compli-cations. . . . It's not that I don't like children. It's that life is complicated by so many other things. It would be hard to pay enough attention to more than one.

So reluctant mothers concluded that one child would disrupt their work far less than two. Indeed, they came to believe that, although two children would invite disaster, one child posed no threat at all. From this high school–educated reluctant mother's perspective, one child imperiled neither her work nor her personal well-being:

A: I know one child won't drive me crazy, and two might. I know I couldn't work and have two; knowing me, I don't think I could handle it.

Q: How do you think having a child will affect your work plans?

A: I don't think it would affect it at all. More than one would; that's one of the reasons I only want one.

The decision to limit fertility to one child almost always involved a downward readjustment from earlier plans. This change required let-ting go of old beliefs about the need for siblings and the pitfalls of being an only child. This change allowed reluctant mothers to rec-oncile their rising work ambitions with their similarly high standards for mothering. This office worker concluded that there were offsetting economic benefits for only children:

A: I feel I can be just as good a mother working as staying home. That's why I want only one child. Before I felt you can't just have one; they need a little brother or sister. I feel now that one child can be just as well adjusted, and a person should have what they can afford.

For some, the decision to bear only one child was part, and often an unintended part, of a strategy of postponement.[1] As time passed and work ambitions rose, deadlines for childbearing neared and the previously unthinkable became not only a probability but a likelihood. This administrative assistant past thirty unwittingly backed into the one-child strategy:

> A: I've always thought you should have at least two children. But the chances are strong we'll have one. I'm too old, and work is too important.

Others found that the experience of motherhood itself sparked the decision to impose a permanent moratorium on childbearing. The experience of rearing her son alone convinced a divorced mother that one child was enough:

> A: The kid has influenced me to the point that I don't want any more kids . . . with just the responsibility, the burden of raising kids. It's kind of held me back to a certain degree, being a single parent, not getting to do what I want to do, having to worry about him first.

In some of these cases, the decision to curtail childbearing plans after only one birth reverberated within the marriage itself. As frustrated mothers clashed with disappointed fathers, marital discord ensued. This high school–educated single mother, for example, chose to divorce rather than to fulfill her husband's desire for more children:

> A: I had my daughter from my first marriage, and [I was] haphazardly wondering if I could hang on to the marriage in the tradition like everybody did. I was raised Catholic, and we didn't believe in divorces. My husband wanted [me] to stay in the marriage, but he wanted a lot of children and I didn't; so we made an understanding that eventually, when I can financially support myself and my daughter, that's what I want to do. And if he wants more children, we would have to think about separating, and his continuing his life with more children, which he has.

---

1. Interestingly, working-class women tended to perceive biological deadlines for childbearing as occurring somewhat earlier than did middle-class women. Both groups, however, tended to adjust these perceived deadlines upward over time as part of a strategy of postponement.

Divorce also limited family size even when more children had been planned. Divorce curtailed childbearing not only for childless women but also for those with one child. Mothers who were invariably left to care for the first child concluded that another child would erode the financial security, personal autonomy, and work prospects they had fought so hard to gain:

Q: What are your main reasons for having only one child?

A: I wouldn't want to raise one out of wedlock, not because of the social stigma—it's nobody's business but mine—but I couldn't see raising two kids on the salary I'm making. It costs a lot of money to raise a kid. Also because I have things that *I* want to do. I have plans.

As the number of women exposed to increased work opportunities, affected by divorce, or engaged in a strategy of postponing child-bearing grows, the one-child alternative appears likely to grow as well. The one-child family has never been a popular choice, and some experts (such as Blake, 1966, 1974) argue that neither childlessness nor having only one child is likely to increase substantially with this generation of women. Certainly, many who plan to limit their fertility to one child may find that, once a child arrives, earlier ambivalence and reluctance subside with the pleasant reality of motherhood. The opposite, how-ever, may also occur, as some who plan for two or more children ultimately decide to stop with one after the first is born.

The larger forces at work make the one-child family a sensible choice. As long as growing numbers of reluctant mothers find themselves caught between the costs of children and the costs of childlessness, a substantial number will be motivated to keep the costs of motherhood down without rejecting it altogether. (Bird, 1979, makes the same pre-diction.) Having only one child, whatever the historic social biases against doing so, is a reasonable and readily accessible strategy for accomplishing this end.

Bringing Men In. Reluctant mothers also lowered the costs of chil-dren by bringing men into the parenting process and the domestic work of the household. Although this entailed a conflictual process that typically produced mixed results, many reluctant mothers made male participation a precondition to accepting the responsibilities of parenthood. Without a participatory father, this professional rea-soned, the benefits of parenthood would not be worth the price:

Q: What if Phillip were not willing to participate equally?

A: I don't know that I would want children under those circumstances. I want the emotional support. I want it for the children, for myself. I want the participation, and without it I don't want children. I don't think it would be a fulfilling experience. Without two people doing it, I think it would be a burden on one person. It's no longer a positive experience; it has lots of negative aspects to it.

Of course, wanting—and even demanding—a partner's equal participation does not guarantee securing it. Inequality in the household division of labor has persisted despite the rise in the proportion of committed women workers with young children. Time budget studies collected over the last thirty years unanimously attest to the intransigence of an unequal sexual division of labor in the home. Recent studies confirm what older studies also found: that whether or not they work, married women tend to perform most of the tasks associated with running a modern household. Working wives generally get more help from their husbands than do full-time homemakers, but the couple that shares household tasks equally remains rare.[2] (Male participation in housework and child care does appear, however, to be on the rise, and the trend is toward increased participation; see Badinter, 1981; Shinn, 1983.)

With historical precedent and structural arrangements organized against it, the struggle to bring men into the process of parenting and caring for a home is thus not likely to succeed unless a woman is both sufficiently motivated to struggle and armed with enough leverage to extract consent from her partner. Domestically oriented women had little reason to push for fuller male participation, and childless women generally lacked the leverage.

Reluctant mothers, however, were more motivated and better positioned to carry out this struggle. These women gained leverage primarily from two sources: their spouses' desire for children and the benefits male partners gained from having a work-committed wife. The husband who pushed his reluctant wife toward childbearing usually found he had to give something to get something. This reluctant mother expecting her first child explained:

> Q: Will you be able to depend upon your husband's participation when the baby is born?
>
> A: I think so. We're in the process of changing. We're even now starting to switch the load, and I think it will be shared much more equally when the baby comes. I was kind of

2. See Berk (1980), Blumstein and Schwartz (1983), Hofferth and Moore (1979), Huber and Spitze (1983), Pleck (1975), Scott (1974), Szalai (1972), Vanek (1974), and Wilensky (1968).

cocky when we first got married, and I thought I could be the perfect wife that I envisioned my mother being and also work. We're having to retrain each other's psyches on that.

Q: And he's going along with that?

A: With the kid, he really is. He wanted this kid more than I did.

The financial benefits men gained from work-committed wives gave reluctant mothers additional leverage in the negotiation of domestic equality. Their important contributions to the economic stability of their households provided a base for demanding fuller male participation in parenting. This accountant found that mutual financial dependence promoted mutual arrangements at home:

Q: How does your husband feel about whether you should work, raise a family, or do both?

A: He feels that you can combine both, and he's willing to help and stuff. I think probably, too, he's thinking of the monetary end of it.

In one rare case, the wife was able to command a greater income as a lawyer than her husband did as a house painter and aspiring novelist. Because she was the primary wage earner, they were preparing for an arrangement once considered unthinkable—a father as primary caretaker:

A: I sort of entered law thinking this is the kind of work you can do on a part-time basis, but I think I might have been wrong. But I'm sure by the time we have a child, Larry should be in a situation where he's mostly writing, and he should be at home. So theoretically, it ought to work out fine. I think he realizes that I will have to work, and I think he also thinks it's important to have one of the parents around most of the time. So I think we're going to have to make some sort of trades and really figure it out well at the time.

Although unusual, their situation demonstrates the powerful impact economic arrangements have on domestic organization. Mothering "predispositions" aside, when economics makes exclusive motherhood too costly, fuller participation by fathers is likely to follow. Analyses that define male interests primarily in terms of male dominance via breadwinning supremacy generally overlook the fact that economically independent women such as these offer men benefits they often cannot afford to ignore. Reluctant mothers, moreover, could convert these benefits into increased decision-making power within the home. The husband of this upwardly mobile high school–educated woman, for example, supported her independence because it increased his independence as well:

> A: My husband is very, very understanding. I never have to listen to anything about "Oh, you're never home; you don't cook for me seven days a week." He's very happy that I'm accomplishing what I'm accomplishing. He doesn't want to be burdened by having to make me happy. When I met him, he knew I had a lot more ambition. He helped me along. He's a manager, and I'm a manager, and we just share ideas and help each other out.

Male partners were thus enlisted in what was once considered "women's work." Few reluctant mothers expected to gain complete domestic equality or to shift the primary child-care responsibility to their spouses, but all became involved in a negotiated process to garner increased male participation in parental caretaking. The more responsibility their partners assumed, the less costly children appeared. Negotiating greater male participation in child care and household work was often an unpleasant process, but it was essential to making motherhood an acceptable choice. Initial male resistance confronted female determination. This aspiring linguist explained:

> A: When we were first living together, I did most of the housework. But I think I changed more and more. I feel like [I wanted to be] very, very certain that nothing happens to me again like what happened in the past with other men, including my father. So at first I would ask him to do half the housework. We would argue about it, and finally I would get him to do half of it. And now I can usually get him to do it by asking him about five times, but we don't have to argue so much about it any more. It's coming to be more fifty-fifty.
>
> Q: Do you think you'll be able to depend upon him for help rearing the children?
>
> A: I think by then we'll have those kinds of things worked out to the extent that he will do half. I don't ask him to do anything alone, including financially, to support the child, but I want half. It's going to be a struggle for me to get him to do it.

Thus, despite initial resistance and the intractable nature of old habits, grudging, but nonetheless significant, change in male partners' behaviors and assumptions usually followed. As these men confronted the terms of the implicit bargain they had struck with their work-committed partners, they began to accept and even take pride in their new responsibilities. This manager described the process of change:

Q: How do you think he'll feel about helping out?

A: I think he'll learn to love it. It's been a shock for him. He never expected to marry anybody like me; but he was attracted to me because of the things I am, which is not the little woman who is barefoot and pregnant in the kitchen. His initial response is to rail against it because he never grew up thinking he was going to have to fold his own underwear. As soon as he understands that that's part of the bargain, he even gets to the point where *he* develops some pride in doing for himself; but it really takes a while. I am sure that with a baby it will also be an educational, development time called, "You want me to do what? No, okay, all right." We go through that.

Of course, powerful barriers also made change difficult and limited the degree and type of male participation. Because structural and social supports for male parental caretaking remain weak and because men have little reason to voluntarily forgo prerogatives at home, reluctant mothers faced protracted and exhausting battles to secure their partners' participation. These battles invariably seemed worth the effort, but over time they took an emotional toll. Exhaustion and self-doubt occasionally accompanied the efforts of reluctant mothers to secure male support:

Q: So you've made demands and he's responded to them?

A: I guess I've gone through periods of getting really depressed about it, because I feel like I'm the evil person. If I complain or ask or demand or get mad, I feel like it's all classified as bitching. . . . I don't like being put in the position of having to make the marriage an equal one and always to have to be willing to struggle. Sometimes I think maybe I'd rather be single than struggle. But I think I've gotten more out of the marriage than the struggle. I think that the positive parts have made it worth it. I think about the loneliness, and I don't want to go back to that. I think in the end it's worth working for. But it's too bad the woman has to put more *thought* into it.

Because most reluctant mothers inherited household responsibilities and attempted later to shift them, victories were often limited in scope. Most retained primary responsibility for seeing that things ran smoothly, even when domestic tasks were divided more evenly. Although male participation increased, it was not equal participation, no matter how much a male partner agreed to do under protest. Despite her partner's desire for children and efforts to change, an upwardly mobile computer programmer still feared that the weight of domestic responsibilities would rest on her shoulders:

> Q: What about your husband? You said he really wants children, but you don't feel comfortable about asking him to share in the child care?
>
> A: I think he is willing to do any job that needs to be done, but I think both of us are still looking too much at what he does as helping the little woman out in the home. If we have kids, it's going to be my primary responsibility and my worry, and he helps out. And I notice this when he does work around the house or just the cooking; I still feel guilty. When he doesn't do the dishes, I'm the one who's embarrassed if someone comes over and walks into *my* kitchen. It's very hard to work this thing through.

Full-time work requirements often barred men from greater parental participation. Even reluctant mothers did not endorse an arrangement that would bring a father more fully into the home if it also pulled him out of the workplace. Few, even among the well-remunerated, commanded incomes that compared favorably with their partners'.[3] This earnings disparity made role reversal impractical as well as unattractive to female as well as male partners. Thus, despite the rise in the number of women workers, the economic system continues to promote sexual inequality in household labor. Because these men generally earned more than their wives and rarely retained the option *not* to work, they could more easily justify their comparatively low participation in domestic chores. And because the workplace itself remains so impervious to change, even men who wished to be active fathers faced considerable barriers to high parental participation. As a result, although nondomestic women took great pride in their own economic self-sufficiency, they rarely equated personal independence with traditional male breadwinning responsibilities. Even the most work-committed women approached the idea of male domesticity, and

---

3. The earnings disparity between men and women generally tends to hold at the level of the individual couple as well. A wife who earns as much or more than her husband thus remains relatively rare. Appendix C shows that this sample reflects the larger social trend. Although many respondents felt supported by a male partner in their career-building efforts, this support usually depended on his sense of security about his own work.

resultant dependence on their own earnings, with trepidation and resistance. This professional woman explained:

Q: How would you feel about being the sole breadwinner so your husband could stay home with the children?

A: I've thought about that before and feel that one of the luxuries I allow myself is that I'm working and I don't have to. It's a real screwy little backwards knob in there somewhere; I know that, if he quit and I was the sole support, there'd be a different feeling, if I had to work. It is not something I'm unwilling to do, be the mainstay of the family for a while—which is different from forever, though.

Even the most conflicted reluctant mothers thus rarely viewed gender role reversal as a palatable or possible alternative. Few wanted or expected fathers to remain home with the children during the day. A "catch-22" of sorts worked to discourage male partners from trading their briefcases or tool boxes for aprons. First, domestically oriented homemakers had no incentive to induce their husbands to withdraw from the workplace to care for children; this group depended on a committed male breadwinner to support their own domesticity. Non-domestically oriented women, however, were also reluctant to challenge traditional models of appropriate male work behavior even as they pushed for new definitions of appropriate female behavior. Those who were unwilling to stay home with their young children were equally reluctant to request or demand of their partners what they refused to do themselves. The great importance they attached to work made it difficult for them to accept the legitimacy of domesticity for male partners as well as for themselves. These women supported dual-earning household arrangements (and the delegation of child care to a paid caretaker), but they generally rejected full-time male domesticity as an acceptable alternative to the traditional household.

In sum, numerous obstacles limited what a woman could extract from her partner in order to shift the costs of childbearing. Reluctant mothers could gain the help and support of their partners, but this generally produced a form of equality more accurately described as less mothering than as more fathering. (The words "less" and "more" refer only to the amount of time spent at home and focused specifically on child care. These respondents distinguished between quantity and quality of care. From their perspective, less *time* devoted to child care did not imply a lower quality of parenting.) These women supported an arrangement in which they would spend less time at home; they were reluctant, however, to support an arrangement in which their partners would spend more. Although male parental participation was expected, paid care was considered the cornerstone of a workable arrangement:

Q: Will your husband help care for the children on a regular basis?

A: I think we'll have somebody do it, since I'll keep working. But the time we're together, we'll more than share.

Although reluctant mothers were more motivated and in a better position to secure their partners' help than were either childless or traditional women, they faced considerable barriers to fully integrating men into the work of parenting. Indeed, some combiners found it easier to do without a spouse than to try to secure the help of one. Single mothers, especially, saw men as a hindrance rather than a help in combining work and motherhood:

A: I've been on my own since 1973, and I miss having a male around, I guess for companionship. But then I think, "Is it really worth it, having a male around the house, having to put up with the hassles of, as soon as you come home, having to cook dinner, picking up his clothes, washing them, being like a maid?"

A strategy of equal male participation was therefore often viewed as the path of last resort, when all other alternatives had been tried and failed:

A: I think that any really different kind of arrangement, different in terms of nontraditional, would only come as a result of my not being able to find a more traditional resolution to the problem. Because otherwise, he won't see that there's a need for it.

Because the conditions that support equal male participation, although becoming somewhat more widespread, remain comparatively rare, reluctant mothers also looked elsewhere for strategies to retain their footing in the workplace, reduce the costs of motherhood, and resolve the contradictions of their situation. If structures were unyielding, there remained another, more accessible avenue for change—in the realm of ideas and personal standards about how best to rear a child.

Altering Child-Rearing Ideologies.   In their search for a way to combine committed work with motherhood, reluctant mothers typically changed their beliefs about the nature of proper child rearing and early childhood development. These ideas were more malleable than the relatively intransigent and slowly responding structures of work and marriage. Bereft of viable structural alternatives, ideological change became the path of least resistance. Caught between pressures to procreate and to achieve at work, reluctant mothers surrendered traditional beliefs that their own mothers had lived by and passed on to them:

> A: I'm the opposite extreme of where I came from . . . where I felt you had to be home full-time in order to raise a child in terms of what the *child* needs. I don't think that's true anymore. Before, I felt a mother, to be a good mother, should be home with her children. Not only is it not necessary, but it might not even be best. Besides, those are the terms on which I'm willing to have a family.

The emerging beliefs of this group of women contrasted sharply with the views and behavioral patterns of their mothers, currently domestic women, and women committed to childlessness. They also represented a break from reluctant mothers' own earlier views. To ease the integration of work and family, reluctant mothers rejected traditional views and challenged the widely espoused notion that working mothers have a deleterious impact on their offspring. This process offered an escape from an otherwise irresolvable double bind, but it also required a difficult break from past assumptions and parental messages. A respondent with high work aspirations explained:

> Q: What brought about the change in your attitude that work and child rearing couldn't be combined?
>
> A: I just don't think it's true. I don't think it was true for [my mother]. I believe that I can manage to combine anything I want to, and I can do it well. I feel like a lot of the messages I got growing up were that, in fact, you couldn't combine career and family, that if I were to marry and have a family, that would be the end of my life. And I think I adopted them without understanding that, and I acted on them. Now that I have begun to separate from my parents' views, and particularly my mother's, I don't think that those are valid for me.

For some, ideological change occurred after their children were born. Faced with the experience of domesticity, they realized that, regardless of the dangers they had been told their return to work would entail, staying home was not acceptable. They thus developed new notions of good mothering that better fit their needs. Ambivalent emotions that included both guilt and a certain fragile confidence that their children would not be harmed emerged side by side. A biologist and mother of three returned to work after the birth of her first child despite her concerns and doubts:

> A: I'd never held a baby in my life, and just the idea of this individual being in my charge was overwhelming. And then I found out there's nothing to it. I went back to work with guilt feelings that I should be home, but I could see that [my children] were great.
>
> Q: Why did you decide at that point that it was okay to work?
>
> A: At that point, I wasn't sure if the children were fine. I was still having tremendous guilt feelings, and I did for the next couple of years. But staying home was not for me. I loved my children dearly, and I felt I was a very good mother. I loved my husband dearly. But I wasn't going to sacrifice my life for these individuals. I wanted something for myself, too.

Fear, guilt, and doubt were especially common among those who lacked the moral and financial support of a male partner. This clerk and single mother, for example, considered desperate measures when divorce left her perched on an economic and emotional precipice:

> Q: Did you ever worry that Laurie would suffer from your working?
>
> A: I did. She was about two when I first separated. She started getting hyper attacks. It really scared me. I thought, "Oh, what have I done?" I was going through a very depressed, worried period, and I wrote my brother and asked if maybe I should give her up for adoption, giving her to a family, because maybe I'm not giving her enough. He said, "No. Your daughter, you keep." I think I would have regretted it. My ideal isn't the way it happened, but I don't regret the way it happened, either. I guess I'd never be happy being a housewife because, to me, there's no way to measure the value of it.

Given their lack of other acceptable alternatives, guilt and doubt, however deeply experienced, did not thwart reluctant mothers' determination to combine work and child rearing. Instead, they emphasized the benefits working mothers offer their children. They turned the traditional ideology on its head and began to develop a new philosophy of mothering that hinged upon the conviction that, at least in some instances, full-time mothering can actually harm children.

Inherited beliefs and prevailing theories notwithstanding, reluctant mothers concluded that their own children would be better off because they would be mothered less.

Reluctant mothers came to believe, first, that an unhappy mother would produce an unhappy child. If full-time mothering produced disastrous consequences for the mother, it would produce disastrous consequences for the child as well. This divorced bank officer concluded that a hired, but happy, caretaker was preferable to a miserable full-time mother:

Q: Has working interfered with your ability to raise a family?

A: No, because if Janet and I had stayed home together, we would have driven each other nuts. I would not have been as good a mother as I am now. Thank God there are all these lovely people who are willing to watch my child when I'm gone and give her certain things that I'm not ready or able to give.

Work-committed mothers also argued that they would bring energies, ideas, experiences, and resources to child rearing that full-time mothers could not offer. An accountant reasoned:

A: Also, I think that, if I'm challenged and alert, it's something I could probably communicate to my children.

Reluctant mothers thus believed that their absence could and would be offset by benefits they were uniquely positioned to provide.

Third, reluctant mothers focused on money. If full-time homemaking would impose financial strains on the household, they reasoned, then a child would suffer more from economic deprivation if its mother stayed home than it would from maternal deprivation if its mother worked. The fact that a working mother could provide money in place of time also justified the choice to work. This lawyer offered the same rationale for working full-time that men have historically relied on to justify their absence during the day:

A: I plan to have children, probably two, and my idea is to take off work, maybe four months, and then go back. I might want to work part-time, but that's just not feasible; so I don't even think about it. I think about going back to work full-time. And you also have to have enough money to make it comfortable, because if you've got economic strains [the child will suffer].

Fourth, reluctant mothers argued that by working they would protect their offspring from the dangers of "overmothering." They directly challenged the belief that children need constant care and attention from one primary caretaker, preferably their biological mother. Instead, they argued that children can be overindulged and overprotected by an ever-present, overzealous mother lacking other major commitments. Reluctant mothers came to believe that their children would actually have a better chance for healthy development precisely because their mothers would be occupied elsewhere:

A: I'm not sure I'm right in saying there's *no* bad in all that comes from being gone all the time during the day. But I had the opportunity to see both families where the parents are at home and the parents aren't at home. To tell you the truth, the kids are better off if they don't have Mommy home all the time, keeping them babies. And I think in a way, too, it might help them to learn responsibility and self-reliance and things like that.

This work-committed mother with another child on the way agreed that her job as a clerk protected her children from the dangers of overinvolved mothering:

Q: Has working interfered with your ability to raise your family?

A: No. I think I've been a much better mother, and also he's around other people, not just me. I think it's a lot better; his adjustment is better. I think it's worked out better than I thought it would.

Finally, reluctant mothers questioned the widely accepted assumption that mothers who do not work shower their children with attention and affection. They argued instead that housework and other activities so preoccupy most full-time homemakers that they are no more likely to attend to their children's needs than are working mothers.

Q: So you don't think the children will suffer if you work?

A: No, I don't think so. You figure that a mother that is home all the time, even though she might be around, is still preoccupied with something else. She spends a lot of her time doing housework or whatever; so I don't see the difference. When a family gets together at night, their main concentration right then is on each other; so I think it's something that *would* work out.

This argument may not be as farfetched as it superficially appears. Bane (1976:15–17) reports that television has become a major baby-sitter for most children, including preschoolers, and that the difference in the amounts of time working and homemaking mothers spend exclusively with their children is "surprisingly small." The average preschooler, for example, watches television about one-third of his or her waking hours, regardless of who is caring for the child. Reluctant mothers concluded that the quality rather than the quantity of time spent with offspring was the decisive criterion for defining good mothering and responsible child rearing. In their view, working did not seriously compromise the overall texture of the relationship between parents and children. They argued instead that working actually improved the quality of familial bonds. This rather simple substitution—of quality for quantity of time a mother spends with her child—opened up the otherwise inaccessible option of combining motherhood with committed work:

> Q: You said that when you were younger, you saw working and raising children as incompatible. Why don't you feel that way any more?
>
> A: Because it's the quality of time that you spend with them, I think. That's where I was a little bit confused. I thought you had to spend all your time with them and be a mother and housewife or just full-time working, but you can do both.

Ideological change required not only a leap of faith into uncharted territory, but a considerable amount of discounting as well. Confronted with a traditional set of beliefs (however ill-supported by evidence) that argues that mothers of young children who indulge their "selfish" desires to work run the risk of producing damaged offspring, reluctant mothers had to struggle to minimize such a possibility in their own minds. Because they were experimenting but would not know the results for some time, they found themselves waiting and hoping that all would turn out well. But they also braced themselves for unanticipated contingencies. Reluctant mothers chose to travel an uncertain path, the outcome of which they knew they could not foresee:

> Q: Will working interfere with your ability to raise a family?
>
> A: I'll try very hard not to let it. But clearly it will be different for my kid than it was for me having a mother at home all the time. Whether that's going to be a positive thing or a negative thing, only time will tell.

Reluctant mothers also discounted the costs children threatened to exact from workplace accomplishment. Although the fear of work costs remained, they struggled to minimize such threats as well:

> Q: Do you think having children will affect your progress at work?

A: I think that is in the back of my mind. . . . Probably the reason why I've never actively gone out to have a kid is that concern. But again, I keep pushing that concern aside and saying that it's not going to affect [anything], which may be foolish.

Whatever their qualms, the process of ideological change lowered the perceived costs of children to a level that made the choice for motherhood possible. In the midst of uncertainty, reluctant mothers developed a strong commitment to creating new ways of integrating work and family life. For this group, there was no other acceptable choice. They concluded, unlike both their domestic and childless counterparts, that responsible mothering and committed work are not incompatible. As this aspiring worker declared:

Q: What are the main reasons you plan to work and raise a child at the same time?

A: Because I don't think just raising kids would be fulfilling for me. If I had to give work up, I don't think I would have children. But I don't see why I would have to give it up. I don't think they're incompatible.

Psychoanalytic theory notwithstanding, beliefs about what constitutes correct child rearing and good mothering are as much ideological constructs as established scientific "fact." There are, of course, some demonstrably wrong ways to rear a child, such as extreme abuse, deprivation, or neglect; but that leaves much room for variety in terms of who cares for the young, how much time is focused upon them exclusively, and how many caretakers are actively involved. Caretaking by the biological mother is neither the only safe option nor a guarantee of a "successful" outcome. It is thus difficult to resist the conclusion that persistent beliefs about the harmful effects of working mothers serve more to control women's behavior than to protect their children. These beliefs can be considered ideologies in the truest sense of the word: important control mechanisms that prevent some women from acting in their own behalf and that induce guilt in those who do.[4]

The argument that modern theories of child rearing are ideologies that serve, to some extent, as mechanisms of social control is supported by the historical record. Full-time mothering is a relatively rare and historically recent social construction, as are the beliefs that support and justify this particular family form. Before the industrial revolu-

---

4. See Schur (1973) for a thorough consideration of how gender norms and the female "deviance" they create operate as systems of social control to regulate the behavior and experience of women.

tion, children were afforded neither maternal indulgence nor constant adult attention, and they were not deemed to need them (Ariès, 1962; Ryan, 1981; and Shorter, 1975). Because these children appear to have developed into healthy, functioning adults, these examples call into question the scientific basis for concluding that all children require a specific and universal form of mothering for proper development.

Despite the power of ideological prohibition, however, reluctant mothers were compelled to change the terms of the discourse about motherhood. They rejected the received wisdom of their childhood and many of their peers and substituted a set of beliefs that better fit their own needs and circumstances.

A vivid illustration of how "theories" of correct child-rearing practices tend to change with social circumstances can be found in the American "bible" for parents, Dr. Benjamin Spock's *Baby and Child Care*. Although this book championed full-time motherhood when it was first released in the late 1940s, the most recent edition rejects Spock's earlier claims that working mothers harm children. It argues instead that women should feel free to work and that men make good parents, too (Spock, 1976). Perhaps Spock has been as much influenced *by* women as he has influenced them.

This process of ideological change among reluctant mothers shows clearly how beliefs about child rearing serve as imperfect mechanisms of social control. Traditional child-rearing ideologies supported some women's preference for domesticity and led others to reject motherhood. Those committed to combining work and parenthood, however, were influenced, but not controlled, by traditional beliefs. Traditional ideologies made their task more difficult, but ultimately these beliefs did not and could not prevent reluctant mothers from breaking the rules they had been reared to believe in.

Armed with the support of a growing group of like-situated women and fearful of the hazards of domesticity, these women brought the weight of collective social change to their struggle. Emerging support groups neutralized the impact of the disapproval they faced and legitimated new alternatives in spite of the structural and ideological forces opposed to change. Eroding supports for domesticity gave strength to those, such as this accountant, committed to change:

Q: What are the main reasons you plan to work and raise children at the same time?

A: I think in our society the whole attitude has changed. There aren't the social groups or anything for nonworking mothers. When I was growing up with my mother being home all the time, she did have a lot of social contact. But that was a different situation from what I'm in. Right now, with most of the women working anyway, there aren't that many women staying home. Like in this apartment building, there isn't anybody who stays home. You would be basically by yourself.

Ideological change, then, helped reluctant mothers cope with the motherhood dilemma. The pressure to challenge traditional beliefs and values, however, would not have been present if larger historical forces had not created a dilemma in the first place. Pressure from changing social structures gave impetus to change in ideas. Once confronted by these structural dilemmas, reluctant mothers had little recourse but to alter their beliefs to better fit their circumstances. This mental reformulation subsequently affected behavior, easing the way toward motherhood while simultaneously justifying a continued attachment to work. Structures created the need and impetus for change, but ideological responses helped shape the specific contours that change assumed. As this process took its course, psychology changed along with social structure. An upwardly mobile reluctant mother thus gradually came to accept herself as both a worker and a parent:

A: Before, had I gotten married, I could have given up something, because that was my psychology at that point. I also think that was the psychology of most of the people I knew, men and women. But now that I've achieved a certain amount, I have time to look around and see what is missing and what I really believe is correct for me.

Childlessness Versus Reluctant Motherhood

Nondomestic women brought different resources and pressures to bear on the motherhood dilemma. Some consequently decided to forgo childbearing altogether; others moved ambivalently and reluctantly toward motherhood.

Those who ultimately chose childlessness lacked both the resources and the pressures to opt for motherhood. Male partners were either absent from their lives or unwilling to become involved, participatory parents. In this context, child rearing seemed a lonely and onerous task. Tenaciously held traditional notions of good mothering reinforced this perception of the demands of child rearing. In the absence of pressure to change this ideological stance, they concluded that opting for motherhood would entail negative consequences for their personal well-being, their careers, and, worst of all, the children they chose to have. Childlessness came to be seen as the only responsible, if not necessarily the most appealing, choice. Ironically, this response is, in part, an unintended consequence of an ideology that has historically promoted female domesticity.

The women who decided against motherhood also engaged in a process of discounting the potential costs of childlessness. They worked to convince themselves that their fate was not without its benefits and that perhaps the joys of motherhood were overrated. Given the general cultural aversion to childlessness, this was not an easy task.

In contrast, reluctant mothers faced strong pressures—especially from their spouses—to bear children. When these pressures were added to the perceived social and psychological costs of childlessness, they prompted reluctant mothers to move haltingly toward motherhood. Reluctant mothers were also better situated to extract a commitment to parenting from their male partners. They thus both faced more pressure to bear children, which increased the perceived costs of childlessness, and brought more resources to bear on the decision, especially in the form of help from their partners, lowering the perceived costs of motherhood.

As some work-committed women moved reluctantly toward motherhood, they developed coping strategies to make child rearing less costly. They decided to limit their family size, struggled to enlist their partners in the parenting process, and gradually changed their personal beliefs concerning proper child-rearing practices. Just as their childless counterparts discounted the costs of childlessness, they discounted the potential costs of motherhood and focused instead on the long-run costs of never having a child.

Reluctant mothers also employed other coping strategies—such as mustering network support from neighbors, relatives, and friends for child care and pressuring employers to accommodate their growing family needs. These strategies, however, varied considerably across the group and were neither uniformly successful nor uniformly desired. Most reluctant mothers did not wish to alter their work schedules for fear a change would lessen their chances for advancement. None worked in settings that provided on-site day care or similar programs for working parents. Most were reluctant to seek help from relatives or friends unless it was voluntarily offered. This occurred infrequently and typically involved other costs (such as becoming obligated to someone) that offset the financial savings. Thus, paid child-care arrangements were overwhelmingly favored by the group. Finally, many of these strategies were employed only *after* the decision to have a child was made, when parents confronted the problems of child rearing within the context of full-time work. Such coping strategies, although important, did not play a significant role in contributing to the decision itself.

The different resources and pressures nondomestic women brought to their fertility decisions affected their perceptions about the relative merits of each option and their subsequent behavior and psychological orientation. Both structural and ideological forces played a part in this process as contrasting structural conditions either promoted or inhibited ideological change. Men were especially important in shaping the conditions that either eased or complicated the process of opting for motherhood. Traditional standards of good mothering played a role, too, whether they were retained or modified. Ironically, those who continued to adhere to traditional beliefs about responsible child rearing were less likely to have or plan for a child than those who responded to the dilemma they faced by redefining their ideological position.

Domestic Versus Nondomestic Responses

We have seen how a group of women facing historically unprecedented circumstances developed new responses to the structural dilemmas arising from their emerging commitment to a life beyond domesticity. Whether they opted for childlessness or moved reluctantly toward motherhood, they constitute the cutting edge of social change. They did not just respond passively to the constraints that confronted them; rather, they took actions that shaped the contours of change as well as the conditions of their individual lives. Whether these women were childless or struggling to combine motherhood with committed work, their choices represent the emergence of new alternatives that, if successfully implemented, inevitably necessitate new social arrangements. Their actions and those of others like them have already promoted changes in family organization, workplace dynamics, and accepted beliefs about good mothering.

Because work arrangements were the most resistant to change, the most concerted efforts focused on changing domestic organization, decisions, and beliefs to better fit the demands of work. If nondomestic women's rising demands and dilemmas are to be met, however, work as well as family organization will have to change—for men as well as for women. As increasing numbers of women find that they cannot or will not turn back to domesticity, the impact of nontraditional choices will mount at home and at work. In some form, it will reverberate throughout the structures of marriage, child rearing, and the workplace, going far beyond occasional isolated changes in women's "roles."

The path of least resistance led all nondomestic women toward relatively less mothering. They reduced both their fertility and the proportion of time spent with offspring. Nondomestic women also subjected men to increasing pressure to parent more, to participate more fully in domestic activities, and to make way for them at the workplace.

As the proportion of women committed to work has climbed, their aspirations have risen and their determination to reject domesticity has solidified. The momentum of these forces has fueled resistance, rebellion, and demands for change. This buildup of forces for social change must eventually find some avenue of expression. If childlessness remains the unpopular choice it has historically been, then new arrangements for rearing children, new beliefs about their care, and new conceptions of men's and women's capacities and behavioral alternatives will become the most viable route to change.

These changes have already generated great opposition and controversy, however. Opposition stems not just from fear of or resistance to innovation. Were these the major sources of opposition, it would dissolve as people grew accustomed to the inevitable. The sizeable number of women, as well as men, whose choices, orientations, and interests remain lodged in traditional arrangements constitute a far more powerful source of opposition.

For those committed to domesticity, security remains rooted in a strict sexual division of labor that maintains a clear separation between parenting and economic responsibilities. Such arrangements may confer prerogatives on men in the form of a patriarchal family structure and a male-dominated workplace; but they also reserve the domestic sphere for women, making female domesticity both possible and socially legitimate. Changes advocated by nondomestic women threaten such arrangements. Thus, despite the growing proportion of women who face alternatives that compel them to push for change, a substantial number remain objectively and subjectively opposed to these efforts. As new options and constraints have developed alongside the old, the contrasts—and conflicts—between them have intensified.

Nondomestic women committed to childlessness retained beliefs about responsible child rearing and women's options that also characterize the more traditional approach. Although their positions were used to justify different actions, childless and domestically oriented women agreed that career and motherhood are incompatible, that children suffer when their mothers are strongly committed to the workplace, and that work is an acceptable option for mothers only as long as it is not defined in terms of career. In contrast to both these groups, those who planned or had already begun to combine committed work with motherhood engaged in a process of ideological as well as behavioral change. They adopted a new set of beliefs that rejected these traditional tenets and supported their own choices, preferences, and situational demands. They also began to reorganize their patterns of domestic labor and to redefine their notions concerning appropriate male behavior. In both thought and action, they diverged from both their childless and domestically oriented counterparts.

Sharply contrasting positions thus form the lines along which political constituencies have already emerged. Nondomestic women, and especially those determined to integrate work and motherhood, challenged old ideas and patterns. Domestically oriented women responded by reaffirming traditional arrangements, as well as the beliefs that legitimate them. These responses deepened the gulf between the two groups. Members of each found themselves denigrating the other's orientations and choices. Domestically oriented women, for example, were typically critical of their more ambitious counterparts. These two homemakers, the first an ex-saleswoman and the second a career housewife, offered nightmarish assessments of occupationally successful women:

> A: Women can become department managers, but it's a blood-and-guts thing. Those who make it are witches because they found out what they had to do to get there. I wouldn't have liked the person I would have become.

Or:

> Q: When you hear about women who don't have children and are making their way in a job or whatever, does that bring out any response in you?
>
> A: I have met a number of them in my husband's company. There are very few I've been impressed with as people. I think a lot of them are still fighting their way up the ladder and feel they're very much in competition with men. You don't have to get married and have children, but I feel they're missing a lot.

Similarly, full-time mothers looked with varying degrees of disdain, pity, or angry concern upon those who eschewed motherhood or remained at the workplace while their children were young. This homemaker and mother of two, for example, resented working mothers who, in her eyes, put their own needs before their children's needs:

> Q: How do you respond to a woman with a young baby who goes to work every day?
>
> A: I have a neighbor like that. She works just because she wants to. I get sort of angry. What I don't like is, you can't have everything! I think what I get angriest at is some of the justifications I hear: "Well, I spend quality time with my

child." I reject that. I think I resent the unfairness to the child. I don't know how to answer the argument why men can have families and work but women can't. Maybe it's not fair, but that's the way it is.

Other domestically oriented women pictured the working mother not as selfish but as an unenviable victim:

Q: How do you feel about women with young children working?

A: Most of the time all I hear from them is griping, and they're tired, and they're frantic to get everything done. It's a shame. I hate hurrying like that.

Virtually all in the domestic group viewed work, no matter how rewarding, as a poor substitute for the mothering experience:

Q: When you see other women about your age who have jobs or careers but don't have children, how does that make you feel?

A: I have mixed emotions, but at the same time I feel like they're missing out on something. If they're going to make a long-term thing of it and never have children, I think they're missing something.

Not surprisingly, nondomestic women, both with and without children, responded with similar aversion to their more domestic peers, whom they viewed with a mixture of superiority and horror:

Q: What is your response when you see other women about your age staying home to care for young children?

A: I feel a little superior in a way. It's terrible, but I have the stereotype—here's this lady jiggling the handles of toilets that aren't flushing.

Or:

A: My reaction is repulsion. Absolute aversion. I can't think of anything I want less. I have no desire. As a matter of fact, I look at my boss's wife—who is the perfect mother—and think, "She is the epitome of everything I never want to be." And she is the perfect mother!

Nondomestic women projected the costs they attached to domesticity onto those who had chosen the path they rejected:

A: To me, they tend to be kind of mentally underdeveloped and not too interesting. Let's face it, it's kind of boring. I guess I don't consider having children as doing something.

Or:

> A: I don't think it seems very interesting. When I see women tugging kids along downtown or dragging children to the laundromat, I don't think it seems very interesting.

Thus, in order to justify their own embattled positions, domestic and nondomestic women denigrated each other's choices. This process has created deep ideological schisms between the two groups that point to two important aspects of women's current social position.

First, whether domestic or nondomestic, all women face an ambiguous set of alternatives in which to some extent they are "damned if they do and damned if they don't." Structural ambiguity ensures that there are few, if any, unambiguously legitimate paths for women. Whatever a woman's choice, she faces social disapproval and significant obstacles to achieving her goals.

Second, ideological conflicts among women are based on deeply rooted structural divisions. No matter how much each group discounts the costs of its own choices and inflates the costs of other choices, both domestic and nondomestic women must make their choices in response to a specific and contrasting set of alternatives and constraints. Ideological schisms will persist as long as the structural conditions that create them persist.

The deepening political conflicts among women reflect and spring from the social and psychological divisions in women's experiences. As long as domestic and nondomestic women face different dilemmas and contradictions, but a shared challenge to the legitimacy of their various choices, each group also retains an interest in opposing the other in order to protect its own social position. Because neither group is likely to disappear or concede defeat, the political ramifications of this conflict will shape the nature of American political life until the legitimacy and viability of both groups are guaranteed.

8 | *The Changing Contours of Women's Place*

We have followed a strategic cohort of women as they made critical decisions about work and family. They developed a variety of behavioral, psychological, and ideological responses to the variable, contradictory contexts they faced. How can we account for the variety of pathways these women took? What do these pathways imply about the social, psychological, and ideological underpinnings of "women's place"? What do they tell us about the logic of human development and the role social structures play in shaping it?

Development, Choice, and Structured Alternatives

The lives examined in the previous chapters suggest a number of general conclusions about how women make work and family decisions. First, change is a dominant motif. Although a minority of the women in this study had the luxury (or, viewed from a different perspective, the misfortune) to carry through the plans and expectations they initially took into adulthood, the more typical experience involved encounters with new, unanticipated situations that deflected women from their early goals. They responded to these events by acting in ways they themselves had not foreseen.

191

In the long run, the life patterns of these women grew out of a series of decisions that interacted in surprising ways. Many decisions were based on limited information concerning the future consequences of present actions; even the most carefully calculated choices often had unintended consequences that led in unanticipated directions. Change occurred not simply because people wished it to, but more fundamentally because seemingly static, discrete, inconsequential decisions had only dimly perceived long-term consequences.[1]

If change is not only a persistent possibility, but also a common occurrence, the orientations, dispositions, and capacities these people brought to adult decisions could not have been irrevocably formed in the early years of life. Rather, individual abilities continued to develop as these women aged, moved into new life stages, and encountered critical choice points. Aging, by its nature, requires change as people move through a series of stages from one set of social and psychological tasks to the next.[2] Transition of some kind must take place. These respondents, however, did not simply progress through a natural, predetermined, and uniform sequence of stages. Their adult development was instead variable, problematic, and typically open-ended.

Neither chance circumstances nor individual personalities determined the paths these women took as they made decisions that shaped the direction of their lives. Their choices reflected instead an interaction between socially structured opportunities and constraints and active attempts to make sense of and respond to these structures. Constraints and opportunities in the immediate social environment limited the range of possible options and channeled motivation to select one option from among this range.[3] In this sense, the work and family

1. For more on the long-run implications of short-run decisions, see Howard Becker's (1964) analysis of building commitment through "side-bets" and Merton's (1957) discussion of the "unintended consequences" of human action. For more on Merton's general perspective, see Stinchcombe (1975).

2. See Erikson (1963) for the classic statement of the problem of psychological development throughout the life course and for a presentation of a developmental schema based on psychoanalytic principles and assumptions. Gerth and Mills (1953) present an overview of competing theories of human development. Kett (1977), Modell et al. (1976), and Modell and Hareven (1973) consider historical variations in life-course structuring and examine the link between social structure and individual developmental processes. For more recent studies of adult development in sociological perspective, see Rossi (1980) and Smelser and Erikson (1980). For a consideration of gender differences in moral development, see Gilligan (1982).

3. Kanter (1976, 1977a) points to the close connection between socially defined options and internally experienced desires in the culture of the corporation. She also documents the sex-neutral nature of this process by pointing out that men exposed to blocked opportunities show the same low morale, lack of motivation on the job, and interrupted career patterns that women facing a comparable structure of incentives exhibit.

decisions of these women were sensible reactions to the socially structured contexts they faced.

Sensible choices, however, are not necessarily conscious choices. The forces that shape options and channel actions, motives, and belief systems are often hidden from conscious awareness. Unconscious motivation is not confined to psychodynamic processes; structural as well as psychological processes mold behavior in ways that the actor barely recognizes. Indeed, structure tends to exert its most powerful influence by shaping one's perception of alternative options. Women respond in contextually sensible ways to their environment without full conscious awareness of the structural forces impinging on them or the overall logic of their choices, just as they may be unaware of subconscious psychodynamic pushes and pulls.

How, then, do social arrangements structure women's choices? First, women are especially subject to the dilemma of "packaged" choices. Not only are they reared with conflicting expectations, but they also confront ambiguous structures that often require them to choose among a number of desired goals. It is particularly difficult for women to build strong bases in both the domestic and the public spheres, and decisions in one sphere limit the range of options in the other. Trade-offs are thus built into the structure of choice: Whether a woman opts for work, motherhood, or some combination of the two, she must accept the costs of what is forgone as well as the benefits of what is chosen ("opportunity costs," in the language of economics). In this sense, women face a set of dichotomous choices in which work and family commitments are posed as competing, alternative commitments. Their work and family decisions are inextricably linked; choices in one sphere depend on the opportunities, incentives, and constraints posed in the other.[4]

The responses of the women in this study to the contradictory, ambiguous, and packaged alternatives they faced developed out of and depended on how they negotiated four especially important factors in their social environment. Taken together, these factors defined the range of options available, determined which among them appeared most (or least) desirable, and ultimately shaped the respondents' definitions of their situations and varied life choices.

First, the building of or failure to build a stable relationship with a male partner, together with this partner's orientations toward bearing and rearing children, had a powerful impact on women's work and family choices. A stable, permanent marriage promoted female

---

4. Glidewell (1970) discusses the problem of dichotomous choice. Kanter (1977b) analyzes the contradictions between work and domestic institutions as they apply to women and men.

domesticity in a number of ways. It fostered a belief in marriage as a safe, secure place that both permits and rewards economic dependency; over time, it tended to narrow a woman's occupational options, as wives' work decisions were subordinated to those of their spouses; and it ultimately offered an attractive alternative to unsatisfying workplace experiences. Similarly, a stable marriage promoted a context in which childbearing came to be seen as a natural outgrowth of the relationship itself. Stable marriage thus not only made female domesticity possible for a number of the respondents, but it also fostered an environment in which bearing children and withdrawing from the workplace to rear them seemed natural, inevitable, and desirable. Indeed, strong pressure or encouragement from a mate was enough to lead some working women to become reluctant mothers, despite their own ambivalence and the potential danger to their work careers.

In contrast, when men were not a stable part of these women's lives, when having children threatened the relationship even when it was stable, or when men rejected participatory fatherhood, women found convincing reasons to choose work over family.

The experience of blocked versus expanding workplace opportunity had a similarly powerful impact on the respondents' choices. Stable marriage tended to pull some women into the home, but constricted work opportunities tended to push them out of the workplace. Blocked work mobility dampened expectations for future work accomplishment, imposed few costs for workplace withdrawal, and enhanced the pull of domestic commitments. In this context, some women tended to opt out of the workplace to embrace domesticity and motherhood as the preferred alternative.

If blocked mobility tended to enhance the pull of marriage, motherhood, and domesticity, then expanding workplace opportunity, unexpected promotions, and the promise of a career ladder reinforced the choice in favor of work even when it had initially been considered temporary. Upward job mobility competed directly with women's domestic pursuits. Rewarding work did more than provide economic independence outside of marriage, although this alone expanded these women's alternatives. It also provided another source of personal identity and social reward. The experience of workplace advancement increased the immediate social, economic, and emotional rewards of working; it fostered a belief in future rewards at work; and it raised the costs of leaving work, even for a short time, to have a child. Upward mobility at the workplace nourished work aspirations and raised the perceived costs of motherhood. Expanding occupational opportunities drew some women into the workplace; eroding domestic supports pushed others out of the home.

Third, when the spouse of a stably married woman was able to provide an income that was perceived as adequate, women were not pushed out of the home or away from domesticity. Male economic support both permitted these respondents to withdraw from work to rear children and sheltered them from exposure to unexpected work opportunities that might have initiated a process of change.

In contrast, women who experienced economic squeezes in the household were likely to be pulled into the workplace, despite their earlier plans or preferences. When this occurred, it often triggered a chain reaction of events that ultimately altered work and family decisions. The perceived need for a second income not only forced some women into the world of work; it also delayed childbearing decisions, limited the number of children a family could afford and the time a mother could devote to their care, and provided a period for unanticipated work opportunities to initiate a reassessment of family as well as work aspirations. Perceived economic squeezes thus led some stably married women to pursue nondomestic pathways and to reconsider their commitments to motherhood as well as to work.

Finally, the perceived rewards and costs of a domestic life-style shaped these women's work and family decisions. Some women found mothering and homemaking the fulfilling experience they had hoped it would be. Others were surprised to find that, contrary to their earlier expectations, the life of homemaking or full-time motherhood was decidedly disappointing. As growing numbers of their neighbors, friends, and peers left the home for work, these women found the increasing isolation and devaluation of full-time mothering and housekeeping too costly to bear. This decline in the social supports for motherhood, together with the rise in supports for alternative choices such as working and childlessness, led many to reject the domestic patterns more typical of earlier generations.[5]

Some or all of these four factors precipitated critical turning points for most of these respondents. At such times, unanticipated events, which ultimately reshaped the course of their lives, intervened. For the individual experiencing them, these events seemed random and their effects idiosyncratic and personal. From a broader perspective, however, this apparent randomness takes on an orderly form. No matter how fortuitous a divorce or new job opportunity may have seemed to the woman confronted with change, these events are rooted in shifts taking place in the structure of American work and family institutions.

The process of individual change was thus closely linked to the social environment in which individual development took place. As

5. See Oakley (1974a) and Gavron (1966) for detailed descriptions of the frustrations of homemaking and confined motherhood in the context of twentieth-century industrialism.

the pace of social change has quickened, the probability has increased that women will be exposed to unanticipated events that promote, and even require, change in their lives. Periods of accelerated social change make individual change not only possible but probable. In such periods, stability becomes as uncertain and difficult to accomplish as change; neither is assured, and both call for explanation.

Despite the forces promoting nondomestic responses, supports and incentives for domestic patterns remain. Because they were exposed to a more traditional set of constraints and opportunities, some women responded to the dilemmas they faced by reproducing domestic patterns. Even among those who veered away from initial goals, the direction of change was not uniform. Although underlying social forces have pushed ever more women into the workplace, obstacles to change have led others to follow a more traditional domestic path. Some women developed high workplace aspirations, aiming for jobs they had once considered out of reach and turning away from domestic orientations, while others reduced their career aspirations and turned instead to traditional feminine pursuits. In negotiating transitions through adulthood, the women in this study veered in different directions, developed divergent orientations, and stressed different abilities even when they started with similar goals, desires, and orientations.

In short, the fact of social change did not determine a uniform outcome in individual lives. These women faced dilemmas, not clear-cut choices. They had to make decisions amid contradictory circumstances, and the process was full of ambiguity and conflict. It involved development and negotiation in which women struggled with and against their employers and male partners to define and control their situations.

These women responded to their dilemmas in genuinely creative ways. Their choices, their struggle to create viable life paths, often led to extensive personal growth. In many respects, these women have been sailing in uncharted waters. Taken together, their efforts are changing the social order as well as their own lives. Their individually creative responses have combined to create new social forms—forms springing from changes in social structure but defined and implemented by individuals. Because these women's biographies have intersected with social structures in transition, they have created history. They have been not just passive receivers of change, but also its authors.

Not everyone, of course, is equally well situated to respond to social change by making creative choices. As young adults, these women represent a group that plays an especially important role in the process of social change, for they are young enough to be able to take advantage of new opportunities, yet old enough to act in an independent and thus creative manner. In early adulthood, work and family options are still open, if only for a limited period. At this age, people must form independent identities that reflect, but do not mimic, parental models and must make life commitments that will have fateful consequences for their future development. In choosing a vocation, a family form, a way of life, and a set of beliefs, these women, like young adults generally, confronted the options made available by their historical period. Because they were constrained in different ways and to varying degrees, they responded to these options in diverse ways. Their seemingly small, personal decisions have, in turn, shaped the development of the social institutions with which they have collided.

These findings about the process by which women negotiate the choice between work and family have a number of important implications for understanding women as a social group. They highlight the inadequacies of theories that posit either that early childhood experiences are the major determinant of women's adult choices or that women's behavior can be fully understood as the result of universal patterns of male domination. Instead, the extent, type, and permanence of change in women's social position must be located in the changing social order and in the process by which different groups of women make different choices in response to variable circumstances.

The Limits of Socialization, Personality, and Dominance Models

To a large extent, prevailing models for understanding women's social position and individual behavior do not take sufficient account of these findings and thus are poorly equipped to explain them. Indeed, these findings suggest that substantial modifications are required of both the socialization and the structural (or male) dominance approaches, the two most widely accepted current paradigms. In particular, any theory that purports to explain women's work and family choices must be able to account for both aggregate variation among women as a group and change over time in the lives of individual women.

Childhood Socialization

For the women in this study, childhood provided the first arena in which psychological orientations, capacities, and conflicts were formed. Early life experiences set the stage for future development, which they influenced in subtle and varied ways. Taken alone, however, childhood messages, models, and relationships were not sufficient to explain women's adult decisions. Recent studies corroborate this finding. Miller and Garrison (1982:250, 252) report that the evidence linking parental behavior in the early years of life with adult outcomes is inconclusive and weak. Their review of the socialization literature reveals that "modeling per se plays a minor role in the development of sex-typed behavior" and that "in the long run structural and family constraints are more relevant to women's occupational achievement" than are mothers' employment statuses. Mnookin's (1979) review reaches a similar conclusion about the indeterminant role childhood experience plays in shaping long-term development.

Childhood experiences are insufficient to explain adult choices for three reasons. First, to the extent that childhood socialization played a role in women's later life choices, it played a different role than gender socialization theories hypothesize. Despite the assumption made by these theories that parents, and especially mothers, consciously and unconsciously socialize their daughters to be feminine (or *not* masculine), these women's childhood experiences tended to be varied. The messages they received as children often provided a set of ambiguous and inconsistent signals. Not only did mothers present multifaceted models; children were also influenced by other figures in their social environment. As a result, these respondents could choose, both consciously and unconsciously, from a variety of models and messages. In the long run, this variety alone led to ambivalence, resistance, and rejection, as well as to emulation.

Second, however parents, and especially mothers, treated their offspring, their behavior alone did not determine the child's reaction to it. Consciously and unconsciously, children responded to their childhood contexts in a variety of ways that were not determined by the context itself. In some cases, parental messages actually "backfired," triggering an opposite reaction in the child. (In psychoanalysis, this response is called "reaction formation.") The child's early orientations thus emerged from the interaction between early messages and her reaction to them—a response that was to some extent indeterminate from the perspective of childhood socialization taken alone.

Third, childhood influences were subject to later revision. Intervening events, especially in late adolescence and early adulthood, when the struggle to establish an independent identity began in earnest, often shook up old assumptions and led many respondents to reassess the parental messages they received. This process of reexamination was never guaranteed, but it remained an abiding possibility. It was more likely to occur when the assumptions, skills, and orientations inherited from childhood left the respondent ill-prepared to deal with social arrangements encountered in adulthood. As Gerth and Mills (1953:158) state the case, "If in a society there are many large differences between the roles expected of the child and the roles of the adult world, then patterns acquired during childhood are less likely to be successful if they persist in the adult." In this context, the person who refuses or is unable to change invites failure. Rapid social change increased the need for and the likelihood of personal change. This change process modified, and even diminished, the impact of early childhood experiences on adult choices. Women's orientations toward, decisions about, and capacities for working and parenting are thus emergent, developmental, and subject to change over time.

In sum, childhood experiences set up the conflicts that formed the starting point from which these women's adult development proceeded. These experiences influenced how conflicts were *experienced* later in life. They did not, however, determine how these conflicts were resolved (or if they could be resolved at all) or how early messages were "used" in adulthood. Whatever importance childhood socialization has for more subtle aspects of personality development, it alone cannot account for the work and family decisions these women made as adults.

Psychological Variation and the "Feminine Personality"

Whatever the role of childhood socialization, it does not appear to have produced a universal "mothering need" present in the same form or expressed in the same way among all women. The finding that all women do not share a universal need to mother, whether rooted in biological predispositions or early childhood socialization, is surely confirmed by other recent studies and historical evidence. (See, for example, the mounting literature on contemporary maternal abuse of children and Badinter's 1981 study of maternal indifference in eighteenth-century France.) Although the women analyzed here faced a number of similar dilemmas, they responded with a varied range of motives, aspirations, and choices. It is difficult, if not impossible, to extract from this variety a distinct "feminine personality" characterized by strong maternal desires or underdeveloped work ambitions. The search to isolate some special psychological quality that binds all women and differentiates them from men thus obscures the differences among women and risks perpetuating the same stereotypes that have served historically to justify gender inequality. This is so, moreover, even when these approaches argue that, in important respects, women are morally or emotionally superior to men. Bringing women down from this pedestal facilitates analyzing how and why women construct their lives in contextually rational ways.

Similarly, at least in terms of these women's perceptions, men do not form a homogeneous group with uniformly undeveloped emotional capacities. The respondents became involved with male partners who held a wide variety of orientations toward parenthood. Many men appeared to possess sufficient relational needs and capacities to parent successfully; as a group, they were perceived as neither substantially less equipped for nor less interested than their female partners in parenthood.[6]

Not only do there appear to be vast differences among women in their orientations toward children and work; there also appear to be fewer sharp differences between men and women in these psychological attributes than theories that stress a "feminine personality" would lead us to believe. Women and men do experience different *conflicts* —not only because they are treated differently as children, but also because they confront different options as adults. But this does not imply that they have inherently different capacities, needs, or desires. Rather, they are offered different avenues for the expression, or thwarting, of these emotional possibilities.

Work and parenthood are structurally difficult to integrate, but the emotional capacities to love and to work are not mutually exclusive. The dichotomy between "productive" labor that generates an income and "reproductive" labor that socializes new human beings—the so-called split between "instrumental" and "expressive" functions—is not based on inherent psychological antagonisms, but rather on malleable structural conflicts and social arrangements. Whatever their responses, women experience psychic conflict over the choice between love and work because structural arrangements make it a choice in the first place.

This psychological and behavioral variation among women dilutes the explanatory power of theories that postulate a distinct feminine personality as the cause of women's mothering behavior. Surely such variation in motives, needs, and capacities cannot explain the general uniformity and intractability in the social assignment of nurturing responsibilities to women. A more intriguing question appears to be,

---

6. Pleck's (1981) trenchant analysis of "the myth of masculinity" demonstrates convincingly that the notion of inherent sex-linked personality traits located at opposite poles on a "masculine-feminine" continuum is more an ideological construct than an accurate description of men and women. This approach to understanding gender differences sets up unrealistic standards of masculinity and femininity that have been used to measure the adequacy or inadequacy of individual behavior and psychological profiles. In short, the idea of distinct masculine and feminine personalities serves more to label and evaluate behavior than to explain it.

if each gender displays such a variety of orientations toward work and parenthood, why is the sexual division of parenting tasks that assigns emotional duties to women and economic duties to men so persistent? The answer to that question lies more in the structuring of options open to women and men than in deep-seated gender differences in motivation or relational capacities.

Finally, regardless of women's personality traits, such psychological attributes are linked to behavior in complex, problematic, and to some extent indeterminate ways. Most human beings experience a set of conflicting emotions, motives, and needs as they move through life. Because women are especially subject to structural ambiguity in which they must choose between incompatible goals, this multiplicity of emotional pushes and pulls does not produce any one specific response. Among the variety of emotional states women experience—from "fear of success" to "fear of failure" or from the "need to nurture" to the "need to achieve"—no one emotion determines behavior. Rather, as women struggle with conflicting emotions, they will overcome some and act on others. Their choices are thus more likely to reflect the mix of structural constraints and opportunities available to them when critical life decisions are made than to represent the preordained unfolding of their "feminine personalities" or the expression of a uniform and distinctly feminine voice.

Structural Dominance and Perceived Interests

If these women did not share a single orientation toward mothering, neither did they share a common, consistent set of interests. As a group, they occupied a variety of social positions, faced a set of ambiguous, often conflicting alternatives, and had unequal access to social resources. Their socially structured "interests" were variable and internally inconsistent, promoting a variety of ideological responses.

Most of these women faced conflicting pressures over the course of their lives that forced them to choose among a number of antagonistic interests. They found considerable difficulty in defining or locating their "true" interests. Although their responses to these contradictions may have appeared at times to reflect "false consciousness," they can more accurately be understood as stances that make sense in terms of an individual's "perceived interests." Once "perceived interests" are substituted for "false consciousness," a whole host of otherwise "irrational" ideologies make sense. Jackson (1984) argues, for example, that "conceived interests" are ideological responses to ambiguous circumstances. Social conflict thus typically involves a process in which actors attempt to identify and define interests that are rarely obvious, unambiguous, or straightforwardly "objective."

Those who chose to affirm traditional arrangements perceived that they had little to gain and much to lose from the erosion of traditional female protections, however much these protections result from underlying female subordination. Their compliance is best understood not as a passive acceptance of domination, but as an active effort to protect their own interests, as they saw them, from the incursions of social change.[7]

Similarly, under the right circumstances, some women developed strategies of resistance to social oppression. Because the arrangements that subordinate women also depend on their participation, this resistance poses a challenge from which few are insulated. This challenge will, of course, produce opposition on the part of those who are threatened, but opposition alone cannot halt resistance that springs from underlying social change. Some women thus acted as a force for change that reverberated throughout the social institutions that impinged on them. In this process, they became far more than passive victims of the social arrangements they inherited.

Because their situations diverged, some women chose to defend traditional arrangements of gender inequality; others became involved in a struggle to overcome them. Whether they resisted or complied, all were nevertheless acting to protect what they perceived to be their interests. These perceptions could hardly be called false in either case. When people possessing different resources face different constraints, they are likely to disagree about where their objective interests lie.

Men's relationships with women were also more complex than a dominance (or coercion) model suggests. Men, like women, were subject to conflicting, divergent, potentially malleable interests, some of which they were forced to affirm at the expense of others. A husband

---

7. See Ehrenreich (1983) for an unconventional analysis of the roots of antifeminism. Briefly, she argues that antifeminists are responding more to men's flight from the family in the last several decades than they are to feminism per se. Antifeminists, like feminists, are concerned with protecting and advancing women's endangered social position. They disagree with feminists, however, over which political strategies and social arrangements are most likely to achieve such an outcome.

The theme of male flight from the family extends back centuries in American culture (Fiedler, 1966; Swidler, 1980). Ehrenreich fails to distinguish this cultural tradition from actual male behavior and also fails to document a rise in either over the last two decades. Although divorce is on the rise, there is no evidence that men are any more responsible for this trend than are women. Her analysis thus cannot explain why antifeminism developed now and not earlier. Surely this is because in the context of recent structural change, feminism presents a significant challenge to the traditional argument that women are best "protected" by male supremacy.

may have greeted his wife's paycheck with ambivalence, for example, because it undermined his authority at home, but he was also likely to welcome this easing of his economic burdens. While some respondents had male partners who were hostile to their work careers, others reported notable support from men who valued their wives' independence. Women's emergent independence does not represent an unqualified defeat to all men. To the extent that the concept of patriarchy assumes universally shared, antagonistic male and female interests and a universal ability and desire on the part of all men to successfully dominate women, it captures neither the diversity nor the complexity of women's and men's relationships, actions, and interests vis-à-vis each other.[8] It oversimplifies men's roles in women's lives. More important, it underestimates women's active roles in constructing their own lives.

Because many men and women require some degree of mutual attachment beyond coercion, male-female relationships develop out of a negotiated process in which both struggle to define and meet their own needs while also trying to provide what the other wants and demands. When these demands are complementary, as was more often the case with domestically oriented women, the sexual struggle is accordingly mild. When interests clash, however, as they were more likely to do between nondomestic women and their male partners, conflicting desires must be negotiated. When women bring increased economic, social, and emotional resources to this negotiation process, they are better positioned to achieve greater equality. Thus, nondomestic women who had gained economic and social independence through work and who had also been able to build committed relationships with supportive partners were in a better position to resist male dominance and gain greater control in their relationships with the men who depended upon them.[9]

8. Willis (1977) argues that "patriarchy" affects male behavior in ambiguous and surprising ways. In his study of British working-class boys, patriarchy operates as a system of beliefs that channels these boys into working-class jobs. Their affirmation of antifeminist, male supremacist, and sexist ideas leads them to reject middle-class occupations that require more "feminine" (from the boys' point of view) behavior in favor of blue-collar occupations based on more "masculine" skills, such as physical strength. In Willis's analysis, patriarchy is less a structure of male dominance than an ideology that encourages working-class men to stay in the less rewarded sectors of the occupational structure.

9. Collins (1971) discusses how sex stratification in affluent market economies takes the form of negotiations between men and women. The outcome of these negotiations, he argues, depends on the relative balance of the various social and economic resources each brings to the relationship and is able to convert into power within it. Although most women command fewer social resources than most men, the more a woman brings to the negotiation process, the greater her ability to control the outcome.

Structural constraints, like patterns of socialization, define the limits of human action; but within these limits, a range of human responses is possible. Existing social arrangements can have unanticipated consequences and provoke unintended reactions, including both resistance and conformity. The critical questions become: What conditions promote resistance rather than compliance? When is resistance likely to succeed?

The experiences of the women in this study suggest that the first question can be answered by looking at the social-structural roots of the events that precipitated critical choice points—and subsequent changes in life paths—in individual lives. These events reflect and stem from larger structural changes now taking place in women's social position.

Work and Family Structures in Transition

Several structural arrangements have coalesced historically to promote domesticity as the path of least resistance for most women. Female domesticity has traditionally depended on the mutually reinforcing effects of four especially consequential social arrangements:

1. A family system characterized by permanent, stable marriage
2. A household economy founded on a one-paycheck, male "family wage"
3. Limited work opportunities for women
4. Sufficient behavioral similarity among women to provide mutually reinforcing support for female domesticity

The combined strength of these factors led to the rise of female domesticity, which was embraced—as an ideal and a reality—during the 1950s. During this period, most women eschewed the workplace in favor of family pursuits, and those who did not or could not were subject to disapproval, pity, or worse.

Even as female domesticity predominated, however, its structural underpinnings had begun to erode. The last thirty years witnessed a gradual decline in the strength of the major institutional supports for women's domesticity. During the 1970s, the pace of change quickened, dramatically altering the balance of pushes and pulls women face inside and outside the home. These changes have exposed increasing numbers of women to nondomestic alternatives and forced many of them to change the direction of their lives.

How pervasive are these changes? How deep do they go? How enduring are they likely to be? Do they portend long-term structural change that promises to affect a wide range of social institutions and to touch the lives of women, men, and children alike? Or are they instead ephemeral, short-term trends, so-called "bumps on the log of history," that will soon reverse, leaving women pretty much where they were before? An examination of these structural changes suggests the answer is more likely to be the former than the latter.

The Decline of Stable Marriage

Perhaps the most critical underpinning of women's domesticity is stable marriage. Permanent marriage makes economic dependency and full-time motherhood possible and contributes to a context in which childbearing and mothering seem natural. But marriage no longer offers the promise of permanence on which female domesticity has historically depended. Figure 4 shows that the rates of marriage, divorce, and remarriage all climbed from about 1920 until the end of World War II, when they began a short-term decline. According to Glick and Norton (1974:303), however, in the mid-1950s, "a critical new development appears. Since the mid-1950s, the first marriage rates have continued to decline while the divorce and remarriage rates have risen sharply."

As a result, the proportion of people marrying today is lower than at any time since World War II, but the proportion of people divorcing is higher. Throughout the 1950s, the divorce rate hovered around 15 per 1,000 married women aged fourteen to forty-four; by 1977, that rate had climbed to a historic high of 37, with no signs of abating. Moreover, the number of separations is actually greater than the divorce rate implies. Some married couples separate but never divorce; many other couples live together out of wedlock and eventually separate (Cherlin, 1981; Weiss, 1975).

The growing tendency to experience marital instability is especially acute among younger cohorts. Cherlin (1981:23) estimates that, among marriages begun in 1950, approximately 30 percent have ended or will end in divorce; among marriages begun in 1970, that figure rises to almost 50 percent. The remarriage rate, although high, is not keeping pace with the divorce rate, and second marriages have a slightly greater chance of ending in divorce (Hacker, 1979).

Although the recent decline in first marriages probably signals an increased preference for postponed marriage and cohabiting, "this downturn in the proportion of early first marriages could eventuate in a substantial increase of lifetime singleness" (Glick and Norton,

Figure 4 *Rates of First Marriage, Divorce, and Remarriage
for U.S. Women: 1921–1977*

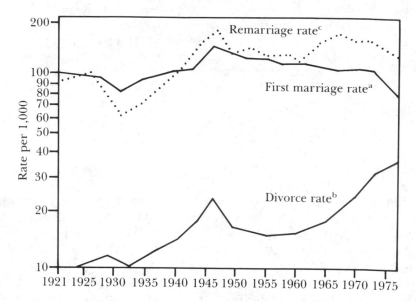

^a First marriages per 1,000 single women 14 to 44 years old.
^b Divorces per 1,000 married women 14 to 44 years old.
^c Remarriages per 1,000 widowed and divorced women 14 to 54 years old.

SOURCE: Glick and Norton (1977:5).

1974:305). The proportion of women, especially young women, likely to experience marital instability, late marriage, or even to be permanently single has increased strikingly in recent years.[10]

The rise in the rate of separation and divorce and the increase in the number of people choosing to postpone or reject marriage altogether have combined to leave an increasing percentage of women, and men, outside the structure of legal marriage. Although almost 80

10. Some analysts (for example, Bane, 1976) argue that divorce has merely replaced death as a form of marital instability. At the purely statistical level, this argument may be correct. However, these two forms of marital breakup differ significantly in their personal and social implications. Emerging forms of instability are more likely to occur early in adulthood, to recur throughout adulthood, to affect young children, and to affect the kinds of decisions women make in these critical young adult years. In addition, divorce and similar events involve choice, at least on the part of one partner; death is imposed and seldom anticipated in the early years of adulthood. Finally, new forms of marital instability coincide with women's increased reproductive control and are thus more likely to influence their fertility decisions.

percent of American households contained husband-wife couples in 1950, this figure had dropped to a little more than 60 percent by 1980 (see Table A.6).

The decline of stable marriage has altered the context in which both single and married women view their options. Younger cohorts of women, in particular, cannot safely equate marital vows with lifetime economic security or assume that any children they might bear will grow up in a household with both parents.[11] For those unwilling or unable to commit themselves to a permanent marital bond, which most still consider a precondition for parenthood, childbearing often appears out of reach. Instability and fragility in heterosexual relationships have thus made economic dependence, domesticity, and even motherhood increasingly elusive options. This changing context has encouraged, and even required, an increasing proportion of women to turn away from traditional domestic commitments toward stronger work ties, fuller economic independence, and higher work aspirations.

The Decline of the Family Wage

A male "family wage" that provides income adequate for the support of an entire household constitutes another critical underpinning of women's domesticity. But the male family wage, so long associated with industrial capitalism, is also in a decline.

A household economy based on a sole male breadwinner emerged only recently in human history—with the rise of the factory system and the consequent separation of the home and the workplace—and has never been achieved by all social strata, even during periods of widespread economic affluence. What constitutes an acceptable standard of living depends on individual tastes; once above a bare minimum, there is no objective measure of an adequate family income. American families in the twentieth century have nevertheless come to expect that a husband's earnings should not only suffice, but indeed provide for a relatively high standard of living. The two decades following World War II witnessed a period of economic growth so rapid

11. These patterns have led to a sharp upturn in the percentage of children spending a portion of their childhood with only one parent. In 1960, 88.5 percent of all children under fourteen lived with both parents; by 1974, that figure had fallen to 82.1 percent. Bane (1976:14) reports that, if present patterns continue, "nearly 40 percent of the children born around 1970 will . . . live in a one-parent family at some point during their first 18 years." The rise in marital instability has thus significantly altered the environment in which the nation's children are growing up.

and widespread that unprecedented numbers of American households from both the middle and working classes could enjoy the luxury of living well on one (male) paycheck.

Since 1970, however, the earning power of the single paycheck has been declining (Blumberg, 1980; Sternlieb et al., 1982). Figure 5 shows that, after controlling for inflation, the size of the weekly earnings of workers with three dependents reached a peak in 1972, after which it began a drop that continued throughout the last decade.

This drop has not yet reached and may never reach immediate post–World War II levels. Its effect on women's behavior, however, must be understood in terms of families' expectations. The economic expansion of the post–World War II era fueled people's expectations as it filled their wallets. A declining living standard, however slight, is therefore experienced as severe because it represents a growing gap between high expectations and the reality of declining affluence. This *perceived* gap between means and wants has had a powerful effect on women's assessment of the relative costs and benefits of committed work versus domesticity.

The one-paycheck household persists, to be sure, but Table A.6 in Appendix A shows that its dominance has eroded over the last three decades. In 1980, husband-wife households were evenly divided between those with a working wife and those without, whereas in 1950 husband-wife households without a working wife outnumbered husband-wife households with a working wife by three to one. An increasing

Figure 5 *Real Disposable Income for Workers with Three Dependents, 1947–1979 (in Constant Dollars)*

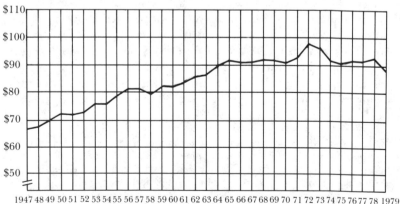

SOURCE: Blumberg (1980:69).

percentage of intact families have concluded that they cannot afford to ignore the income a woman can provide (Masnick and Bane, 1980; Oppenheimer, 1982; Vickery, 1979). These perceived economic squeezes have pushed a growing proportion of stably married women into the workplace to bring home earnings on which their children and husbands also depend.

The Ambiguous Expansion of Work Opportunities

The expansion of the clerical and service sectors of advanced, "postindustrial" economies has been largely responsible for the rise of the woman worker in the twentieth century (Oppenheimer, 1970). Located at the bottom of bureaucratic hierarchies, offering salaries well below those typical for male-dominated occupations, and characterized by flat mobility routes, these female-dominated occupations have been organized to encourage loose, tenuous work ties. Across the class structure, female pink-collar labor ghettos have historically discouraged high work ambitions that might detract from the pull of home and children. Nurses, primary school teachers, and librarians, like saleswomen and clerical workers, tend to arrive early in their "careers" at a point above which they cannot expect to rise.

The vast majority of women workers remain crowded into this narrow range of female-dominated occupations, where relatively low pay and constricted advancement opportunities still prevail (Barrett, 1979; Blau, 1979). Two recent trends suggest, however, that job opportunities for women have begun to change in ways that are changing the nature of women's ties to the workplace across the class structure.

The most dramatic change has occurred among college-educated women, who entered traditionally male occupational preserves in unprecedented numbers during the last decade. Table A.7 shows that, while the proportion of women in most female-dominated professions and occupations remained stable or increased slightly, the proportion of women lawyers, administrators, and the like rose markedly during the 1970s.[12] Of greater significance, as demonstrated in Tables A.8

---

12. Amsden (1980:12) argues, however, that, in terms of *overall* sex segregation, "there has been little movement of women into male-dominated fields over the past decade," that despite the dramatic rise in women's paid employment, occupational inequality between men and women remains static. In Chapter Nine, I consider the nature and implications of this apparent contradiction between rising opportunities for some women and static work prospects for most women. Strober (1983:9) reports that, when male-dominated occupations are defined as those with 60 percent or more men, the proportion of all employed women working in these occupations rose only slightly— from 9 percent in 1972 to 10 percent in 1978. Most of the increase has occurred in

and A.9, the proportion of first professional degrees and Ph.D.s awarded to women in male-dominated fields rose at an even faster pace during this period. Because younger cohorts account for most of the observed change, the proportion of women in the highly selective, prestigious occupations historically dominated by men should continue to rise for some time to come.

The mere presence of women in occupations that remain firmly male dominated does not, of course, imply equality, especially if these occupations begin to decline in prestige and pay as women enter them.[13] Sexual equality remains a distant, elusive possibility. The influx of women into middle-class professions once considered "for men only" is nevertheless a first, necessary step toward equality and signals the direction in which change is likely to continue.

Although the prospects for working-class women are even less bright, a small but notable proportion of this group has also benefited from new pressures and opportunities at the workplace. As women have filled the growing pool of jobs in the rapidly expanding service sector, they have begun to recognize the permanent nature of their ties to paid work, and their aspirations have risen accordingly. This change in attitude has begun to place unprecedented pressures on male-dominated institutions not only to make more highly rewarded male occupational categories accessible to women, but also to reward female-dominated occupations with better working conditions, higher pay, and greater upward mobility. The general climate created by women's awakening aspirations, coupled with affirmative action pressures, has induced, or forced, some employers to restructure the career ladders open to women, allowing advancement out of clerical ranks into managerial and quasi-managerial positions. The gains thus far achieved are limited, but they are not inconsequential and point toward working women's growing determination to improve their position at work (see Table A.7).

Although most women workers remain segregated into a small number of dead-end occupations, a growing number of women across

---

"integrated" occupations with no more than 60 percent of either sex, where the proportion rose from 16 to 22 percent. Only time will tell whether or not occupational sex segregation decreases more significantly as successive cohorts of younger women join the labor force and those now in it move into new positions over time. We are likely to witness a bifurcation of the female labor force as some women move up while most remain stuck in low-level positions.

13. For example, in the Soviet Union, where women account for a majority of physicians, medical doctors' pay and prestige are on a par with the pay and prestige of American schoolteachers. Similarly, when clerical occupations first arose in the late nineteenth century, the first secretaries, who were predominately male, were comparatively more respected and better remunerated than are female secretaries today.

the class structure are seeking expanded work opportunities. Mobility routes remain limited and obstacles differ by class position, but exposure to unanticipated opportunities has had a significant impact on the work and family decisions of both groups. As working women increasingly recognize that they can no longer view paid work as an intermittent, part-time, or secondary commitment, the pressure of their demands for upward mobility and occupational equality will mount.

The Erosion of Domestic Supports

Declining marital stability, increasing economic squeezes, and expanding workplace opportunities have combined to exacerbate a historic dilemma—with few exceptions, women have been the primary caretakers of children, yet work associated with child rearing and the private sphere has been systematically devalued. This dilemma predates the industrial revolution but was intensified by the rise of the factory system. Industrial capitalism promotes the devaluation of child rearing and homemaking by remunerating only work performed outside the home; it also encourages the isolation and social exclusion of those who perform these activities through the physical separation of the home and the workplace. Structural isolation and social devaluation have thus been the hallmarks of "women's place" since the rise of the industrial system.

Historically, few women have been able to escape this contradiction. Thirty years ago, there was a dominant pattern of female development. Most young adult women in the late 1940s and early 1950s married in their twenties, bore at least two children soon thereafter, and withdrew from work, at least temporarily, to devote themselves to home, husband, and children. In this context, female domesticity reigned as both the dominant ideology and the predominant model. The domestic option reinforced itself through the examples women set for each other and the stigma this similarity attached to non-domestic options. Similarity among women also produced networks of neighborhood support to offset the potentially isolating effects of confinement to the private sphere.

The rise of nondomestic alternatives has allowed mounting numbers to reject women's traditional developmental pattern. Those who for whatever reasons have eschewed the domestic model have unwittingly set in motion a self-reinforcing process that changes the situation for all women. As women have increasingly vacated the home for the workplace, those left behind have found themselves having to defend an increasingly devalued way of life. These conditions have induced others to seek the social integration of the public sphere, leaving those who remain at home more isolated than before. No matter how intrinsically satisfying or important their work may be, full-time "career mothers," no less than working mothers and childless women, find themselves embattled, forced to justify a position once considered sacrosanct.

Similarly, as women have entered the workplace, they have made it progressively easier for others to join them, while those who have postponed or rejected motherhood have been able to build networks of support for these once maligned choices.[14] The socially reinforced norm has shifted its center of gravity as new alternatives have gathered momentum. Old patterns persist, to be sure; but as new options have become more viable, they have undermined the supports for traditional ones as well.

Across the class structure, divisions have emerged between those who opt for mothering as a career and those who do not. To some extent, all women—including full-time mothers, working mothers, and permanently childless women—face a set of alternatives that are inherently contradictory and ambiguous. Adherents to each pattern have had to struggle to legitimate their responses to the structural contradictions between work and motherhood. This struggle between domestic and nondomestic women, whether it takes the form of battles over abortion rights, equal rights for women, affirmative action policies, or publicly provided day care, is likely to continue as long as the structural conditions that support it remain.[15]

Conclusion

Our analysis of the life histories of a carefully selected group of homemakers, working mothers, and childless workers from a variety of class, educational, and occupational backgrounds has uncovered

14. Kanter (1977a) analyzes the effect of numbers on women's aspirations, behavior, and position within hierarchical, bureaucratic firms. Ferree (1976a) reports that networks of support at the workplace promote and diffuse a feminist ideology among working women.

15. Lo (1982) presents an overview of recent research on countermovements and conservative movements in the contemporary United States. Luker (1984) analyzes the social-structural bases of "pro-life" and "pro-choice" abortion activism.

reasons why some women developed nondomestic orientations while others moved toward domesticity in adulthood. This analysis shows that childhood socialization provides an inadequate explanation of women's adult decisions, that notions of "feminine personality" do not do justice to the complexity and variety of women's orientations toward mothering and work, and that structural dominance models oversimplify the active role women take in shaping their lives and resisting the social arrangements they confront. Women's adult choices are neither the predetermined result of early childhood socialization nor mere reflections of static, purely coercive social structures, although each of these factors plays a role.

Women's decisions for or against motherhood and for or against committed work ties develop out of a negotiated process whereby they confront and respond to constraints and opportunities, often unanticipated, encountered over the course of their lives. The process is dynamic, not stable and fixed. It depends on how women define and perceive their situations as well as on the objective circumstances that structure these perceptions. Because the structural arrangements that channel women's motivations, perceptions, and behavior are ambiguous and contradictory, decision making involves a difficult struggle to define and act on situational interests.

Experiences with work and family structures in flux shaped these women's adult choices and led many of them to change the direction of their lives. The social arrangements that shape women's choices are undergoing transition, thus restructuring the alternatives women face. Marriage no longer necessarily offers the stability and economic security it once promised. More one-paycheck households are experiencing an erosion of their standard of living severe enough to make the benefits of two paychecks outweigh the complications of two workers. Workplace opportunities are expanding, albeit in limited ways, for both middle-class and working-class women. Female domesticity no longer enjoys the structural and ideological support it commanded thirty years ago. Finally, increased economic self-sufficiency, coupled with a growing acceptance of sex outside marriage, has provided women with an expanded set of alternatives to traditional marriage.

These structural changes in the economy, the organization of the workplace, and the nature of private life have combined to create new avenues for women outside the home, to erode the supports for female domesticity, and to intensify the split between those reproducing old patterns and those riding the currents of social change. Women develop differing choices and orientations toward motherhood and work, moreover, because some have been exposed to these structural changes while others have been insulated from them.

The old contradictions between home and market work remain, but shifts in family and work institutions have created new dilemmas, required new resolutions, and engendered new social cleavages and conflicts. Neither the type nor the extent of change is entirely clear or predetermined. Changes across structures are nevertheless mutually reinforcing; change in one structure tends to promote a chain reaction of readjustments in the others. These patterns are thus likely to become more deeply anchored over time, for they are rooted in social trends extending back into the last century.

The combined effect of all these changes has a number of important implications for women's lives. Most obvious, a growing proportion of women—even among those who were raised to prepare themselves for a life centered around full-time mothering—are increasingly likely to find their lives centered as much on the workplace as on the home. Personal independence and commitments outside the home will continue to take on greater importance in women's lives, and motherhood is not likely to command the central place in the vast majority of women's lives that it did thirty years ago. Many women will continue to travel the well-worn domestic paths of their mothers and grandmothers, but the relative size of this group is likely to continue to fall. In its place will rise a burgeoning group of working mothers, childless women, and career-committed women from both the middle and working classes searching for new forms of intimacy outside traditional marriage.

Second, women, as well as men, are increasingly likely to experience change over the course of their lives. The rise in marital instability and nontraditional household forms, along with changes in the structure of workplace opportunities, means that women, and especially young women, have become increasingly likely to move in and out of a diversity of work and family arrangements throughout adulthood. Among women coming of age today, there is no single, dominant pattern of adult development. The adult life course has become more fluid, more diverse, and less stable, exposing an increasing number of women to unanticipated events that are likely to induce and even perhaps require change. As Alonso (1980:42) notes:

> It is not only that there has been a diminution of the proportion of the population in the traditional family of husband-wife-children; there has also been a marked increase in the fluidity of family arrangements, so that individuals change their circumstances far more often.

Interactive and reinforcing structural changes in work and family institutions have thus created new alternatives for women. Unless these changes suddenly reverse, these new life patterns are here to stay. In spite of these new developments, however, old patterns will persist—

not only because many still find the structural supports for them, but also because obstacles to progressive social change often make old patterns preferable to the new. Structural changes in the position of women have done more than create new options for women; when coupled with persistent gender inequality, they have also created new and intensified personal dilemmas and social conflicts.

Finally, the social-structural circumstances that have promoted resistance to both traditional notions of femininity and traditional second-class citizenship for women in the labor force will probably persist in doing so. As social change promotes individual change, it also increases women's incentives to bring pressure to bear on the social institutions around them. This much appears certain. Exactly how successful this pressure will be in achieving greater gender equality is much less clear. More likely, gender stratification at home and in the workplace will remain deeply entrenched, although the forms it takes and the dilemmas it poses will continue to become more variable and complex.

The Politics of Parenthood

> Consider: Anyone can turn his hand to anything. This sounds very simple, but its psychological effects are incalculable. The fact that everyone between 17 and 35 or so is liable to be "tied down to childbearing" implies that no one is quite so thoroughly "tied down" here—as women, elsewhere, are likely to be—psychologically or physically. Burden and privilege are shared out pretty equally; everybody has the same risk to run or choice to make. Therefore nobody here is quite so free as a free male anywhere else.
>
> Ursula Le Guin, *The Left Hand of Darkness*

The Limits of Change and the Conflict Among Women

This book has charted the process by which a small but strategic group of women who came of age in the 1970s made inextricably linked decisions about work and family. As women on the cutting edge of social change, this group is especially well situated to illuminate the causes, contours, and likely consequences of women's changing social position. They were born into a period of rapid social change and thus had to make work and family decisions in a changing historical context. Through their choices, these women became unwitting molders of social change as well.

Although reared to pursue domestic goals, some women moved away from motherhood and toward careers as they found unexpected opportunities at work and encountered unpleasant experiences in marriage. In contrast, many of those reared with nondomestic aspirations found the road to work success blocked and opted instead for domesticity despite their earlier plans. Those who developed nondomestic orientations sought to restructure the sexual division of labor at home and at work and also to redefine traditional ideologies of child rearing. They met opposition from domestically oriented women who found it in their interest to preserve traditional arrangements and beliefs. The study found emerging divisions among women that promise to add to the social turmoil generated by women's changing social position. Despite the small sample size, there are good reasons to believe that the relationships uncovered here reflect larger social trends and point toward future social developments.

This group of women has been exposed to the kinds of structural changes that are likely to affect an increasing proportion of women throughout the class structure. Because women at the lower rungs of the class ladder are especially likely to confront eroding domestic supports in the form of marital instability and economic constraints, poor women are susceptible to the same forces propelling women in general to follow nondomestic pathways. Indeed, traditional patterns of female domesticity are becoming increasingly the luxury of the more affluent pockets of the middle class. Thus, despite the sample's racial homogeneity and bias upward in class position, these respondents illustrate dynamics that apply to their generation as a whole. Their lives provide some important clues about the future alternatives women as a group are likely to confront, where others that follow are likely to go, and what women's choices are likely to imply for processes of social change versus social reproduction.

Appendix B presents a full description of how the sample was selected, why and to what degree it can be considered representative of larger social trends and relationships, and its major limitations. Because the goal of this study has been to discover, rather than to verify theory, my conclusions can be only suggestive. They should be considered in the context of corroborative findings from larger, more representative samples.

Demographic analyses based on such larger samples do in fact support the findings presented here. Although low birthrates, high rates of female labor force participation, and associated trends surfaced dramatically only recently, they have been developing for many decades. Aside from the post–World War II period, which now appears to be an aberrant reversal of long-term historical trends, women's movement out of the home has been steadily gaining momentum since at least the turn of the century. Although recent changes in the position of women represent new developments that differ in important respects from past patterns, these developments nevertheless extend earlier trends.

The emergence of new life patterns for women is not peculiar to the American context. To some extent, these patterns characterize all the developed, postindustrial nations, whatever their political or economic system. Despite cultural and social differences, women's participation in the paid labor force appears to be endemic to the structure of all advanced, industrial societies.

Women's changing commitments stem from underlying structural changes that are widespread, are deeply rooted, and tend to reinforce each other over time. These structural changes—such as increased marital instability, pressures for greater female workplace opportunity, and a heightened need for women's earnings—have rearranged the options and incentives many women face. The reversal of these mutually reinforcing trends, although possible, seems unlikely. Thus, despite the perils of social forecasting, there are good reasons to believe that a sizeable proportion of women will continue to follow nondomestic paths as old doors close and new doors open. Alonso (1980: 45–46) concludes:

> I have three reasons for thinking that these changes are permanent indications of a new social reality. First, they represent a consistent story that has been evolving for many decades, with only the temporary anomalies of the baby boom. Second, comparable changes are being experienced in every developed country, so it is unlikely that temporary local peculiarities are at work. And third, these changes are deeply anchored and mutually reinforcing. . . . I cannot believe, given the coherence of these interrelated strands, that we can return to the high fertility and low labor force participation rates that pertained to women of a generation ago.

Some form of change appears inescapable, but its contours are less clear. The dual process of change and resistance to change that is under way promises to engender continuing social unrest and deepening personal and social dilemmas.

The Nondomestic Alternative

Despite the historical aversion to high rates of childlessness and one-child families, the percentage of women remaining childless or limiting their fertility to one child seems likely to remain high. For a variety of reasons, some chosen and some involuntary, fewer women will find themselves well situated for bearing even two children, much less the three or more commonly borne by earlier generations. Childless households and those with only one child are increasingly likely to replace the larger household of a generation ago. According to Masnick and Bane (1980:43), demographic analyses of childbearing patterns among younger female cohorts suggest that "the speed with which the generation is moving toward small families indicates that

40 percent or more of these women born in the 1950s may end up childless or with only one child." Even if this prediction proves to be exaggerated by as much as 10 percentage points, this still leaves almost one-third of all women in this age group opting for a very different kind of life than their mothers, who spawned the baby boom.

Alongside this increased preference for childlessness and only children, the number of committed women workers, with and without children, is also likely to remain high. First, as younger cohorts age, the percentage of all women of working age who are in the labor force will probably increase (Smith, 1979a, 1979b). Even more significant, an increasing number of these women workers are likely to move from tenuous, limited work participation to full-time, long-run work attachment. Masnick and Bane (1980:9) conclude: "Recent trends toward year-round, full-time and continuous work, especially among younger women, make this revolution [in women's work attachments] seem likely."

These strengthened work ties among younger women have important implications for the structure of the workplace and the household. The demand—and the need—for increased occupational and economic equality for women will persist, although obstacles to achieving gender equality at the workplace remain formidable.

Similarly, the rise of the committed woman worker necessitates some form of change in accepted ways of child rearing. However difficult the task may be, increasingly more women have little choice but to combine child rearing with committed, continuous work. For most women, this option still implies the proverbial "double burden" of household work added to paid work. The rise of the working mother nevertheless challenges some of the culture's most cherished ideas about proper child rearing and correct maternal behavior. At the very least, the notion that full-time mothering is the only responsible form of mothering faces continued challenge from those who by necessity or preference remain at the workplace throughout their children's preschool years.

Whether or not this ideological challenge weakens the obstacles that now make integrating work and parenthood so difficult remains an open question. The growth of new work and mothering patterns among women nevertheless promises to have repercussions that reach beyond the individual women generating them, requiring additional adjustments in how children are reared, how the family is organized, and how work is structured for both women and men.

In important respects, this growing group of nondomestic women represents a kind of quiet rebellion against the continuing dilemmas and contradictions of women's place. These women are to some extent on strike against a set of structural arrangements that provides meager social supports and rewards for child rearing and a set of beliefs that pits the interests of the mother against the interests of the child. As long as child rearing remains an undervalued occupation that is automatically assigned to women without substantial aid from men or the larger society, a sizeable proportion of women will reject full-time motherhood in favor of more highly rewarded alternatives.

The Domestic Challenge

Despite the rise of new alternatives for women, many remain committed to domesticity. This commitment to preserving past arrangements and opposing new ones makes sense in the context of persistent gender inequality, which makes the nondomestic road rough and uncertain.

Gender inequality persists on a number of related fronts, all of which combine to place obstacles in the paths of those women who lose or would reject the traditional protections of domesticity. First, although women's nondomestic aspirations have risen, inequality at the workplace remains deeply entrenched. Although college-educated women have joined male-dominated professions in unprecedented numbers, their climb to the upper ranks of these exclusive occupations has proven harder to accomplish. Despite some gains in nontraditional jobs, most women workers remain crowded into a relatively few female-dominated occupations. In 1979, for example, over 60 percent of all women workers were employed in either clerical, service (including private household), or sales jobs (U.S. Department of Labor, 1980:9). The proportion of men in most predominantly female occupations, moreover, has decreased slightly in recent years (U.S. Department of Labor 1980:10–11). Thus over 80 percent of all clerical workers and over 97 percent of all private household workers in 1979 were women (U.S. Department of Labor, 1980:9).

This pervasive sex segregation at the workplace has fostered widespread economic inequality between men and women. Despite the rise in the number of women seeking stable employment in highly responsible jobs, the male-female earnings gap has not diminished. Indeed, "the ratio of median earnings of full-time, year-round women workers to male workers actually dropped from about 63 percent in the mid-1950s to below 60 percent in the mid-1960s and 1970s" (Barrett, 1979:32). Even controlling for age, educational level, prior work experience, and number of hours worked, women's earnings remain well below men's earnings in all major occupational categories (Barrett, 1979; Wikler, 1981).

Although women have poured into the workplace, the sexual division of labor at home has been slow to respond to this change. Regardless of whether or not a woman works, housework remains a primarily female task (see Berk, 1980). Recent studies show that some men are spending more time in child care and housework than was typical in previous decades (Badinter, 1981; Pleck, 1979, 1982; Shinn, 1983); but those who bear children still find it difficult to make fathers equal partners in the daily work of parenting. Whatever a couple's preferences, few men are able to withdraw from the workplace to care for a newborn. Given the pervasiveness of male-female earnings differentials, few families could afford to substitute male for female caretaking even if employers were willing. The organization of household labor has thus been slow to respond to changes in the household economy. Women remain caught between the home and the workplace while most men remain second partners in the private sphere.[1]

Workplace organization also still assumes a traditional family model, even though only a minority of American households now fits this pattern. Paternity leaves, flex time, job sharing, and other arrangements that might increase the options open to women and men are available to only a few. Day-care programs, whether public or private, are notable in the United States primarily by their absence. Employers and policymakers have done little to confront, much less alleviate, the dilemmas households face when women attempt to combine work and parenthood.

Finally, widespread inequality between women and men makes the growing instability of marriage particularly dangerous for women. In the event of divorce, women tend to assume increased economic and social responsibility for their children even as they lose the economic support of a male earner. When divorce occurs, child custody is still awarded overwhelmingly to the woman (Wikler, 1981). Although joint custody arrangements are on the rise, Hacker (1982) reports that the number of divorced fathers with sole custody of their children has actually decreased in the last decade. Given the relatively low earnings and constricted occupational options most women command, the loss of male economic support usually brings a lower standard of living and for many brings economic disaster. The economic impact of divorce

---

1. If women's work patterns look increasingly like those of men, men's work patterns have also begun to more closely resemble women's (Hirschhorn, 1977). The trend toward shorter working hours and lower work participation among men, coupled with cultural changes in definitions of appropriate male behavior, may make greater male participation in homemaking and child rearing more feasible, if not more likely. Men, like women, are a varied group in which some are retaining traditional breadwinning patterns, others are assuming more parenting duties, and still others are rejecting family ties altogether (see Badinter, 1981; Ehrenreich, 1983; Gerson, 1984).

tends to be highly unequal according to gender. Cherlin (1981:82) reports, for example, that, after adjusting for changes in need, the income of women who separated or divorced between 1968 and 1973 dropped by an average of 7 percent. Their male counterparts' incomes actually increased by an average of 17 percent. Weitzman (1981) and Wikler (1981) report similar findings. More than half of all families currently below the poverty level are maintained by women (National Advisory Council on Economic Opportunity, 1981). This feminization of poverty is the direct result of the burgeoning proportion of female-headed households that drop below the poverty level because of the loss of or failure to secure male economic support.

In light of the male-female earnings disparity, the persistence of constricted opportunities for women in the labor force, the intransigence of the sexual division of household labor, and the relative paucity of social programs for working parents of either sex, it is easy to understand why the traditional pattern continues to attract adherents. Occupational and economic inequality between women and men makes the nontraditional route dangerous for women. Despite its dangers, however, a growing number of women face no other or better alternative.

Cleavages, Conflicting Interests, and Contradictory Trends

Alternatives for women have expanded, but gender inequality persists. Some women have benefited from the expansion of avenues outside the home, but many have not gained access to such felicitous circumstances. For these women, eroding domestic supports undermine their traditional protections without offering offsetting gains. These dual trends underscore the paradoxical nature of changes in women's position: Some have gained; some have lost; and most have gained in some respects and lost in others.[2] The contradictory nature of these changes has created new social cleavages, new sets of opposing interests, new political conflicts, and new social problems.

Although most analyses focus on how men and women form separate interest groups, this view is too simple. As the historically superordinant group, men have much to lose from sexual equality. As fathers and breadwinners, however, men do stand to benefit from some offsetting gains. Female equality offers them the chance to engage more fully in parenting, including its pleasures as well as its difficulties. Sexual equality also implies a shared responsibility for the financial

2. This process is somewhat analogous to the changing position of black Americans, where a sizeable middle-class stratum has emerged alongside a persistent and larger group of the extremely poor (Wilson, 1978).

support of the family, thus easing the economic pressures on men (and especially those with marginal earnings capacities). Because men, like women, are a heterogeneous group, some benefit, some lose, and most benefit in some ways and lose in others from changes in women's social position.

The deepening divisions among women and between traditional and nontraditional households throughout the class structure are as significant as conflicts between men and women. The contradictory nature of change ensures that differently situated women will disagree about where their best interests lie.

Domestic women, whose interests remain lodged in traditional family forms, understandably fear the erosion of the protections offered by traditional arrangements. This group, however, cannot go untouched by the changes taking place around it. As historical forces create new options and growing numbers choose them, those who follow established patterns face new challenges to their way of life. Female opposition to feminist political goals can be more easily understood in the context of persistent gender inequality, which leaves many women, as well as men, opposed to the changes around them.[3]

Nondomestic paths for women, however, are too long in the making and too deeply rooted to dissolve in the face of this opposition. They also guarantee that women's demands for equality will continue. These demands stem as much from new forms of female economic and social vulnerability as from a more general desire for liberation. Divisions between those who embrace new patterns and those who oppose them will thus continue to generate intense political conflict over women's, men's, and children's proper places in the social order.

The pressure for change in the organization of work and family life will persist, and some form of social change is assured, but change will not necessarily lessen the dilemmas women face. To the contrary, some changes in family organization, coupled with limits to change in the workplace, have intensified women's economic vulnerability, the social cross-pressures on them, and the psychological conflicts they experience.

3. Gender equality is a controversial policy goal precisely because women, like men, stand to lose as well as gain. Although sexual equality would strip men of their historic economic and occupational advantages, it would also strip women of their historic protections, such as exemption from the draft, the right to be supported economically, and legal claims over the custody and control of children. Equality always implies double-edged consequences, for it involves equal responsibility along with equal opportunity. Yet, given the choice, most socially disadvantaged groups have welcomed the right to trade the so-called "protections" of second-class, dependent status for the full responsibilities and rights of citizenship.

Gender Equality, Social Policy, and the Role of the State

The diversity of women's perceived interests makes the formulation of social policy on issues of gender inherently problematic. Policies aimed at achieving gender equality and diminishing the obstacles to combining work and parenthood will threaten those women, and men, who stand to lose from the erosion of traditional arrangements. Similarly, policies that promote female domesticity and make nontraditional options harder to implement will please the domestic group but provoke strenuous protest from those who have chosen or been forced to leave the domestic sphere. These conflicting stances make it difficult, if not impossible, to construct a coherent set of policies for women that meet the needs of all groups. Most policies, whatever their content, will face opposition from one group or another.

Political conflict between opposing interest groups forms the context in which change takes place. Opposition to change limits the degree and type of change possible, but it cannot stifle change in some form. For a variety of reasons far beyond anyone's control, the emerging diversity among women is here to stay. Because some type of change appears inevitable, public policy becomes a critical ingredient in determining whether social change reduces or exacerbates the problems women experience. We must ask at this point which social policies would be more effective in easing the contradictions women face.

Although women's interests diverge in the short run, in the long run, gender equality in income, occupational opportunities, and domestic options would lessen the contradictions all women face and expand the range of choices open to women and men alike. Children, moreover, would be the ultimate beneficiaries of policies that mandate sexual equality at work and in the home.

Policy Goals

Inequality at the workplace inhibits equality in the sexual division of parenting responsibilities; inequality in parenting inhibits occupational and economic equality.[4] Effective social policy must thus address sexual inequality on both fronts.

---

4. Polatnik (1973) analyzes the circular nature of gender inequality. In her explanation of why men do not rear children, she argues that male dominance is perpetuated and reinforced by the interaction between male advantages at work and women's responsibilities for rearing the young.

In the public sphere, the fundamental underpinning of workplace inequality is job segregation by sex. This system facilitates other forms of occupational inequality, such as the lower earnings and blocked mobility routes that characterize female-dominated occupations. Reducing workplace inequality requires diminishing job segregation by sex, providing equal pay for jobs of comparable worth, and restructuring female-dominated occupations to provide upward mobility over time as well as the social and financial rewards associated with a career.

This study shows that upward mobility and the associated benefits it provides are essential aspects of a satisfying work experience. Women, no less than men, are increasingly unwilling to settle for anything less. But improvements in women's work prospects and conditions are not likely to occur unless employers face political pressure not simply from women as individuals but, more important, from state policies. These women's lives show that affirmative action does make a difference, especially for working-class women who lack the economic freedom and educational resources to force change from below or look elsewhere for nourishing work.

Equality at work would have a number of consequences for women and men. First, it would reduce income disparity between them. This in turn would give women greater leverage to draw men more fully into household and parenting responsibilities and also improve the economic position of female-headed households.

Second, making female-dominated occupations more socially and economically attractive would lessen the devaluation of women's work and might ultimately draw more men into female-dominated jobs. Genuine workplace equality requires not only that women have access to traditionally male positions, but also that men become better integrated into traditionally female ones. Stasz (1982) points out that, despite the influx of women into male-dominated fields, a significant decrease in sex segregation depends upon a parallel movement of men into female-dominated job categories. Current efforts to secure equal pay for jobs of comparable worth may facilitate this process by narrowing the earnings gap between male-dominated and female-dominated occupations. If these efforts do not succeed in reducing occupational sex segregation by attracting more men into female-dominated occupations, however, the problem of gender asymmetry at the workplace will remain. History has shown that separate usually leads to unequal and that identifiably "women's work" will tend to be undervalued no matter what its content (Rosaldo, 1974; Treiman and Hartmann, 1981). Because much of the work women do is associated with children, providing increased social and economic rewards for women's work might have the added benefit of increasing the quality of care available for children.

Finally, if jobs became more sexually integrated and the disparity between male and female earnings narrowed, women and men would find it more economically rational to share equally in parenting. They would at least have a wider range of choice in deciding who would be the primary breadwinner. The increased time made available to fathers to care for their children would offset the loss of caretaking time available to work-committed mothers. Changes in workplace organization should reverberate into the private sphere, where inequality in the household could more easily diminish. Reducing domestic inequality would, in turn, give women greater freedom to pursue nondomestic goals.

Occupational equality will have a limited impact, however, unless the obstacles to integrating work and child rearing are reduced for both sexes. As long as employers penalize workers who are responsible for the care of children, male breadwinners will find it difficult to become involved fathers and mothers will find it difficult to become successful workers. Traditional households and childless workers will retain an advantage over those who would try to combine committed work with involved parenthood until parenthood is defined as a right and not just a privilege of all workers, regardless of gender.

Two types of social policies would reduce the barriers working parents face. First, legislation requiring employers to offer paid parental leave to both men and women on request (much as employers are now required to offer sick leave) would increase the options open to dual-earner households, help women workers who wish to bear children to remain in or rejoin the labor force, and make it easier for childless couples to opt for parenthood without endangering their financial solvency or occupational goals. Of no less importance, such policies would improve the chances that children of working parents will receive the care they need in the crucial first months of life. Such policies are not without precedent. Sweden, for example, guarantees the right to parental leave with job protection for up to eighteen months for parents of either sex.

Similarly, the development of a wide range of child-care services, programs, and facilities would help mothers and fathers better integrate their work and family lives. This range could, and should, include tax incentives to promote private sector alternatives such as neighborhood and workplace-based day care as well as publicly funded programs. The European example is also instructive here, for most northern European countries provide public day-care programs to the poor and nonpoor alike as a matter of course. The United States lags far behind European nations in providing government-supported child-care services. Indeed, this country stands in a minority among the rich, industrial nations in its failure to construct a coherent family policy that recognizes the rights and needs of working parents throughout the class structure. (See Kahn and Kamerman, 1975; Kamerman and Kahn, 1981; Wilensky, 1975, for overviews of welfare policies among the advanced industrial nations.)

In addition to promoting gender equality, these measures would increase the range of choice for working and child rearing open to both women and men. They would also help alleviate the dilemmas faced by nondomestic women of all social classes. Although social programs are important, legislative efforts to promote affirmative action, to secure equal pay for jobs of comparable worth, to prohibit discrimination against parents of either sex, and to provide new means of child care for overburdened parents are equally critical. Innumerable other policies might be added to this agenda, but those outlined here go to the roots of gender inequality and deserve central attention.

The State and Social Change

Given the existing diversity among women and men, no consistent set of policies can meet the various, often conflicting interests of differently situated groups. Those who continue to follow traditional patterns are especially likely to oppose the social arrangements the policies outlined here would promote.

The various groups who oppose state efforts to support gender equality and the development of alternative family forms offer three arguments to support their position: that such policies would bestow an unfair advantage on women and nontraditional arrangements; that state intervention in family life will hasten the "decline" of the family; and that children will suffer from women's movement out of the home. Each of these arguments has serious flaws.

First, affirmative action and other policies that mandate equal opportunity at the workplace do not discriminate against men. Rather, they redress a former imbalance by giving women some of the rights and privileges men have historically enjoyed. Because men have had the privilege of not having to compete with qualified women, they will experience these changes as unfair. In the long run, however, the sexual integration of occupations in the better rewarded sectors of the economy will remove the undeserved advantage now given to mediocre men and render the system more, not less, meritocratic.

Similarly, policies that ease the conflicts between work and family do not outlaw traditional arrangements or even make them significantly harder to implement. Rather, they acknowledge the fact of irreversible social change and address the problems thus created. To this extent, they challenge the social and economic advantages traditional forms have been afforded and compel them to compete on fairer terms with other alternatives.

Second, some maintain that, if women forsake the home for the workplace, they will usher in increased state and expert intrusion into family affairs, a sphere of life better left to parents (read: women) alone. Even some New Left critics (for example, Lasch, 1977, 1980) find themselves uncharacteristically aligned with conservatives who bemoan the dangers of state interference in private life and the unwarranted injection of experts into the process of child rearing. Although Lasch claims he has been misunderstood, he has become an influential spokesman in defense of the patriarchal family. He argues that the rise of child-rearing experts and public programs has undermined the paternal authority on which the modern nuclear family was built. As a result, the father is no longer able to provide the strong figure around which children can form oedipal struggles and conflicts. This robs children of the opportunity to rebel and resolve their oedipal conflicts as they mature, leading to destructive psychodynamic consequences.

This is, indeed, a contorted and curious defense of the privatized, bourgeois family *and* female subjugation. Lasch fails to discuss the cornerstone of this system of paternalism: women at home caring for children and families. Lasch thus appears to fear the destructive impact of socially based efforts to ease the plight of women on *men's* authority and *men's* psychodynamic development. But the consequences of these efforts, even in his argument, are likely to be liberating for women.

This argument against state support for nontraditional families also contains a logical flaw. The rise of the state and the rise of experts are both by-products of advanced industrialism (or postindustrialism); they are outcomes of the same social forces, but they are not caused by one another and are not the same phenomenon. Experts in the "helping professions," in particular, are an endemic aspect of postindustrial society, with or without a coherent family policy.

State policies that promote gender equality and provide support services for child rearing will not hasten the so-called decline of the family, lower the quality of family life, or destroy family privacy and independence. To the contrary, such policies are likely to have the opposite effect. Given current realities, policies that recognize the irreversibility of women's movement out of the home and provide needed support services are more likely to improve family life than to harm it. (See Joffe, 1977, for a well-reasoned discussion of these issues.)

It is, moreover, erroneous to equate weak or hidden state policy with the absence of policy. When the state fails to intervene on behalf of social justice, it is implementing policy as surely as when it does so.

This is the fallacy of "benign neglect." The very reluctance of the American state to provide universally available child care or mandate female equality at work has been as much a form of state policy as any so-called interventionist or strong family policy might be. For better or for worse, the state will shape private life in some way. The issue is not the degree of state involvement, but rather the form it takes.

Ruggie's (1982:10) contrast between policies toward women in Sweden and England shows that the state's efforts or failure to promote "a universal framework" of family and work policies can make a critical difference. There are, however, those who believe that, whether or not a coherent state policy regarding the family is desirable, its formulation is impossible. Steiner (1981) argues that there are too many different types of state policies affecting the family—from taxation to education—to make it either possible or desirable to coordinate them toward one goal or end. This argument is probably correct, but it is beside the point. The difficulty in coordinating all state policies does not preclude a concerted state effort to redress the grievances of women. Moreover, policies that take account of the diverse needs of a variety of households (without discriminating against or in favor of any one type) should be directed at providing a range of options, not consistently promoting only one option. Surely our traditional national commitment to tolerance and diversity requires no less from us.

There is no evidence to support the argument that state participation per se weakens the fabric of family ties or contributes to the family's demise. The forces that are changing private life as we have known it will have their impact regardless of the state's response. Policies can either ease these changes or make them more difficult to live with, but they cannot prevent some type of change from occurring. Families in some form will always be with us; no known society, past or present, has been without them. The question concerns their form and quality. Policies that recognize and address the new constraints and dilemmas many families face can inject new vitality into our private lives.

Finally, perhaps the most widespread fear, even among those most disposed to support and follow new paths, is the danger to children posed by women who work. Concern over the welfare of the nation's children is justified, but the blame for children's plight is misplaced. It is not women's equality that threatens children's welfare, but rather the social and economic devaluation of children and those who would care for them. Until we value our children enough to provide them with the services they need and reward those entrusted with their care, we cannot expect women to shoulder the burden our political and economic systems refuse to accept. The new vulnerabilities children face because of changing family structures have not ultimately been caused by women, and they cannot ultimately be solved by women alone. For reasons far beyond their individual control, working mothers cannot and will not return to the home; decreeing that women belong at home and refusing to ease their movement out of it will not stem the tide of women, with and without children, moving into the world of work.

Indeed, in the face of this massive social change, female inequality is the greatest threat to children's welfare. As long as we undervalue those who care for childen, we will undervalue children and their needs. If we are committed to improving the quality of children's lives, we will increase the rewards to those who provide both paid and unpaid care to children, provide supportive structures and services for families with children, and promote economic equality for women, who increasingly must support children without the aid of men.

Of equal importance are policies that allow and promote participatory fatherhood. Such policies increase the number of parents available to the child and the number of options available to families. A child thus stands a better chance of receiving care from a concerned, committed, and competent caretaker—rather than one who has been forced into the job. Mothers and fathers might both approach the job of child rearing with greater enthusiasm if they felt they had more choice concerning how to go about it. And whatever losses children might incur from a decrease in time spent with their mothers would be more than offset by the benefits they gained from an accompanying decline in "paternal deprivation".[5]

The reproduction and regeneration of a society through its offspring is inherently a social, and not merely a female, task. Social policy must recognize that parenthood is a shared endeavor and that children are ultimately a social as well as a private responsibility. Because men and women will increasingly share in the economic responsibilities of rearing children, it is appropriate that they more equitably share in the emotional and nurturing responsibilities as well. At the most fundamental level, we must move beyond outdated concepts that define "mothering" as a specific style of interpersonal caring and "fathering" as limited to the acts of procreation and breadwinning. These gender-biased definitions do not accurately describe what fathers and mothers can and often do give their children, nor do they fit the circumstances facing growing numbers of parents. We would do well to recognize that both genders possess the human capacities to nurture and to work.

We need not fear a world in which men and women shoulder equal burdens in the home as well as at work. The range of human cultures

5. For still rare, but increasingly frequent discussions of paternal deprivation and the role of the father in child development, see Fein (1978), Lamb (1982), Lynn (1974), Parke (1981), Pedersen (1980), and Rapoport et al. (1977).

makes clear that beliefs about the proper place of women and the proper way to rear children result more from social circumstances than from scientific fact. Throughout human history, societies have constructed their family lives, reared their children, and even defined childhood in a variety of ways without high levels of social disorganization or mental breakdown (see, for example, Ariès, 1962; Badinter, 1981; Gordon, 1978; Kagen, 1976; Laslett, 1972). These variations confirm that there is no one "correct" family form and attest to the resilience of women, men, and children.

We should fear, however, the consequences of *not* moving toward gender equality. Although the economic and political costs of such policies are likely to be high, the costs of ignoring, punishing, or trying to prevent the changes now under way are likely to be even higher. If we fail to approach current changes in women's position with a respect for diversity and a concern for women's plight, the individual and social problems spawned by these inevitable changes will surely grow more severe.

The conflicts and dilemmas women face will not diminish, despite women's changing social position, until the costs and rewards of working and parenting are more equally distributed by gender. As long as the social costs of parenting fall more heavily on women than men, women with good workplace prospects will continue to resist full-time motherhood. Similarly, as long as women are denied equal access to the rewards of working, those with poor prospects will cling to economic dependence within marriage as their only protection from alienating work. A growing number, however, will be forced to combine work with child rearing, despite the obstacles that lie in their path. The biggest losers, of course, are those who lose their economic, social, and emotional base at home and cannot offset this loss with genuine opportunities for rewarding work.

In the absence of a social policy that respects the variety of paths a woman can take and recognizes that this diversity is here to stay, women will remain ambivalent about their choices, whether for work, motherhood, or some combination of the two. Many will be forced to opt for childlessness or less parenting, despite the negative sanctions opponents of social change would like to attach to these outcomes. Others, choosing domestic paths, will find these equally conflict-laden. The level of conflict among women and between women, men, and the institutions of government and work will surely persist and will likely rise.

However appealing past patterns may appear, they are simply not viable alternatives for many, for their structural underpinnings are eroding. The most humane and sensible choice, then, is to take the difficult, conflict-laden steps toward gender equality at work and in the home. To do so will not ensure human liberation, but the failure to do so will promote increasing personal and social discontent, and not for women alone.[6]

Those who would mourn the past we have lost would do well to recognize that social change is an inherently ambivalent process in which some things are lost and some things are gained. As Hirschhorn (1977: 448–49) notes: "Yet we know that each time people resolve the ambivalence they are the richer for it; . . . that, just as they experience losses, so they develop the capacities to cope with those losses." The women we have met in these pages testify to this human capacity to prevail over and not just survive the challenge of change. It is appropriate to ask our political and social institutions to do so as well.

6. There are those who argue that gender equality, especially in parenting, would bring with it genuine human liberation as psychodynamic asymmetry was eradicated or "feminine" and "masculine" personalities became integrated. (See, for example, Dinnerstein, 1976.) It is, however, possible to imagine a world in which women are equal that is still unequal, unjust, and inhumane in other ways. Unfortunately, there is little evidence to suggest either that women with power behave more morally than male power holders or that the human race would be psychologically transformed by gender equality. Nevertheless, even if equality between the sexes is unlikely to create utopia, it is surely a worthy goal in itself.

APPENDIX A | *Tables*

Table A.1 *Female Labor Force Participation Rates by Marital Status, Children in the Household, Age, and Percent of Full-Time Workers, 1950–1980*

	1950	1960	1970	1980[a]	Percentage Increase
Single[b]	40.6%	41.8%	45.6%	52.5%	29.3%
Married, husband present	21.6	30.5	40.8	49.4	128.2
No children in household[c]	30.3	34.7	42.2	46.7	54.1
Children under 6 in household[c]	11.9	18.6	30.3	43.2	263.0
Children 6–17 in household[c]	28.3	39.0	49.2	59.1	108.8
Aged 20–24	46.0	46.1	57.7	67.7	47.2
25–34	34.0	36.0	45.0	65.4	92.4
35–44	39.1	43.4	51.1	65.5	67.5
45–54	37.9	49.8	54.4	59.6	57.3
55–64	27.0	37.2	43.0	41.7	54.4
Percent of women workers who work year-round full-time	—	36.9	40.7	43.7[d]	18.4[e]

[a] For married women and women with children in the household, percentages refer to 1979.
[b] Includes never married, separated, divorced, and widowed.
[c] For women who are married with husband present only.
[d] Data for 1978.   [e] Base year is 1960.
SOURCE: U.S. Department of Labor (1980:14,16, 22, 28).

Table A.2 *Future Births Expected by Births to Date, All Women Aged 18–34*

Number of Births to Date	Number of Future Births Expected					
	0	1	2	3	4+	Total
0	26.0	10.1	46.5	12.0	5.4	100
1	41.8	42.0	12.8	2.5	0.9	100
2	83.3	12.6	3.4	0.4	0.2	100
3	90.3	8.3	0.6	0.4	0.3	100
4+	91.7	4.7	2.5	0.4	0.7	100

SOURCE: U.S. Bureau of the Census (1980a: Table 4A).

Table A.3 *Female Labor Force Participation Rates, 1955–1979, of Birth Cohorts by Year of Birth, Five-Year Intervals*

Year of Birth	Age in 1979	Participation Rate at Age										
		20–24	25–29	30–34	35–39	40–44	45–49	50–54	55–59	60–64	65–69	70 & over
1956–60	(20–24)	69.1										
1951–55	(25–29)	64.1	65.7									
1946–50	(30–34)	57.8	57.0	61.8								
1941–45	(35–39)	50.0	45.2	51.7	63.4							
1936–40	(40–44)	46.2	38.9	44.7	54.9	63.9						
1931–35	(45–49)	46.0	35.7	38.2	49.2	56.8	60.4					
1926–30	(50–54)		35.3	36.3	43.5	52.9	55.9	56.5				
1921–25	(55–59)			34.7	40.8	48.5	55.0	53.3	48.7			
1916–20	(60–64)				39.2	46.8	51.7	53.8	47.9	33.9		
1911–15	(65–69)					44.1	50.7	50.1	49.0	33.3	15.3	
1906–10	(70–74)						45.9	48.8	47.1	36.1	14.5	4.7
1901–05	(75–79)							41.5	42.2	34.0	17.3	4.8
1896–1901	(80–84)								35.6	31.4	17.4	5.7

SOURCE: U.S. Department of Labor (1980: Table 5).

Table A.4 *Cumulative Birthrate for Female Cohorts by Year of Birth, 1900–1959*

Year of Birth	Age in 1980	Birthrate at Age							
		15–19	20–24	25–29	30–34	35–39	40–44	45–49	50–54
1955–59	(21–25)	.087	.56						
1950–54	(26–30)	.084	.58	1.21					
1945–49	(31–35)	.098	.71	1.44	1.89				
1940–44	(36–40)	1.130	.91	1.81	2.31	2.57			
1935–39	(41–45)	1.040	.94	2.09	2.71	2.95	3.00		
1930–34	(46–50)	.089	.82	1.95	2.74	3.09	3.19	3.13	
1925–29	(51–55)	.071	.66	1.64	2.43	2.87	3.02	3.04	2.99
1920–24	(56–60)	.065	.57	1.40	2.12	2.58	2.77	2.80	2.80
1915–19	(61–65)	.060	.50	1.22	1.86	2.28	2.48	2.52	2.52
1910–14	(66–70)	.070	.52	1.14	1.69	2.09	2.28	2.32	2.32
1905–09	(71–75)	.070	.59	1.25	1.74	2.07	2.26	2.30	2.30
1900–04	(76–80)	.067	.62	1.40	1.94	2.28	2.44	2.48	2.49

SOURCES: U.S. Bureau of the Census (1980a: Table 7A); U.S. Department of Health, Education and Welfare (1976).

Table A.5 *Percent Childless for Female Cohorts at Different Ages by Year of Birth, 1900–1959*

Year of Birth	Age in 1980	Percent Childless at Age							
		15–19	20–24	25–29	30–34	35–39	40–44	45–49	50–54
1955–59	(21–25)	92.5	63.5						
1950–54	(26–30)	93.1	61.3	36.8					
1945–49	(31–35)	92.4	56.4	29.5	19.8				
1940–44	(36–40)	91.2	50.3	23.3	14.2	12.1			
1935–39	(41–45)	91.8	47.7	19.3	11.5	9.3	10.1		
1930–34	(46–50)	92.7	52.4	20.9	12.3	9.8	9.2	10.5	
1925–29	(51–55)	94.1	57.0	25.3	14.4	11.4	10.6	10.5	10.5
1920–24	(56–60)	94.5	63.3	29.9	16.5	12.5	11.5	11.3	11.3
1915–19	(61–65)	94.9	67.2	38.2	22.7	17.5	16.0	15.8	15.8
1910–14	(66–70)	94.1	66.9	43.0	28.3	22.0	20.2	19.9	19.9
1905–09	(71–75)	94.0	62.6	40.0	29.1	23.8	21.7	21.4	21.4
1900–04	(76–80)	94.3	61.3	35.5	25.5	21.8	20.4	20.1	20.1

SOURCES: U.S. Bureau of the Census (1980a: Table 7A); U.S. Department of Health, Education and Welfare (1976).

Table A.6 *Composition of U.S. Households, 1950–1980*

	Husband-Wife Households		Other Households			Total
	Traditional[a]	Working Wife[b]	Female-Headed	Primary Individuals[c]	Other[d]	
1950	59.4%	19.6%	8.4%	10.8%	1.8%	100%
1955	54.2	21.7	8.8	12.8	2.5	100
1960	51.2	23.2	8.5	14.9	2.5	100
1965	47.0	25.6	8.7	16.7	2.0	100
1970	41.6	28.9	8.8	18.8	1.9	100
1975	36.6	29.2	10.0	21.9	2.3	100
1980	30.3	30.6	10.8	26.1	2.2	100

NOTE: For husband-wife families, breakdown by presence of children was not available. The traditional group would be smaller if presence of children were included. The larger figure is probably more accurate, however, because it includes those families in which children are planned or have already left the household.

[a] Husband-wife families with wife outside labor force.
[b] Husband-wife families with wife in labor force.
[c] Single adult living alone or with unrelated persons.
[d] Primarily male-headed families with no wife present.

SOURCES: Hirschhorn (1977:437); U.S. Bureau of the Census (1981: Tables A and 18).

Table A.7 *Women as a Percentage of Total Employed Workers, for Selected Occupations, 1972 and 1978*

	1972	1978
Professional, technical, and kindred (male-dominated)		
Accountants	21.7%	32.9%
Computer specialists	16.9	23.1
Designers	18.3	28.5[a]
Drafting technicians	6.3	14.8[a]
Engineering and science technicians	9.1	13.4
Lawyers and judges	3.8	12.4[a]
Life and physical scientists	10.0	18.0
Personnel and labor relations	30.7	43.7
Pharmacists	12.8	24.4[a]
Physicians, dentists, and related practitioners	9.3	10.5
Psychologists	38.0	50.0[a]
Public relations workers	29.9	43.8[a]
Religious workers	11.0	14.8
Social scientists	21.3	33.7
Teachers, college and university	28.0	33.8
Writers, artists, and entertainers	31.7	35.6
Professional, technical, and kindred (female-dominated)		
Health technologists and technicians	69.3%	70.9%
Librarians and kindred	81.7	81.1
Registered nurses, dieticians, and therapists	92.6	92.9
Social and recreation workers	54.9	61.0
Teachers, except college and university	70.0	71.0
Managers and administrators	17.6%	23.7%
Bank officers and financial managers	18.9	30.4
Health administrators	47.0	46.2
Office managers, not elsewhere classified	41.9	65.0
Public administrators and officials, not elsewhere classified	20.3	24.8
Sales managers and department heads	15.6	22.4
Sales workers	41.6%	44.8%
Demonstrators and peddlers	77.0	85.0
Insurance agents, brokers, and underwriters	11.6	20.3
Real estate agents and brokers	36.7	45.1
Sales clerks, retail trade	68.9	71.5
Clerical and kindred	75.6%	79.6%
Bank tellers	87.2	91.5
Bookkeepers	87.9	90.7
Cashiers	85.8	87.2

Table A.7 *(continued)*

	1972	1978
Receptionists	97.0	96.9
Secretaries, stenographers, and typists	98.1	98.4
Shipping, stock, and receiving clerks and storekeepers	19.1	37.4
Telephone operators	96.7	93.9

NOTE: In some male-dominated occupations, the trend toward increased female participation began before the 1970s. For an overview of these trends from 1950 to 1979, see U.S. Department of Labor (1980:10–11).

ᵃThese figures are for 1979.

SOURCES: Scientific Manpower Commission (1981: Table G-WF-3) and U.S. Bureau of the Census (1980d:63).

Table A.8 *Proportion of First Professional Degrees Awarded to Women, for Selected Professions, 1970–1971 and 1978–1979*

	1970–1971	1978–1979
Law	7.3%	28.5%
Medicine	9.2	23.1
Architecture	12.0	25.8
Theology	2.3	13.1
Dentistry	1.2	11.9
Veterinary medicine	7.8	28.9
Optometry	2.4	13.1
Osteopathy	2.3	15.7
Podiatry	2.0	7.2
Pharmacy	25.2	39.9

SOURCE: Scientific Manpower Commission (1981: Table G-PRO-3).

Table A.9 *Proportion of Ph.D. Degrees Awarded to Women, 1972 and 1982*

	1972	1982
Physical sciences	6.6%	13.4%
Engineering	0.6	4.7
Life sciences	14.8	27.7
Social sciences	18.8	36.7
Humanities	27.0	42.4
Professional fields	12.0	32.7
Education	23.2	48.8
All Ph.D.s	16.0	32.4

SOURCE: National Research Council for the National Science Foundation (1983:6).

APPENDIX B | *Methodology*

This study began with two related questions. At the general level, it sought to explain how women make inextricably linked decisions about work and family. At a more specific level, it sought to explain the emergence of the subtle revolution in women's work and child-bearing patterns over the last decade or so. Because the generation of women who were in their prime childbearing years during the last decade is most responsible for these dramatic changes in women's life patterns, a close examination of this strategic group promised to offer the best method for uncovering the causes and consequences of both the subtle revolution and women's more general decision-making processes.

From the outset, the research questions called for an exploratory study designed to discover, not verify, theory. No well-developed (or, at least, convincing) theory was available to guide analysis, specify critical variables, or generate hypotheses. (See Chapter Two for a discussion of why prevailing theories of women's behavior do not adequately address the questions posed by this study.) Nor had data collected by earlier investigators anticipated the vast social changes now under way. Existing data thus could not satisfactorily address the questions as formulated. Indeed, specifying the right questions became as important as finding their answers.

I chose a "grounded theory" approach as the most appropriate research strategy. (See Glaser and Strauss, 1967. Luker, 1975, applies this approach to the explanation of contraceptive risk taking.) Open-ended, in-depth interviews with a carefully targeted sample of women would facilitate the process of discovery by enabling theoretical concerns to emerge and develop throughout the interview stage of research. In this way, the study stood the best chance of avoiding the Scylla of qualitative research that is descriptively rich, but lacks analytic precision, and the Charybdis of quantitative research that is causally precise, but lacks the data necessary to uncover process or answer the critical questions. Locating a sample and constructing an interview schedule that would fulfill the goal of developing better theory became the study's major methodological tasks.

Sampling

Study design required a sample that focused on a specific cohort of women who varied in their work experiences, class positions, and choices concerning work and family. The sampling procedure thus had to locate a group of women within a delimited and somewhat narrow age range who nevertheless varied in class background and occupational position, including homemakers and workers (both childless and with children) in a variety of job settings. Accomplishing this task efficiently while preserving the principles of randomness proved to be difficult. Sample requirements rendered traditional procedures, such as random sampling within census tracts, sampling from the workplace, and snowball sampling, either unworkable or unacceptable.

Random sampling within census tracts, the preferred strategy for securing an unbiased, representative group, was impractical in this case. Recent census statistics quickly revealed that the age range within specified local census tracts in the San Francisco Bay Area was too large and too varied to permit neighborhoods to be targeted efficiently on the basis of age. Going door to door in selected neighborhoods in order to locate the few eligible respondents on a particular street would have been too time-consuming and costly to be worth its benefits.

Sampling from the workplace would have made it easier to locate the proper age group, but this procedure had other, equally undesirable drawbacks. Because a major goal of the study was to uncover the forces that lead some women into the workplace and others out of it, the sample had to include nonworking as well as working respondents in a variety of occupations. Sampling from one or two or even three workplaces would exclude homemakers and provide only a limited range of occupational groups. This procedure could not yield the full range of respondents necessary to the analysis.

Abandoning the principle of randomness altogether and using a snowball or network method to generate a pool of respondents or simply seeking out potential respondents where they are likely to congregate, such as supermarkets, shopping centers, and other public places, would have yielded the correct mix of respondents. However, such methods involve other unacceptable risks: The potential for self-selection and thus for building unmeasurable but systematic bias into the analysis would have compromised the findings too severely. These less stringent sampling methods were therefore also rejected.

Largely through a process of elimination, an acceptable sampling strategy emerged.[1] The procedure involved choosing respondents randomly from two pools: a list of alumnae from a local university and a list of recent female enrollees in business, technical, and general interest courses at a local community college. The university sample consisted of women who had attended and in most cases graduated from a four-year college. They were thus relatively educationally advantaged. Community college respondents were drawn from enrollment lists of a community college located in a working-class area and designed to serve the needs of local residents who lacked a college education (and in some cases, a high school diploma) and wished to return to school for a course or two. Although the community college offered some liberal arts courses leading to a two-year degree, respondents were randomly selected only from those divisions offering technical training (for example, accounting, stenography, and typing) or general nondegree courses (for example, exercise classes and undeclared general majors). The sample was thus expanded to include women with limited educational backgrounds and comparatively modest economic resources. To avoid confounding sources of variation, racial and ethnic variation was kept to a minimum. The sampling procedure produced no black respondents.

For a number of reasons, this procedure proved especially effective. First, because educational institutions generally keep accurate, up-to-date records on their students and alumni, a reliable list of names was available. Second, generating a random list of names that covered roughly the correct age cohort was a simple matter because these names could be selected according to year of graduation (in the case of the university sample) or year of birth (in the case of the community

1. Kristin Luker's strategic advice was critical at this stage of the research. Ann Van de Pol also helped locate the community college.

college sample). An initial telephone screening eliminated those few names that did not fall within the correct age range. Third, lists of this kind did not systematically exclude important groups within the research design. This procedure yielded a diversity of women, including mothers, childless women, homemakers, and workers in a wide variety of occupations. Fourth, sampling from two pools stratified by education provided a good mix of class backgrounds as well as work and educational experiences. The university sample also increased the chances of locating some professional career women, a group that is statistically small but theoretically important. Finally, and of no small consequence, these samples were accessible. Because educational institutions are sympathetic to university-based research, I was able to secure cooperation from the first two institutions I approached.

The sample generated by this procedure efficiently targeted appropriate pools of respondents and enabled random selection from among them. It also generated a high response rate, at least in part because I was able to contact named respondents directly (see Appendix C, Table C.1). It nevertheless contains some biases worth noting. Although it produced variation in occupational experience, class background, and current class position, this sampling strategy excluded those who did not complete high school or receive any post–high school training. Although not strictly representative of all white working-class and middle-class women, the sample nevertheless focuses the analysis on a group representing a large and theoretically important category of women. (Appendix C presents a selected statistical description of the sample and compares it to the general population of white American women in a roughly similar age group. I refer those not convinced that students at two-year colleges are primarily from the working class to Karabel, 1972, and Brint and Karabel, 1981.)

The reader may object that a sample of comparatively well-educated respondents focuses on a self-selected group that is more disposed toward nondomestic patterns than the general population. To some extent, this is so. The bias in favor of emergent or nontraditional patterns takes on less significance, however, because the study aimed to explain not only why new life paths for women are emerging, but also why old ones persist. The aim is not to predict the proportion that can be expected to follow one path or another, but to uncover the social forces that lead women to choose whatever path they take. The insights and conclusions of this analysis can and, I hope, will be applied to and tested among other groups of women in different social environments and of other races and age cohorts.

The exploratory nature of the study also limited the sample size. Long, probing interviews (three to four hours on the average) conducted exclusively by the author precluded selecting enough respondents to meet quantitative standards for statistical reliability. Although, everything else being equal, a large sample is preferable to a smaller one, in this case, the benefits of collecting qualitative, in-depth information outweighed the sacrifice in sample size. (The response rate of 87.5 percent suggests that there is negligible bias in self-selection of respondents; see Appendix C for complete details.) Conducting interviews one at a time enabled me to follow new leads as they emerged. At the same time, a structured interview schedule ensured that I collected comparable information on each respondent. Through this "constant comparative method" (Glaser and Strauss, 1967), I developed and refined a theoretical perspective at every stage in the research process. The final five to ten interviews offered no more "surprises" that required investigation in succeeding ones. "Saturation" was thus achieved, and additional interviews promised to be only marginally useful.

The ideas discovered by this method await more systematic verification on larger samples. But without this stage of small-scale, exploratory research, the findings presented here would probably not have been uncovered.

Finally, for practical and financial reasons, I confined the sample to a single metropolitan region, the San Francisco Bay Area. Because this region is sometimes considered atypical and perhaps a bit ahead of the nation as a whole, I made every effort to overcome this potential source of bias. I drew respondents from a variety of geographically dispersed and socially diverse locations, including inner-city, outer-city, and suburban neighborhoods. I automatically excluded areas I considered too aberrant from the national norm (for example, Berkeley and the University of California environs) from the sampling pool. In the end, the study's findings are consistent with national trends that have been documented by census statistics and findings from other studies. (See, for example, Alonso, 1980; Masnick and Bane, 1980; Smith, 1979a, 1979b.) The subtle revolution among women is not confined to a single geographical area, and the San Francisco Bay Area does not appear to be significantly different from other metropolitan areas across the nation in this respect.

Although their numbers are small and biased slightly upward in the social structure, the respondents selected for this study represent an important segment of their generation. As a group, they have been exposed to a wide variety of structural forces that are likely to affect increasing numbers of women throughout the class structure and in generations to come. The kind of relationships found among this group are thus also likely to hold for others who find themselves facing a similar set of structural opportunities and constraints. To the extent that the social conditions propelling these women down their various paths, whether domestic or nondomestic, endure, these respondents not only illuminate the forces that have shaped the choices of their generation, but also signal the directions that succeeding generations will be likely to take.

The Interview

The interview schedule was developed over a period of months, during which twelve pretests helped transform a series of vague questions into a structured interview. This phase made it clear that a structured interview format was necessary not only to encourage theoretical insight, but also to guide the respondent through what would otherwise have been a thoroughly confusing experience.[2]

Even before the official phase of data collection began, this process of interview construction raised several unanticipated questions: How does a woman with a domestic orientation at twenty become a childless career woman at thirty-five? And, conversely, how does someone with high work ambitions in adolescence become a committed homemaker at thirty? These early pretests made it clear that women's decisions could not be fully understood in terms of either static, coercive structures (which I had been inclined to emphasize) or earlier childhood experiences. Rather, work and family choices were cumulative, interactive, and developmental. The interview schedule gradually assumed the form of a life history questionnaire that guided the respondents through their personal "life lines" and focused on mobility routes through work and family events.

The final interview schedule was structured to guide the interview and ensure comparability across groups; it was open-ended to allow for probing and discovery of the range of possible answers and to accommodate new theoretical insights as they occurred. Only a few minor changes were required after the official data collection began. All interviews were taped and subsequently transcribed verbatim. In the presentation of quoted material, occasional quotes have been edited slightly for clarity and all names have been either removed or changed to ensure respondent anonymity. To facilitate the flow of the argument, one or two quotes were typically chosen to support a point, even though numerous examples were available.

2. This process was aided by the painstaking guidance of Charlotte Coleman, an interview designer at Berkeley's Survey Research Center. The interview schedule is reproduced in Appendix D.

The reader may nevertheless fairly object that the reliance on interviews per se introduces bias into the research. To some extent, this must be true. Self-reporting always runs the risk that the respondents will present what they deem to be desirable rather than accurate pictures or, worse, will be unable to articulate unconscious motives and causes. These inherent problems with self-reporting are compounded when, as in this case, the respondents are also asked to describe events that happened in the past and consider actions they may take in the future. Such methodological perplexities can never be entirely overcome. Their impact on the study's findings were, however, kept to a minimum.

Care was taken to achieve a sense of rapport and trust with the respondents. The interviews took place at times and in settings deemed most comfortable by the respondents. This nonthreatening environment usually put the respondent at ease and encouraged intimate disclosure—to which only the interview material itself can testify. No observers (including spouses and older children) were allowed in the room during the interview, although on rare occasions a toddler or infant was present. No personal information about the interviewer was given until the interview was completed. In these ways, the respondents were encouraged to respond openly and were reassured that there were no correct or incorrect answers.

At the end of the interview, I was often asked to reveal my own choices and plans, especially concerning childbearing. I replied by asking the respondent what she imagined my situation to be. In each case, the respondent concluded that my decisions were similar to her own. This response underscores the degree to which trust was gained, for both mothers and childless women typically assumed I was like them.

Of course, even the most conducive environment cannot eliminate the danger of bias in retrospective reporting. In the abstract, this difficulty is serious; in the concrete situation, however, it proved to be less troublesome. With remarkably little prodding, most respondents recalled their pasts with ease, confidence, and even enthusiasm. This is less surprising for those whose lives had not changed significantly over the years and whose childhood experiences seemed in no apparent contradiction with their present orientations. Those who had undergone significant change since childhood also expressed the same clarity, however. Retrospective recall was thus not biased in favor of consistent or against inconsistent life histories. As a result, there is less reason to suspect that the interview structure itself significantly altered the nature of the results.

Although making predictions about the future is especially unreliable, this too is less problematic than it superficially appears. Many respondents may have changed their plans after the interview was completed. The study itself predicts that such changes would occur under conducive circumstances. Like past changes, future changes would not be arbitrary but would result from changes in the underlying structure of a respondent's alternatives. In the long run, moreover, barring large reversals at the structural level, changes among individual respondents are likely to even out; so individual changes will not necessarily lead to changes in the group as a whole. As Stinchcombe (1968:67–68) explains, this tendency toward group stability in the face of individual change makes it possible to do research that inquires into the future as well as the past:

> The pollster who takes a "snapshot" of the population at a given time is not really measuring the ephemeral and changing characteristics of individuals. Instead, he is measuring a balance of causal forces characterizing the group. This group property is usually much more stable and reliable than the characteristics of the individuals. . . . The stability of a population proportion only very rarely depends on the stability of the individual characteristics on which it is based. A great deal of stability of social phenomena depends on such equilibria of forces of change.

We can thus discount systematic bias in predictions about the future just as we can in retrospective reporting.

Finally, some might object that self-reports necessarily underestimate the role of unconscious motivation in determining individual behavior. The job of an interviewer and data analyst, however, is precisely to overcome this problem. Like the psychoanalyst, the researcher relies on self-reports for evidence, but she or he is also equipped with methodological and conceptual tools that make analysis of unconscious causation possible. Among these tools are a comparative perspective that is gained by interviewing many respondents, a set of concepts and theories to interpret what may appear to the respondent as self-evident, a skeptical eye, and the ability to probe. Self-report interviews are not confined to the exploration of conscious processes; they can uncover structural and psychological causes of which the respondent may remain unaware. The women in this study did not view their actions in terms of the framework presented here. Yet although they were unaware of the logic of their behavior, they provided information to help explain it.

APPENDIX C | *Sample Characteristics*

Table C.1 *Results at Each Step in Sampling Procedure*

Sample	Total Names Drawn	Did Not Fit Sample Criteria[a]	Unable to Locate[b]	Eligible for Interview			Response Rate
				Agreed	Refused	Total	
University	72	15	17	35	5	40	87.5%
Community college	51	4	15	28	4	32	87.5
Total	123	19	32	63	9	72	87.5

NOTE: The sample was selected via a three-step procedure. First, names were randomly selected from lists of women provided by the sources described in Appendix B. The university list was constructed by year of graduation, with age inferred; the community college list was constructed by date of birth. Next, letters were mailed to all randomly selected names describing the study and announcing that addressees would soon be contacted by phone. Third, a phone call screened out ineligible respondents, gathered basic demographic information from eligible respondents, and made an appointment with those who agreed to participate to conduct the interview.

[a]In most cases, too old to be in the cohort under study.
[b]For example, moved out of area, phone disconnected, or letter returned.

Table C.2 *Marital History: Comparisons Between Study Sample and All White Women Aged 25 to 34*

	Study Sample (N = 63)	All White Women Aged 24–35[a] (N = 14,863,000)
Single	28.6%	25.8%
Never married	15.9	12.8
Divorced	12.7	8.8
Separated	—	3.7
Widowed	—	.5
Married, husband present	71.4%	74.2%
First marriage	60.3	64.0[b]
Remarried	11.1	10.0[b]

[a]Source: U.S. Bureau of the Census (1980b).
[b]Estimates based on 1977 figures.

Table C.3 *Number of Children Born: Comparisons Between Study Sample and All White Women Aged 25 to 34*

	Study Sample (N = 63)	All White Women Aged 25–34[a] (N = 14,561,000)
No children	52.4%	27.5%
1 child	14.3	21.4
2 children	23.8	30.1
3 or more children	9.5	21.0

[a]Source: U.S. Bureau of the Census (1979a).

Table C.4 *Birth Expectations: Comparisons Between Study Sample and All White Women Aged 25 to 34 Who Completed Four Years of High School or More*

	Study Sample (N = 63)		All White Women Aged 25–34 Who Completed 4 Years of High School or More[a] (N = 11,633,000)	
No children	22.2%	38.1%	11.1%	24.8%
1 child	15.9		13.7	
2 children	49.2		46.6	
3 or more children	12.7		28.6	

[a]Source: U.S. Bureau of the Census (1979a).

Table C.5 *Years of School Completed: Comparisons Between Study Sample and All White Women Aged 25 to 34*

	Study Sample[a] (N = 63)	All White Women Aged 25–34[b] (N = 14,860,000)
3 years of high school or less	—	14.8%
4 years of high school	22.2%	43.7
1 year of college	9.5	8.3
2 years of college	11.1	9.0
3 years of college	1.6	3.5
4 years of college	20.6	13.9
5 years of college or more		6.8
Teaching credential	12.7	
Other	22.2	

[a]Includes time spent in business or technical schools.
[b]Source: U.S. Bureau of the Census (1979b).

Table C.6 *Occupational Breakdown of Female White-Collar Workers: Comparisons Between Employed Women in Study Sample and All White Women in White-Collar Jobs*

	Employed Women in Sample Study (N = 46)	All White Women in White-Collar Jobs[a] (N = 24,572,000)
Predominantly male professions[b]	10.9%	7.6%
Predominantly female professions[c]	15.2	17.2
Managers and administrators	17.4	9.6
Clerical, sales, and kindred workers	56.5	65.6

NOTE: 65.5 percent of all employed women in 1978 occupied white-collar jobs. The rest were either blue-collar workers (14.3 percent), service workers, including private household workers (18.8 percent), or farm workers (1.4 percent).

[a]Source: U.S. Bureau of the Census (1980d).
[b]Professions in which men constitute more than 50 percent of the employed workers.
[c]Professions in which men constitute less than 50 percent of the employed workers.

Table C.7   *Annual Work Experience: Comparisons Between Study Sample and All White Women Aged 25 to 34, 1977 and 1970*

	Study Sample (N = 63)	All White Women Aged 25–34[a] 1977 (N = 16,858,000)	1970 (N = 12,901,000)
Not employed	27.0%	31.9%	43.5%
Employed part-time[b]	7.9	16.7	16.2
Employed full-time[c]	65.1	51.4	40.3

[a]Source: U.S. Bureau of the Census (1980d).
[b]Fewer than 35 hours a week in the majority of weeks worked.
[c]Thirty-five hours a week or more in the majority of weeks worked.

Table C.8   *Total Family Income: Comparisons Between Study Sample and All White Households with Household Head Aged 25 to 34*

	Study Sample (N = 63)	All White Households with Household Head Aged 25–34[a] (N = 11,368,000)
0–$4,999	—	6.1%
$5,000–$9,999	4.8%	11.8
$10,000–$14,999	17.5	17.9
$15,000–$19,999	9.5	22.4
$20,000–$24,999	11.1	19.5
$25,000–$29,999	17.5	
$30,000–$39,999	22.2	20.9
$40,000–$49,999	7.9	
$50,000 and over	9.5	1.6

NOTE: This table excludes single male–headed households.
[a]Source: U.S. Bureau of the Census (1980c).

Table C.9   *Personal Earnings: Comparisons Between Study Sample and All White Women Aged 25 to 34*

	Study Sample (N = 63)	All White Women Aged 25–34[a] (N = 14,861,000)
None	14.3%	18.4%
$1–$4,999	17.5	37.2
$5,000–$9,999	14.3	23.6
$10,000–$14,999	25.4	14.9
$15,000–$19,999	11.1	4.3
$20,000–$24,999	9.5	1.0
$25,000 and over	7.9	.7

[a]Source: U.S. Bureau of the Census (1980c).

Table C.10 *Ethnic Background by Sample Source*

	University Sample (N = 35)	Community College Sample (N = 28)	Total (N = 63)
Northern European	77%	64%	71%
Southern European	6	15	10
Eastern European	17	7	13
Asian	—	7	3
Hispanic	—	7	3

NOTE: The exact wording of the question was, "From what countries or part of the world did your ancestors come?" When more than one region was named, the one named as predominant was used to categorize the respondent. In the case of a tie, the category closer to the bottom of the list was chosen.

Table C.11 *Father's Occupation by Sample Source*

	University Sample (N = 35)	Community College Sample (N = 28)	Total (N = 63)
White collar	92%	15%	58%
Professional, technical, and kindred	29	—	16
Managers and administrators	34	4	21
Sales workers	29	11	21
Blue collar	3%	57%	27%
Craftsmen and kindred	—	7	3
Operatives, except transport	—	18	8
Transport equipment operatives	—	18	8
Laborers, except farm	3	14	8
Service workers, except private household	3%	21%	11%
No steady employment	3%	—	1%
Don't know (father deceased, divorced, or otherwise not present)	—	7%	3%

NOTE: The exact wording of the question was, "What was the best job your father ever held while you were growing up?"

Table C.12 *Husband's or Partner's Occupation by Sample Source*

	University Sample (N = 35)	Community College Sample (N = 28)	Total (N = 63)
White collar	60%	32%	47%
Professional, technical, and kindred	40	7	25
Managers and administrators	14	18	16
Sales workers	6	7	6
Blue collar	9%	37%	20%
Craftsmen and kindred	3	4	3
Operatives, except transport	3	11	6
Transport equipment operatives	—	4	2
Laborers, except farm	3	18	9
Service workers, except private household	6%	7%	6%
No steady employment	6%	—	3%
No partner (or no information on partner)	20%	25%	22%

NOTE: The exact wording of the question was, "What kind of work does your (husband/partner) do?" *(If Necessary:* "Tell me a little more about what he actually does in that job. What are some of his main duties? What is his job title?")

Table C.13 *Incidence of Abortion by Sample Source*

University sample	11.4% (N = 35)
Community college sample	7.1 (N = 28)
Total	9.2 (N = 63)

Table C.14 *Husband-Wife Earnings Differentials by Sample Source*

	University Sample (N = 26)	Community College Sample (N = 20)	Total (N = 46)
Husband earns more	69%	70%	69%
Earnings about equal	19	25	22
Wife earns more	12	5	9

NOTE: Table excludes single respondents without partners and with partners who were not living in the household.

Table C.15 *Religious Background by Sample Source*

	University Sample (N = 35)	Community College Sample (N = 28)	Total (N = 63)
Protestant	60%	43%	52%
Catholic	20	35	27
Jewish	14	—	8
Other	—	3	2
None	6	18	11

NOTE: The exact wording of the question was, "Were you raised in a particular religion?" If yes: "Which one?"

Table C.16 *Present Religious Affiliation by Sample Source*

	University Sample (N = 35)	Community College Sample (N = 28)	Total (N = 63)
Protestant	34%	54%	43%
Catholic	12	14	13
Jewish	14	—	8
Other	6	3	4
None/don't know	34	29	32

NOTE: The exact wording of the question was, "Do you consider yourself a [religion] today?" If no: "Do you consider yourself a member of any [other] religion?"

Table C.17 *Party Affiliation by Sample Source*

	University Sample (N = 35)	Community College Sample (N = 28)	Total (N = 63)
Democratic	37%	14%	27%
Republican	29	7	19
Independent			
Closer to Democratic party	14	43	27
Closer to Republican party	3	18	10
Closer to neither party	17	14	16
Don't know	—	4	1

NOTE: The exact wording of the question was, "In politics, generally speaking, do you usually think of yourself as a strong Democrat; a not very strong Democrat; an independent, closer to the Democratic party; an independent, closer to neither party; an independent, closer to the Republican party; a not very strong Republican; or a strong Republican?"

Table C.18 *Political Orientation by Sample Source*

	University Sample (N = 29)	Community College Sample (N = 27)	Total (N = 56)
Liberal	48%	26%	37%
Middle-of-the-road	31	59	45
Conservative	21	15	18

NOTE: The exact wording of the question was, "In politics, would you say that you are radical, liberal, middle-of-the-road, conservative, or a strong conservative?" (No one selected the extreme options of radical or strong conservative.) Six cases are missing because the question was added after some interviews had already been conducted.

Table C.19 *Number of Children Ever Born by Sample Source*

	University Sample (N = 35)	Community College Sample (N = 28)	Total (N = 63)
No children	54%	43%	49%
First pregnancy[a]	6	—	3
1 child	9	21	14
2 children	17	32	24
3 children	14	4	10

[a]Two respondents were pregnant with their first child at the time of the interview. (Two respondents were involuntarily infertile. One had adopted two children; the other had chosen to remain childless.)

Table C.20 *Age of Respondent by Sample Source*

	University Sample (N = 35)	Community College Sample (N = 28)	Total (N = 63)
27–29 years	26%	54%	38%
30–32 years	31	29	30
33–35 years	21	18	24
36–37 years	14	—	8

Table C.21 *Percent Currently Childless by Age of Respondent and Sample Source*

	University Sample (N = 35)	Community College Sample (N = 28)	Total (N = 63)
27–29 years	67%	40%	54%
30–32 years	72	63	68
33–35 years	30	20	27
36–37 years	40	—	40

Table C.22 *Future Plans by Sample Source*

	University Sample (N = 35)	Community College Sample (N = 28)	Total (N = 63)
Childlessness	23%	21%	22%
Combining work and motherhood	28	32	30
Erratic work	26	19	22
Full-time homemaking	23	28	25

APPENDIX D | *Interview Schedule*

WORK-FAMILY COMMITMENT STUDY

I.D. No.: _____

Name: _____

Address: _____

_____

Phone: _____

Date of Interview: _____

Date Transcribed: _____

Interview No.: _____

RECORD OF CALLS

Call #	Date	Result of Call
1		
2		
3		
4		
5		
6		

ENUMERATION

I. First, I'd like to get an idea of who lives in this household.
   1. What are the names of all other adults who live here?
   2. Now, how about the children? I'd like their names in order, beginning with the oldest. (Any others?)
   3. Is there anyone else who usually lives here, like a roomer or boarder?
   4. Have I missed anyone who is away temporarily? Any babies?

II. *For each person listed, ask as necessary and record in table:*
   1. How is _____ related to you?
   2. Is _____ a (male/female)?
   3. How old was _____ on (his/her) last birthday?
   If over sixteen:
   4. Is _____ now married, divorced, separated, or has (he/she) never been married?
   5. Is _____ now employed full-time or part-time? [*Count thirty hours or more per week as full-time.*]

   If not employed: Is _____ looking for work or on lay-off from a job?

ENUMERATION TABLE [*Fill in respondent information from screening form.*]

Name	Relation to Respondent	Sex	Age	Marital Status	Labor Force Status
	Respondent	F		1. Mar	1. Emp full
				2. Sep	2. Emp part
				3. Wid	3. Looking
				4. Div	4. Lay-off
				5. NvM	5. Not emp
	1. Spouse/S.S.	1. M		1. Mar	1. Emp full
	2. Child	2. F		2. Sep	2. Emp part
	3. Parent			3. Wid	3. Looking
	4. Other relative			4. Div	4. Lay-off
	5. Not related			5. NvM	5. Not emp
	1. Spouse/S.S.	1. M		1. Mar	1. Emp full
	2. Child	2. F		2. Sep	2. Emp part
	3. Parent			3. Wid	3. Looking
	4. Other Relative			4. Div	4. Lay-off
	5. Not related			5. NvM	5. Not emp
	1. Spouse	1. M		1. Mar	1. Emp full
	2. Child	2. F		1. Sep	2. Emp part
	3. Parent			3. Wid	3. Looking

| 4. Other relative | | 4. Div | 4. Lay-off |
| 5. Not related | | 5. NvM | 5. Not emp |

1. Spouse	1. M	1. Mar	1. Emp full
2. Child	2. F	2. Sep	2. Emp part
3. Parent		3. Wid	3. Looking
4. Other relative		4. Div	4. Lay-off
5. Not related		5. NvM	5. Not emp

[Continue for each member of household.]

CHILDHOOD AND PERSONAL HISTORY

Now, I'd like to ask you about yourself when you were growing up.

P.1.a. Were you living with both parents most of the time up to age sixteen?

        Yes [*Skip to P.2.*]   1

        No   2

  b. *If no:* Who were you living with most of the time up to age sixteen? [*Circle all that apply.*]

        Father   1

        Mother   2

        Stepfather   3

        Stepmother   4

        Other [*Specify:* _____]   5

  c. Was your (father/mother) deceased—or what?

        Father deceased   1

        Mother deceased   2

        Parents divorced   3

        Other [*Specify:* _____]   4

  d. How old were you when your (father/mother/parents) (died/were divorced)?

        Age _____

      If father deceased and no surrogate, skip to P.4.

P.2.a. What was the best job your (father/stepfather) ever held while you were growing up?

  b. About how old were you when he got this job? Age _____

  c. How many years did your father hold this job? Years _____

    If held job for less than two years: What was the best job your father had most of the time while you were a teen-ager?

d. How do you think he felt about his job—did he like his work or do you think he would have preferred to do something else?

Liked job	1
Preferred something else	2

Comments:

P.3. What was the highest grade or year your (father/stepfather) completed in school?

Grade school: 1 2 3 4 5 6 7 8
High school: 9 10 11 12
College: 1 2 3 4
Graduate school: 5 +   [*Specify highest degree received:* _____]

P.4. How old was your mother when you were born?

Age _____

If mother deceased and no surrogate, skip to P.9.

P.5.a. Did your (mother/stepmother) work at all when you were young? (*If necessary:* When you lived with your parents?)

Yes	1
No [*Skip to P.7.*]	2

b. *If yes:* Was that full-time or part-time?

Full-time	1
Part-time	2

c. Has she ever worked?

P.6.a. What kind of work did she do?

b. How old were you when she started to work?

Age _____

c. How long did she work? (*Round to nearest year.*)

Number of years _____

P.7.a. Do you think she preferred (working/not working) outside the home, or do you think she would rather have (stayed home/worked outside the home)?

Preferred working	1
Preferred staying home	2

Comments:

b. How did *you* feel about her (working/not working) outside the home—did you like it or dislike it (when she started to work/that she didn't work)?

Liked it	1
Disliked it	2
Indifferent/Never considered	3

Comments:

P.8.   What was the highest grade or year your (mother/stepmother) completed in school?

Grade school: 1 2 3 4 5 6 7 8

High school: 9 10 11 12

College: 1 2 3 4

Graduate school: 5+ [*Specify highest degree received:* _____]

P.9.a.   How many brothers and sisters do you have? None [*Skip to P.10.*] _____

Number of brothers _____

Number of sisters _____

  b.   (Is he/Is she/Are they) older than you or younger than you?

  c.   *If over sixteen:* What is (he/she) doing now? (*If necessary*: Is [he/she] married? Does [he/she] have children? Does [he/she] work?)

#1.

#2.

#3.

#4.

#5.

P.10.a.   When you were growing up, say, just moving into your teens and start-ing to think about the future, what did you think you'd be doing at the age you are now? (*Probe:* Did you think you'd be married and have children? Did you think you'd be working, or doing anything in particular?)

  b.   What about when you were twenty-one or so—what did you think you'd be doing at this age when you were in your early twenties?

P.11.a.   What do you think your parents expected you to be doing at this age? (*Probe:* Did they expect you to be married and have children? Did they expect you to work or have a career?)

  b.   Was there *ever* a time when you wanted to have a (child/career)? *If yes:* When was that? Why didn't you?

P.12.a.   What is the highest grade or year you completed in school?

Grade school: 1 2 3 4 5 6 7 8

High school: 9 10 11 12

College: 1 2 3 4

Graduate school: 5+ [*Specify highest degree received:* _____]

Technical/trade/

business: *Specify:* _____

  b.   What were your grades like in high school—excellent (that is, mostly As), good (Bs), average (Cs), or below average (Ds)? What were they like in college?

	High school	*College*
Excellent	1	1
Good	2	2
Average	3	3
Below Average	4	4

If received higher degree, skip to P. 15.

P.13.a. Did you want to go on for a higher degree?

Yes	1
No	2

b. Why did you leave school at the time you did?

P.14.a. Do you have any desires or plans to go back to school?

Yes	1
No [*Skip to husband section.*]	2

b. *If yes:* What would you like to do?

Skip to husband section.

P.15. *If received higher degree:* What were the main reasons you decided to get a degree in (*type of degree received*)?

HUSBAND OR PARTNER AND MARITAL HISTORY

Some questions now about (your husband/the man in your life/your marital history).

H.1.a. Let's see. You said you were (married/divorced/separated/widowed/never married), is that right?

Married [*Skip to H.2.*]	1
Divorced	2
Separated	3
Widowed	4
Never married	5

b. *If not presently married:* Are you seeing someone steadily right now? (*If necessary:* Is there one special person you are seeing a lot of?)

Yes, living with someone [*Skip to H.3.*]	1
Yes, seeing steadily [*Skip to H.3.*]	2
No, not involved [*Skip to H.9.*]	3

H.2.a. *If married:* How long have you been married?

Number of years _____

b. How long did you know each other before you got married?

Number of years (months)_____

c. What were the main reasons you got married at that time?

d. Is this your first marriage?

Yes [*Skip to H.4.*]	1
No	2

e. *If no:* How many times have you been married? (*Probe:* What happened with that marriage?)

Number of times _____

Skip to H.4.

H.3.a. *If living together or seeing steadily:* How long have you been (living together/seeing each other steadily)?

   b. Do you have any plans to get married (or live together)? (*Probe:* Why [not]?)

Yes, get married	1
Yes, live together	2
No [*Skip to H.4.*]	3

   c. *If yes:* Are you pretty sure you will (get married/live together), or are you just thinking about it?

Pretty sure	1
Just thinking	2

H.4. What is the highest grade or year (your husband/the man in your life) completed in school?

Grade school: 1 2 3 4 5 6 7 8

High school: 9 10 11 12

College: 1 2 3 4

Graduate school: 5 +   [*Specify highest degree received:* _____]

Technical/trade/business: *Specify:* _____

H.5. You said (your husband/the man in your life) is (working full-time/working part-time/not working)—is that right?

Full-time	1
Part-time	2
Not working [*Skip to H.7.*]	3

H.6.a. *If working:* What kind of business or industry does he work for? (*Probe:* What do they do or make there?)

   b. What kind of work does he do? (*If necessary:* Tell me a little more about what he actually does in that job. What are some of his main duties? What is his job title?)

   c. About how many hours does he usually work in an average week?

Number of hours _____

   d. Is that a 9-to-5 schedule—or what?

   e. How long has he been (working at that job/in that line of work)?

Number of months _____

Number of years _____

Skip to H.8.

H.7.a. *If not working:* What does he spend most of his time doing—going to school, unable to work, keeping house, looking for work, or something else?

Going to school	1
Unable to work	2
Keeping house	3
Looking for work	4
Something else [*Specify:*	
_____]	5

   b. When did he last work?

   c. What kind of work did he do? (*Probe:* Does he have a regular line of work?)

   d. Why did he leave that job? (*Probe:* Does he have any plans to return to work?)

H.8.   How do you think (your husband/the man in your life) feels about (his job/what he is doing)—does he find it satisfying or do you think he would prefer to be doing something else? (*If necessary:* What is that?)

If married only once, skip to employment section.
If never married, skip to H.10.
If ever divorced, skip to H.11.

H.9.   *If not presently involved:* What are the main reasons you are not seeing someone steadily right now?

If never married, skip to H.10.
If ever divorced, skip to H.11.

H.10.   *If never married:* What are the main reasons you have never married? (*Probe:* Have you ever been seriously involved with someone or lived with someone? What happened with that relationship?)

Skip to employment section.

H.11.a. *If ever divorced:* How long ago were you divorced?

   b. And how long were you married (that time)?

   c. What were the main reasons you got a divorce? (*Probe:* Why did you get married in the first place?)

EMPLOYMENT

I'd like to find out about the kinds of jobs you've held since you left school.

If employed, skip to E.2.

E.1.   *If not employed:* Have you worked at all since you left school?

Yes	1
No [*Skip to E.12.*]	2

E.2. How many different jobs have you had since you left school (including your present job?)

Number of jobs _____

E.3. What was the *first* job you had just after you left school? (*Probe:* What did you do at that job? What did they do or make there?)

Go to E.4. and ask question series for each job held up to present job.

If still employed in first job, go directly to E.5.

If necessary, explain: Now I'm going to ask you some questions about each job you've held.

E.4. *For each job, ask:*
   a. What did you do at that job? (*Probe:* What did they do or make there?)
   b. Was that full-time or part-time?
   c. How long did you work at that job? (*If necessary:* How old were you when you started and left?)
   d. How did you feel about that job—on the whole, did you like it or dislike it?
   e. What were your main reasons for choosing that line of work?
   f. What were your main reasons for leaving that job?
   g. What did you do after you left that job? (*If necessary:* What was your next job?)

Repeat questions for all jobs up to present.
For present job, skip to E.6.

Job #1:
   a. Job description:
   b. Full or part (hrs/wk):
   c. Years at job (ages started and left):
   d. Feelings about job:
   e. Reasons for choosing:
   f. Reasons for leaving:

Job #2:
   a. Job description:
   b. Full or part (hrs/wk):
   c. Years at job (ages started and left):
   d. Feelings about job:
   e. Reasons for choosing:
   f. Reasons for leaving:

Job #3:
   a. Job description:
   b. Full or part (hrs/wk):
   c. Years at job (ages started and left):

  d. Feelings about job:

  e. Reasons for choosing:

  f. Reasons for leaving:

Continue for each job.

Go to next page for present job.

If not currently employed, skip to E.12.

Now let's talk about your present job.

  E.5.a. You are working (full-time/part-time)—is that right?

Full-time   1

Part-time   2

  b. What kind of business or industry do you work for? (*Probe:* What do they do or make there?)

  c. What kind of work do you do? (*If necessary:* Tell me a little more about what you actually do in that job. What are some of your main duties?)

  d. About how many hours do you usually work in an average week?

Number of hours _____

  e. Is that a 9-to-5 schedule—or what?

9-to-5   1

Different [*Specify:*

_____]   2

  f. How long have you been (working at that job/in that line of work)?

Number of months _____

Number of years _____

  E.6.a On the whole, would you say that your job is really interesting, would you say that it's okay, or would you say that it's boring?

Interesting   1

Okay   2

Boring   3

  b. Why do you say that?

  E.7.a. What are the things you like most about your job?

  b. What are the things you dislike most about your job?

  E.8.a. What are the main reasons you are working now?

  b. What are the main reasons you chose that line of work? (*If necessary:* Why that job in particular?)

  E.9.a. Different people want different things out of their jobs. What are the things you yourself feel are most important in a job? [*Probe:* Why do you say that? *If necessary:* What about (1) advancement; (2) the people you work with; (3) the type of work; (4) the pay; (5) amount of independence; (6) amount of prestige?]

  b. Are you getting these things in your present job?

If employed full-time, skip to E.10.b.

  E.10.a. Imagine that you had a full-time job right now. How do you think that would affect your life? (*Probe:* Do you think your mental outlook would be better or worse?)

b. Imagine for a moment that you were not working (but had a child instead). How would you feel about that? (*Probe:* Do you think your mental outlook would be better or worse if you were not working? What if you had children instead of working?)

c. Has working affected your feelings about yourself in any way?

E.11.a. If you could arrange things just the way you wanted, what would you prefer to be doing right now—working at your present job, working at another job, or not working at all?

Present job [*Skip to E.11.c*]	1
Another job	2
Not working	3

b. *If prefers different job:* What would you like to be doing instead? (*Probe:* Why would you prefer this to what you are doing now?)

c. If you had it to do over again, would you choose the same line of work?

Yes [*Skip to instructions below*]	1
No	2

d. *If no:* Why not? What would you have chosen instead? (*Probe:* Why didn't you choose that at the time?)

If childless and currently employed, skip to question C.1.
If has children and currently employed, skip to question C.14.
If not currently employed:

E.12.a. What do you spend most of your time doing—are you keeping house, going to school, looking for work, or doing something else?

b. What are the main reasons you are *not* working right now? (*Probe:* (1) barriers to working; (2) aspects of working.)

E.13. On the whole, do you really like staying home or would you prefer to be working (if you could arrange things just the way you wanted)?

Like staying home	1
Prefer to work [*Skip to E.15.*]	2

Comments:

E.14.a. *If likes staying home:* What do you like most about staying home?

b. Is there anything you really dislike about staying home?

Skip to E.16

E.15.a. *If prefers to work:* What kind of job would you like to have if you did go to work? (*If necessary:* Would that be full-time or part-time?)

b. What do you dislike most about not working?

c. Are there things you especially like about staying home?

E.16. Imagine for a moment that you had a full-time job. How do you think that would affect your life? (*Probe:* Do you think your mental outlook would be better or worse if you were working? What if you *didn't* have children, but were working instead—how would you feel about that?)

E.17.   Do you think *not* working has affected your feelings about yourself in any way?

If never worked, skip to E.21.a.

E.18.a.   *If has worked previously:* When you worked, on the whole would you say you found your last job really interesting, that it was okay, or would you say that it was boring?

Interesting	1
Okay	2
Boring	3

   b.   Why do you say that?

   c.   What did you like most about working at that job?

   d.   What did you like least about working at that job?

   e.   When you *did* work, did working affect your feelings about yourself in any way?

E.19.a.   Different people want different things out of their jobs. What are the things you yourself feel are most important in a job? [*Probe:* Why do you say that? *If necessary:* What about (1) advancement; (2) the people you work with; (3) the type of work; (4) the pay; (5) amount of independence; (6) amount of prestige?]

   b.   Did you get these things in your last job?

E.20.a.   If you had it to do over again, would you choose the same line of work, or would you prefer to have done something else?

Same work [*Skip to children section.*]	1
Different work	2

   b.   *If different:* Why not? What would you have chosen instead? (*Probe:* Why didn't you choose that at the time?)

Skip to children section.

E.21.a.   *If never employed:* Have you ever thought about going to work? (*Probe:* Why not?)

   b.   If you went to work, what are the things you feel would be most important to have in a job? [*Probe:* Why do you say that? *If necessary:* What about (1) advancement; (2) people you work with; (3) type of work; (4) pay; (5) amount of independence; (6) amount of prestige?]

CHILDREN, OVERVIEW OF CHOICE, AND FUTURE PLANS

If has children, skip to C.14.

I'm going to switch the subject now and ask you some questions about children and your future plans for work, children, and those kinds of things.

C.1.   *If childless and working:* What are the main reasons you haven't had children up to now? (*Probe:* Have you ever considered having a child—instead of working?)

C.2.a.   Have you ever been pregnant?

Yes	1
No [*Skip to C.3.*]	2
Pregnant now [*Skip to C.3.*]	3
Don't know, might be pregnant now [*Skip to C.3.*]	4

   b.   *If yes:* What happened with that pregnancy? (*If applies:* Why did you [have an abortion/put the child up for adoption]?)

C.3.   Imagine for a moment that you had children right now. How do you think your life would be different? (*Probe:* Do you think your mental outlook would be better or worse if you had children? Would you be working if you had children?)

C.4.a.   What are the best things about not having children right now?

   b.   Is there anything you dislike about not having children right now?

C.5.   Over the next five to ten years, do you plan to continue to devote most of your time to working, do you plan to have children and devote most of your time to raising a family, or do you plan to combine working with raising a family? (*If necessary:* At present, then, you [do plan to/do not plan to/don't know whether you will] have children, is that right?)

Plans work only [*Skip to C.7.*]	1
Plans children mainly	2
Plans both	3
Not sure, undecided [*Skip to C.7.*]	4

C.6.a.   *If plans children mainly or plans both:* How many children do you plan to have?

   Number of children _____

   b.   When do you plan to have your first child?

   c.   Why do you plan to have children at that time in particular?

   d.   Why do you plan to have that number of children?

C.7.   How definite are your plans to (have/not have) children—very definite, somewhat definite, or not very definite? (*Probe:* What do you think are the chances that you will change your mind?)

Very definite	1
Somewhat definite	2
Not very definite	3

   Comments:

C.8.   By what age do you think you have to make a final decision?

If plans work only, go to C.9.
If plans family mainly, skip to C.22.
If plans both, skip to C.29.

C.9. *If plans work only:* What are the main reasons you plan to devote your time to work and (don't plan to/don't know whether you will) have children? (*Probe for costs of children and benefits of work.* Why no children? Why work?) (*If necessary:* Do you or don't you want children? Why [not]? Do you or don't you want a career? Why [not]? Is work a factor in your decision not to have children? Has there ever been a time when you wanted children or when you didn't want a career?)

C.10. What are the main things you would like to get out of your work over the next ten to fifteen years? (*Probe:* What would you like to be doing ten to fifteen years from now?)

C.11.a. About how long do you expect to be working at your present job?

b. What do you expect to be doing after you leave this job?

c. Considering all the positions you've had or will have, what would be the best job you expect to have in your lifetime? (*Probe:* If you never have children? Is that realistic or a fantasy?)

C.12.a. How do you think having children would affect these plans for work? (*Probe:* Would raising children interfere with your ability to work outside your home or pursue a career? *Probe for long-term and short-term consequences.*)

b. How do you think having children would affect your life in general? (*Probe:* Do you think you would have to give up anything important in order to have children and raise a family?)

c. Do you think having children would affect your feelings about yourself in any way? (*Probe:* What if you weren't able to work?)

C.13.a. What do you think will be the best things about *never* having children?

b. Is there anything about never having children that bothers you or worries you?

c. Do you think you (will have/have had) to give up anything important in order to work or pursue a career? (*Probe:* Like children or a family?)

d. What do you think your life would be like if you had not chosen to work (or pursue a career) and had had children instead? (*Probe:* How would you feel about that?)

e. If you could start all over again, would you still choose to devote most of your time to work, or would you choose to raise a family, or would you combine working with raising a family? (*Probe:* Thinking back over your life, are there any choices you have made that you regret or that you think you may regret someday?)

Skip to resources section, R.8.

If has children: I'm going to switch the subject now, and ask you some questions about children and your future plans for work, children, and those kinds of things.

C.14. You said you have (*number of children*), is that right?

Number of children _____

C.15.a. How old were you when you got pregnant with your first child?

Age _____

b. At the time you got pregnant, were you working, going to school, staying at home, or what?

Working	1
Going to school	2
Staying at home	3
Other [*Specify*: _____]	4

c. Thinking back to when you (had your first child/first got pregnant), what were your main reasons for having a child at that time? (*Probe:* Did you consider working or doing anything else instead? Did you want to have children at that time?)

d. Was it planned or unplanned? (*Probe:* Were you using contraceptives at that time? Did you consider an abortion?)

If only one child, skip to C.16.d.

C.16.   *If more than one child, repeat questions for each.*

a. How old were you when you got pregnant with your (second/third/ . . .) child?

b. When you got pregnant with your (second/third/. . .) child, were you working, going to school, staying at home, or what?

c. What were your main reasons for having *that* child at that time? (Did you want a child then?)

Second child:

Third child:

Fourth child:

d. Have you ever been pregnant, but terminated the pregnancy?

Yes	1
No [*Skip to C.17.*]	2

If yes: Why did you have an abortion that time?

C.17.a.   Are you currently planning to have any more children?

Yes	1
No [*Skip to C.17.d.*]	2
Can't say, undecided [*Skip to C.18.*]	3

b. *If yes:* How many?

Number of children _____

c. When do you plan to have your next child?

d. How definite are your plans to (have another child/not have any more children)—very definite, somewhat definite, or not very definite? (*Probe:* What are the chances that you will change your mind?)

Very definite	1
Somewhat definite	2
Not very definite	3

Comments:

e. What are your main reasons for (not) having another child?

C.18.a.   What do you think are the best things about having (a child/children)?

b. What are the worst things about having (a child/children)? (*Probe:* Is there anything you dislike about having [a child/children]? Any drawbacks?)

C.19.a. Imagine for a moment that you had *not* had (a child/children). What do you think you would be doing right now? (*Probe:* How would your life be different? Would you be working [more] if you didn't have children?)

b. Do you think your mental outlook would be better or worse if you didn't have children? (*Probe:* Why do you say that?)

C.20.a. What do you think are the major effects having (a child/children) has had on your life?

b. Has having (a child/children) affected your feelings about yourself in any way?

C.21. Over the next five to ten years, do you plan to devote most of your time to raising your family, or do you plan to combine raising your family with working outside your home?

Plans mostly family	1
Plans to combine work and family [*Skip to C.29.*]	2

C.22. *If plans family mainly:* What are the main reasons you plan to (devote most of your time to raising a family/have children and stop working for a while)? (*Probe for benefits of children and costs of work.* Why children? Why not work?) (*If necessary:* Are your children a factor in your decision not to work? Do you or don't you want a career? Why [not]? Has there ever been a time when you didn't want to have children or did want to have a career?)

If currently working, skip to C.24.

C.23. *If not currently working:*
a. Do you have any plans to work in the future?

Plans to work	1
Does not plan to work	2
Can't say	3

b. *If plans to work:* When do you plan to return to work? *If does not plan to work or can't say:* Why not?
c. What do you plan to do? (*Probe:* How will not working affect your chances of getting the kind of job you want?)

Skip to C.25.

C.24. *If currently working:*
a. Do you plan to stop working in order to raise your child(ren)?

Yes	1
No	2

b. *If yes:* For how long? *If forever, skip to C.25.*

c. *If plans to return to work:* What do you think you will do when you return to work? (*Probe:* How do you think stopping work will affect your chances of finding the kind of job you want?)

Skip to C.25.

d. *If no:* What do you plan to do?

C.25. (Would/Does) working outside your home interfere with your ability to raise a family? (*Probe:* Do you think working outside the home or having a career [would involve/involves] *any* sacrifices for you or your family?)

Yes	1
No	2
Don't know	3

Comments:

C.26.a. How do you think having children (will affect/has affected) your plans for work? (*Probe for long-term and short-term consequences.* [Will it/Has it] interfered with your ability to work or pursue a career?)

b. (Have you had to/Will you have to) give up *anything* important in order to have children and raise a family? (*Probe:* Is there anything about not working or pursuing a career that bothers you?)

If has children, skip to C.28.

C.27.a. *If childless:* What do you think will be the best things about having (a child/children)?

b. Is there anything you think you will dislike about having (a child/children)?

c. What do you think are the major effects having (a child/children) will have on your life?

d. Do you think having (a child/children) will affect your feelings about yourself in any way? (*Probe:* How?)

C.28.a. How do you think you would feel if you (had) never had children?

b. What do you think your life would be like if you (chose/had chosen) to pursue a career and (had) postponed or decided not to have children? (*Probe:* How would you feel about that?)

c. If you could start all over again, would you still choose to devote most of your time to your family, or would you choose something different, like working or combining work and family? (*Probe:* Thinking back over your life, are there any choices you have made that you regret or would have done differently?)

Skip to resources section, R.8.

C.29.a. *If plans both family and work or doing both:* When your children (are/were) born, (will you/did you) work and raise children at the same time or (will you/did you) stop working or cut back from work in order to care for your child(ren)?

At same time [*Skip to C.30.*]   1

Stop work for a while   2

Cut back   3

b. *If stop or cut back:* For how long (will/did) you (stop/cut back from) work?

C.30.   What are the main reasons you plan to work and raise children (at the same time)? (*Probe:* Why do you want children? Why do you want to work? Why [not] at the same time? Do you or don't you want a career? Why [not]? Will there any special problems? Has there ever been a time when you didn't want to have children or didn't want to have a job or career?)

C.31.a. What would you like to be doing ten to fifteen years from now? (*Probe:* What are the main things you would like to get out of your work over the next ten to fifteen years?)

If not currently employed, skip to d.

b. About how long do you expect to be working at your present job?

c. What do you expect to be doing after you leave this job?

d. Considering all the positions you've had or will have, what would be the best job you expect to have in your lifetime?

e. How (does/will) having (a child/children) affect these plans? (*Probe:* Would that be different if you never had children or had fewer children? *Probe for long-term and short-term consequences.*)

C.32.a. (Has/Will) raising a family interfere(d) with your ability to work outside your home or pursue a career? (*Probe:* Do you ever feel that having children and raising a family [has prevented/will prevent] you from doing other things you would like to do or entailed *any* sacrifices for you?)

Yes   1

No   2

b. *If yes:* In what ways?
If no: Why not?

C.33.a. What about the other way around—(has/will) working outside your home interfere(d) with raising your family? (*Probe:* Do you ever feel that working outside your home or pursuing a career [has prevented/ will prevent] you from doing other things you would like to do or entailed *any* sacrifices for you?)

Yes   1

No   2

b. *If yes:* In what ways?
If no: Why not?

C.34.a. *If childless:* What do you think will be the best things about having (a child/children)?

b. Do you think there will be anything you won't like about having (a child/children)? (*Probe:* Any drawbacks?)

c. What do you think are the major effects having (a child/children) will have on your life?

d. Do you think having (a child/children) will affect your feelings about yourself in any way? (*Probe:* How?)

C.35.a. How do you think you would feel if you (had/never had) children? (*Probe:* What would be the best things? The worst things?)

b. What do you think your life would be like if you had (not) chosen to work (or pursue a career)? (*Probe:* How would you feel about that?)

c. What do you think your life would be like if you (had not had/do not have) children? (*Probe:* How would you feel about that?)

d. If you could start all over again, would you still choose to combine working with raising a family, or would you choose to work only, or would you raise a family only? (*Probe:* Thinking back over your life, are there any choices you have made that you regret or that you would have done differently?)

RESOURCES

If planning only one of either family or work, or doing one: skip to R.8.

If planning both family and work or doing both: I'd like to ask some questions now about how you (will) arrange things so that you (can/will be able to) both work and raise a family at the same time. (*Probe for availability and willingness to use.*)

R.1.a. (Are you/Do you think you will be) able to depend upon (your husband/the man in your life) to help look after the house?

Yes	1
No	2

b. *If no:* Why not? (*Probe for availability and willingness.*)

If yes: Realistically, how much help (are you/do you think you will be) able to depend upon him for? (*Probe:* What kinds of things [does/will] he do around the house?)

c. *If married or living with someone:* Who usually does each of the following household tasks—mainly you, mainly your (husband/housemate), both equally, or someone else?

	R mainly	partner mainly	both equally	someone else
				(Specify)
(1) cleaning the house	1	2	3	4 _____
(2) cooking the meals	1	2	3	4 _____
(3) shopping for food	1	2	3	4 _____
(4) cleaning up after meals	1	2	3	1 _____
(5) doing the laundry	1	2	3	4 _____
(6) anything else?	1	2	3	4 _____

d. (Does/Will) he help care for the child(ren) on a regular basis?

Yes   1

No [*Skip to g.*]   2

e. *If yes:* When (does/will) he look after the children? (*Probe:* How many days a week? How many hours a day? What time of day?)

f. (Does/Will) this help interfere with his job or involve any sacrifices for him?

g. How (does/will) he feel about (not) helping out? (*Probe:* How do *you* feel about his [not] helping out?)

h. How does (your husband/the man in your life) feel about whether you should work, raise a family, or do both? (*Probe:* How would he feel if it meant he had to work less or do more around the house?)

i. How do you feel about the idea of (your husband/the man in your life) working less and each of you spending part of the day taking care of the house and children? (*Probe:* How would you feel about supporting the family while [your husband/the man in your life] stays home?)

If childless, skip to R.3.a.

R.2.a. *If has children:* Do you have any childcare arrangements at the present time?

Yes   1

No   2

b. *If yes:* What kind of arrangements do you have?
If no: Why not? (*Probe for availability and willingness.*)

R.3.a. (Are you/Will you be) able to depend upon help from a relative, friend, neighbor, or someone else you know to help look after the children or the house on a regular basis?

Yes   1

No   2

b. *If yes:* Who is that?
If no: Why not? (*Probe for availability and willingness.*)

c. What kinds of things (will/do) they do? (*Specify childcare or housework.*)

d. When (will/do) they help out? (*Probe:* How many days a week? How many hours a day? Is that paid or unpaid?)

R.4.a. (Do/Will) you have any (other) paid help to look after the child(ren) and the house on a regular basis?

Yes, house and children   1

Yes, house only   2

Yes, children only   3

No   4

b. *If yes:* What (do/will) you rely upon paid help for? (*Probe:* What kinds of things [will/do] they do? How many days a week? How many hours a day?)

If no: Why not? (*Probe for availability and willingness.*)

c. (Will/Does) your child(ren) go to a daycare center?

Yes	1
No	2

d. *If no:* Why not? (*Probe for availability and willingness.*)

If yes: When (does/will) your child(ren) go there? (*Probe:* At what age? How many days a week? How many hours a day? What kind?)

If not working, skip to R.6.

R.5.a. *If working:* What about your job—(have you been able/will you be able) to change your schedule or cut back on your hours?

Yes	1
No	2

Comments:

b. What (did/will/would) you lose (if/when) you cut back on your job? (*Probe:* Apart from the money?)

c. *If yes:* Can you tell me about these arrangements?
   If no: Why not? (*Probe for availability and willingness.*)

d. Do you feel your work (will suffer/suffers) at all from these changes? (*Probe:* Why [not]? How?)

Suffers	1
Does not suffer	2

R.6.a. What about your family—do you feel that they (will suffer/would suffer/suffer) from the use of (help in your home/daycare/your husband), instead of your being home full-time?

Suffers	1
Does not suffer	2

If yes: How?
If no: Why not?

R.7. If you could have an ideal arrangement, what would it be for you? *If employed part-time:* Would you want to work full-time if you thought you could manage it without your family suffering? Is there any arrangement which would allow you to work full-time?

Skip to network section.

If planning work or children. I'd like to ask some questions now, about what you *would* do if you (did have a child/did go to work). (*Probe for availability and willingness.*)

R.8.a. If you (had a child/went to work), would you be able to depend upon (your husband/the man in your life) to help look after the house?

Yes	1
No	2

b. *If no:* Why not? (*Probe for availability and willingness.*)
   If yes: Realistically, how much help do you think you would be able to depend upon him for? (*Probe:* What kinds of things would he do around the house?)

c. *If married or living with someone:* As things are now, who usually does each of the following household tasks—mainly you, mainly your (husband, housemate), both equally, or someone else?

	R mainly	partner mainly	both equally	someone else
				(Specify)
(1) cleaning the house	1	2	3	4 _____
(2) cooking the meals	1	2	3	4 _____
(3) shopping for food	1	2	3	4 _____
(4) cleaning up after meals	1	2	3	4 _____
(5) doing the laundry	1	2	3	4 _____
(6) anything else?	1	2	3	4 _____

d. If you (had a child/went to work), would he help care for the child(ren) on a regular basis?

Yes   1

No   2

e. *If yes:* When would he look after the child(ren)? (*Probe:* How many days a week? How many hours a day? What time of day? How much would you be able to count on him for?)
If no: Why not? (*Probe for availability and willingness.*)

If childless, skip to g.

f. *If has children:* What does he do to help care for the child(ren) now?

g. If you (had a child/went to work), how do you think he would feel about helping out with the child(ren) and the house?

h. Would it interfere with his work or entail any sacrifices for him?

i. How does (your husband/the man in your life) feel about whether you should raise a family, work, or do both? (*Probe:* How would he feel if he had to work less or do more around the house?)

j. How do *you* feel about the idea of (your husband/the man in your life) spending less time at work and spending part of the day taking care of the house and child(ren) so that you can work and raise a family at the same time? (*Probe:* How would you feel about supporting the family while [your husband/the man in your life] stays home?)

If childless, skip to R.9.c.

R.9.a. *If has children:* Do you have any childcare arrangements at the present time?

Yes   1

No   2

b. *If yes:* What kind of arrangements do you have?
If no: Why not? (*Probe for availability and willingness.*)

c. If you (had a child/went to work), would you be able to depend upon help from a relative, friend, neighbor, or someone else you know, on a regular basis?

Yes	1
No	2

d. *If yes:* Who is that?
   If no: Why not? (*Probe for availability and willingness.*) [*Skip to R.10.a.*]

e. What kinds of things would (she/he/they) do? (*Specify:* childcare, housework, or both?)

f. When would (she/he/they) help out? (*Probe:* How many hours a day? What time of day? How many days a week?) (*If necessary:* Would you be able to depend upon [her/him/them] regularly or just once in a while? Would that be paid or unpaid?)

R.10.a. Would you use any (other/more) *paid* help to look after the child(ren) or the house on a regular basis?

Yes, childcare and housework	1
Yes, housework only	2
Yes, childcare only	3
No	4

b. *If no:* Why not? (*Probe for availability and willingness.*)

c. What would you rely upon paid help for? (*Probe:* What time of day? How many hours a day? How many days a week? How would you feel about using paid help?)

R.11.a. Would your child(ren) go to a daycare center?

Yes	1
No	2

b. *If no:* Why not? (*Probe for availability and willingness.*)
   If yes: When would your child(ren) go there? (*Probe:* At what age? What time of day? For how many hours a day? How many days a week? How would you feel about using this care?)

If not working, skip to R.13.

R.12.a. *If working:* What about your job—would you be able to change your schedule or cut back on your hours? (*If no:* Why not? *If yes:* Can you tell me about these arrangements?)

b. Would your work suffer or not, if you had a child? (*Probe:* What if you used arrangements such as daycare, help in your home, or your husband's help?)

Would suffer	1
Would not suffer	2

c. What would you lose if you cut back on your job? (*Probe:* Apart from the money?)

R.13.a. Do you feel your family would suffer or not, if you (had a child/went to work) and used arrangements such as daycare, help in your home, or your husband's help (instead of staying home full-time)?

Would suffer	1
Would not suffer	2

   b. *If yes:* How?
      If no: Why not?

R.14.a. Is there any arrangement which would, *if* available, make it possible
        for you to combine working full-time outside your home with raising
        your family? (*Probe:* How would you feel about using this arrangement?)

   b. Would you want to (go to work/have a child) *if* you could manage it
      without your (family/work) suffering?

NETWORK

I'd like to get an idea now about how your family and friends feel about your
decision.

N.1.a. (Often people rely on the judgment of someone they know in making
       important decisions about their lives.) Is there anyone whose opinion
       you considered in making a decision about whether to have children,
       work or pursue a career, or do both? (*Probe:* What about your *husband?*
       Your parents? Your in-laws? Your friends? Your doctor? *If working or
       worked:* The people you [know/knew] at work? Do you feel any pressure
       from *anyone* to have a child or stop working? To work instead of having
       a family?)

                          Yes   1
                          No [*Skip to N.2.*]   2

   b. *If yes:* Who is that? (*If necessary:* How are you related to them? How do
      you know them?)
         Name   *Relationship*   *Type of Influence (Work, Children)*
         1. Husband: _____

         _____

         2. Others: _____

         _____

If plans family mainly, skip to N.3.

N.2.   *If plans work only or both:*

   a. How do your parents feel about your decision to (not have any chil-
      dren/work and raise children at the same time?) (*Probe:* [Was/Is] there
      any parental opposition? How strong [was/is] their opposition? How
      [did/do] they express their feelings?)
      Where do they live?

   b. *If married:* How do your in-laws feel about this decision? (*Probe:* same
      as a.)
      Where do they live?

   c. Do you have any other relatives who you feel especially close to or who
      live nearby?
                          Yes   1
                          No [*Skip to N.4.*]   2
   d. *If yes:* Who is that? Where do they live?

e. How do they feel about your decision to (not have any children/work and raise children at the same time)?

Skip to N.4.

N.3. *If plans family mainly:*

a. How would your parents feel if you decided to (go to work/not have any children)?
Where do they live?

b. *If married:* How would your in-laws feel if you (went to work/never had children)?
Where do they live?

c. Do you have any other relatives who you feel especially close to or who live nearby?

Yes	1
No [*Skip to N.4.*]	2

d. Who is that? Where do they live?

e. How would they feel if you decided to (go to work/not have any children)?

N.4.a. Who are the women that you think of as your closest friends? (*Probe:* What about the people that you get together with to have a good time? What about the people you confide in? Are there any neighbors you see a lot of?) (*If necessary:* What are their first names?)

b. *If working:* Are there women that you see a lot of at work or talk about work with? (*If necessary:* What are their first names?)

c. *For each name, ask:*

(1) Does she work? (*If no:* Does she plan to work?) (*If yes:* What does she do?)

(2) Does she have children? (*If no:* Does she plan to have children? Is she married?)

(3) About how old is she? How long have you known her?

(4) Where does she live? (*If necessary:* How did you meet her?)

Name	Relationship (location)	Work Status	Child Status (marital status)	Age (when met)

d. (Does/Did) knowing any of these people affect your attitudes toward having children, working, or doing both? (*If yes:* Who? How were your attitudes affected?)

e. *If necessary:* Do you know *anyone* who is (raising a child/working and raising a child at the same time)?

N.5. *Ask as appropriate:*

If childless, ask a.
If full-time mother, skip to b.
If works and has children, skip to c.

a. *If childless:* When you see other women about your age who have young children but don't have jobs or careers, does that bring out any response in you? (*Probe:* What do you imagine their lives to be like? Does it make you feel lucky, envious, or what?)

What about when you see working women with young children?

b. *If full-time mother:* When you see other women about your age who have jobs or careers but don't have children, does that bring out any response in you? (*Probe:* What do you imagine their lives to be like? Does it make you feel lucky, envious, or what?)

What about when you see working women with young children?

c. *If works and has children:* When you see other women about your age who have full-time jobs or careers but don't have children, does that bring out any response in you? (*Probe:* What do you imagine their lives to be like? Does it make you feel lucky, envious, or what?)

What about when you see women who are staying home full-time to raise their children—does that bring out any response in you? (*Same probes.*)

OPINIONS

Now, I'd like to ask you your opinion on various matters concerning men and women.

O.1. Would you say that abortions should be legal whenever a woman wants one, legal only under certain circumstances, or always illegal?

Always legal	1
Under circumstances	2
Always illegal	3

O.2. How do you feel about husbands and wives splitting the housework—things such as cooking, cleaning, and so forth? Do you think that they should each do about half the work that has to be done around the house, or do you think the wife should do most of it?

Each should do about half	1
It depends	2
Wife should do most	3
Wife should do all	4

O.3. How do you feel about a woman with young children working even if her family doesn't need the money? Would you say that it is generally okay or generally not a good idea? (*If necessary:* Before the children start school?)

Generally okay	1
It depends	2
Generally not a good idea	3

O.4.a. On balance, who do you think has it better—men or women?

Men	1
Women	2
Both equal or can't say	3

b. Why do you say that? (*Probe:* What about the fact that men are expected to work and women are expected to care for the children?)

MORALE

Now, I have some short questions, about how you're feeling these days. Then we're almost finished. (*Hand card*)

	A lot of the time	Some of the time	Only once in a while	Never
M.1. About how often do you feel unhappy or a bit depressed these days—a lot of the time, some of the time, only once in a while, or never?	1	2	3	4
M.2. How often do you feel overwhelmed—that is, there is too much going on in your life for you to handle—a lot of the time, some of the time, only once in a while, or never?	1	2	3	4
M.3. How often do you wish there were more people you felt really close to these days?	1	2	3	4
M.4. How often do things get on your nerves so much that you feel like losing your temper?	1	2	3	4
M.5. How often do you find that you have time on your hands with little to do?	1	2	3	4
M.6. How often do you feel that things are going the way you want them to?	1	2	3	4
M.7. How often do you feel nervous, fidgety, or tense these days?	1	2	3	4
M.8. How often do you feel pleased with what you're doing these days?	1	2	3	4

BACKGROUND

Just a few background questions, and then we'll be finished.

D.1.a. Were you raised in a particular religion?

Yes	1
No [*Skip to d.*]	2

b. *If yes:* Which one?

Was your mother a (*Religion*)?   Yes   No: _____

Was your father a (*Religion*)?   Yes   No: _____

c. Do you consider yourself a (*Religion*) today?

Yes [*Skip to D.2.*]	1
No	2

d. *If no:* Do you consider yourself a member of any (other) religion?

Yes [*Specify:* _____]	1
No	2

e. When it comes to religion, do you consider yourself

Very religious	1
Somewhat religious	2
Not at all religious	3

D.2. Where did you live most of your life up to age sixteen? (*If necessary:* Would you call that a large city, a small city, a suburb, a small town, or what?)

D.3. From what countries or part of the world did your ancestors come?

(1) Father's ancestors: _____

(2) Mother's ancestors: _____

D.4.a. In politics, generally speaking, do you usually think of yourself as

A strong Democrat	1
A not very strong Democrat	2
An independent, closer to the Democratic party	3
An independent, closer to neither party	4
An independent, closer to the Republican party	5
A not very strong Republican	6
A strong Republican	7

b. In politics, would you say that you are

Radical	1
Liberal	2
Middle-of-the-road	3
Conservative	4
A strong conservative	5

D.5.a. Please look at this card (*Hand R Income Card*) and give me the letter of the group that includes (your total family/your) income before taxes. This figure should include all of the family income—wages, salaries, interest, dividends, (child support), and all other incomes. (*If uncertain:* What would be your best guess?)

A.	None or loss	00	J.	$15,000 to $19,999	09
B.	Less than $3,000	01	K.	$20,000 to $24,999	10
C.	$3,000 to $3,999	02	L.	$25,000 to $29,999	11
D.	$4,000 to $4,999	03	M.	$30,000 to $34,999	12
E.	$5,000 to $5,999	04	N.	$35,000 to $39,999	13
F.	$6,000 to $7,999	05	O.	$40,000 to $49,999	14
G.	$8,000 to $9,999	06	P.	$50,000 to $74,999	15
H.	$10,000 to $11,999	07	Q.	$75,000 and over	16
I.	$12,000 to $14,999	08			

Total Income Code: _____

b. Which group includes your own *personal* income before taxes (last or most recent year)?

Personal (or Salary) Income Code: _____

D.6. Is there anything you would like to add, anything you haven't said you would like to say, or any questions you would like to ask me?

That's all! Thank you very much.

Interviewer Observations:

BIBLIOGRAPHY

Alonso, William. 1980. "The Population Factor and Urban Structure." In *The Prospective City*, edited by Arthur P. Solomon. Cambridge: MIT Press.

Amsden, Alice H. 1980. "Introduction." In *The Economics of Women and Work*, edited by Alice H. Amsden. New York: St. Martin's Press.

Ariès, Philippe. 1962. *Centuries of Childhood: A Social History of Family Life*. Translated by Robert Baldick. New York: Knopf.

Badinter, Elizabeth. 1981. *Mother Love: Myth and Reality*. New York: Macmillan.

Bane, Mary Jo. 1976. *Here to Stay: American Families in the Twentieth Century*. New York: Basic Books.

———. 1978. "The American Divorce Rate: What Does It Mean? What Should We Worry About?" *Family Policy Note* 10 (November). Cambridge: Joint Center for Urban Studies of M.I.T. and Harvard University.

Baron, Ava. 1981. "Woman's 'Place' in Capitalist Production: A Case Study of Changing Job Structures and Class Relations in the Nineteenth Century Newspaper Printing Industry." Ph.D. diss., New York University.

Barrett, Nancy S. 1979. "Women in the Job Market: Occupations, Earnings, and Career Opportunities." In *The Subtle Revolution: Women at Work*, edited by Ralph E. Smith. Washington, D.C.: Urban Institute.

Bart, Pauline. 1970. "Portnov's Mother's Complaint." *Trans-Action* 8 (November-December): 59–74.

Becker, Gary S. 1960. "An Economic Analysis of Fertility." In *Demographic and Economic Change in Developed Countries*, a report of the National Bureau of Economic Research. Princeton: Princeton University Press.

———. 1965. "A Theory of the Allocation of Time." *Economic Journal* 80 (September): 493–517.

———. 1981. *A Treatise on the Family*. Cambridge: Harvard University Press.

Becker, Howard S. 1964. "Personal Change in Adult Life." *Sociometry* 27: 40–53.

Becker, Howard S., and Anselm L. Strauss. 1956. "Careers, Personality, and Adult Socialization." *American Journal of Sociology* 62 (November): 253–63.

Benston, Margaret. 1969. "The Political Economy of Women's Liberation." *Monthly Review* (September): 13–25.

Berk, Sarah F., ed. 1980. *Women and Household Labor*. Beverly Hills, Calif.: Sage Publications.

Bernard, Jesse. 1972. *The Future of Marriage*. New York: Bantam Books.

———. 1974. *The Future of Motherhood*. New York: Penguin Books.

Bird, Caroline. 1979. *The Two-Paycheck Marriage*. New York: Pocket Books.

Blake, Judith. 1966. "Ideal Family Size Among White Americans: A Quarter of a Century's Evidence." *Demography* 3(1): 154–73.

———. 1968. "Are Babies Consumer Durables? A Critique of the Economic Theory of Reproductive Motivation." *Population Studies* 22 (March): 5–25.

———. 1974. "Can We Believe Recent Data on Birth Expectations in the United States?" *Demography* 11 (February): 25–44.

Blau, Francine. 1979. "Women in the Labor Force: An Overview." In *Women: A Feminist Perspective*, 2nd ed., edited by Jo Freeman. Palo Alto, Calif.: Mayfield.

Blaxall, Martha, and Barbara Reagan, eds. 1976. *Women and the Workplace: The Implications of Occupational Segregation*. Chicago: University of Chicago Press.

Bloom, David E. 1981. "Traditional Family Strained by Childlessness, Divorce, Planned Remarriage." *San Francisco Examiner* (May 3):16A.

Bloom, David, and Anne R. Pebley. 1982. "Voluntary Childlessness: A Review of the Evidence and Implications." *Population Research and Policy Review* 1 (3): 203–24.

Blumberg, Paul. 1980. *Inequality in an Age of Decline*. New York: Oxford University Press.

Blumstein, Philip, and Pepper W. Schwartz. 1983. *American Couples: Money, Work, Sex*. New York: Morrow.

Bowlby, John. 1969. *Attachment*. New York: Basic Books.

Brim, Orville G., Jr. 1968. "Adult Socialization." In *Socialization and Society*, edited by John A. Clausen. Boston: Little, Brown.

Brint, Steven, and Jerome Karabel. 1981. "The Transformation of the Two Year Colleges: From Liberal Arts to Vocational Training." Center for Applied Social Science Research, Reprint No. 83-E1. New York: New York University.

Broverman, Inge K., S. Vogel, D. Broverman, F. Clarkson, and P. Rosenkrantz. 1970. "Sex Role Stereotypes and Clinical Judgments of Mental Health." *Journal of Consulting and Clinical Psychology* 34:1–7.

Brownlee, W. Elliot, and Mary M. Brownlee. 1976. *Women in the American Economy*. New Haven, Conn.: Yale University Press.

Caplow, Theodore. 1954. *The Sociology of Work*. Minneapolis: University of Minnesota Press.

Carter, Hugh, and Paul C. Glick. 1976. *Marriage and Divorce*, rev. ed. Cambridge: Harvard University Press.

Cherlin, Andrew J. 1981. *Marriage, Divorce, Remarriage*. Cambridge: Harvard University Press.

Chinoy, Ely. 1955. *Automobile Workers and the American Dream*. New York: Random House.

Chodorow, Nancy. 1974. "Family Structure and Feminine Personality." In *Woman, Culture, and Society*, edited by Michelle Z. Rosaldo and Louise Lamphere. Stanford, Calif.: Stanford University Press.

———. 1978. *The Reproduction of Mothering: Psychoanalysis and the Sociology of Gender*. Berkeley and Los Angeles: University of California Press.

———. 1979. "Mothering, Male Dominance, and Capitalism." In *Capitalist Patriarchy and the Case for Socialist Feminism*, edited by Zillah R. Eisenstein. New York: Monthly Review Press.

Chodorow, Nancy, and Susan Contratto. 1982. "The Fantasy of the Perfect Mother." In *Rethinking the Family: Some Feminist Questions*, edited by Barrie Thorne. New York: Longman.

Clarke-Stewart, Alison. 1982. *Daycare*. Cambridge: Harvard University Press.

Clausen, John A. 1968. "A Historical and Comparative View of Socialization Theory and Research." In *Socialization and Society*, edited by John A. Clausen. Boston: Little, Brown.

———. 1972. "The Life Course of Individuals." In *Aging and Society: A Sociology of Age Stratification*, vol. 3, edited by Matilda W. Riley, Marilyn Johnson, Anne Foner et al. New York: Russell Sage Foundation and Basic Books.

Collins, Randall. 1971. "A Conflict Theory of Sexual Stratification." *Social Problems* 19: 3–21.

———. 1975. *Conflict Sociology: Toward an Explanatory Science*. New York: Academic Press.

Condry, John, and Sharon Dyer. 1976. "Fear of Success: Attribution of Cause to the Victim." *Journal of Social Issues* 32 (Summer): 63–83.

Coser, Rose L. 1974. "Authority and Structural Ambivalence in the Middle-Class Family." In *The Family: Its Structures and Functions*, edited by Rose L. Coser. New York: St. Martin's Press.

———. 1981. "On the Reproduction of Mothering: A Methodological Debate." *Signs: Journal of Women in Culture and Society* 6 (Spring): 487–92.

Cott, Nancy F., and Elizabeth H. Pleck., eds. 1979. *A Heritage of Her Own: Toward a New Social History of American Women*. New York: Simon & Schuster.

Daniels, Arlene Kaplan. 1983. Personal communication.

Daniels, Pamela, and Kathy Weingarten. 1977."Parenthood: Now or Later?" Wellesley, Mass.: Wellesley Center for Research on Women. Photocopy.

Davis, Kingsley. 1940. "The Sociology of Parent-Youth Conflict." *American Sociological Review* 5 (August): 523–35.

Demos, John. 1970. *A Little Commonwealth: Family Life in the Plymouth Colony*. New York: Oxford University Press.

Demos, John, and Sarane S. Boocock, eds. 1978. *Turning Points: Historical and Sociological Essays on the Family*. Chicago: University of Chicago Press.

Denmark, Florence, ed. 1974. *Who Discriminates Against Women?* Beverly Hills, Calif.: Sage Publications.

Dinnerstein, Dorothy. 1976. *The Mermaid and the Minotaur: Sexual Arrangements and Human Malaise*. New York: Harper & Row.

DiTomaso, Nancy. 1982. "Sociological Reductionism from Parsons to Althusser: Linking Action and Structure in Social Theory." *American Sociological Review* 47 (February):14–28.

Dowling, Colette. 1981. *The Cinderella Complex: Women's Hidden Fear of Independence*. New York: Summit Books.

Easterlin, Richard A. 1973. "Relative Economic Status and the American Fertility Swing." In *Family Economic Behavior: Problems and Prospects*, edited by Eleanor B. Sheldon. New York: Lippincott.

—————. 1978. "Fertility and Female Labor Force Participation in the United States: Recent Changes and Future Prospects." Paper presented at the International Union for the Scientific Study of Population conference, "Economic and Demographic Change: Issues for the 1980's," Helsinki, August.

—————. 1980. *Birth and Fortune*. New York: Basic Books.

Easton, Barbara. 1978. "Feminism and the Contemporary Family." *Socialist Review* 8 (May–June): 11–36.

Ehrenreich, Barbara. 1983. *The Hearts of Men: American Dreams and the Flight from Commitment*. Garden City, N.Y.: Anchor Press/Doubleday.

Eisenstadt, S. N. 1956. *From Generation to Generation: Age Groups and Social Structure*. New York: Free Press.

Eisenstein, Zillah. 1979. "Developing a Theory of Capitalist Patriarchy and Socialist Feminism." In *Capitalist Patriarchy and the Case for Socialist Feminism*, edited by Zillah R. Eisenstein. New York: Monthly Review Press.

Elder, Glen H., Jr. 1974. *Children of the Great Depression: Social Change in Life Experience*. Chicago: University of Chicago Press.

—————. 1978a. "Approaches to Social Change and the Family." In *Turning Points: Historical and Sociological Essays on the Family*, edited by John Demos and Sarane S. Boocock. Chicago: University of Chicago Press.

—————. 1978b. "Family History and the Life Course." In *Transitions: The Family and the Life Course in Historical Perspective*, edited by Tamara K. Hareven. New York: Academic Press.

—————. 1979. "Historical Change in Life Patterns and Personality." In *Life-Span Development and Behavior*, edited by P. B. Baltes and Orville G. Brim, Jr. New York: Academic Press.

Epstein, Cynthia F. 1970. *Woman's Place: Options and Limits in Professional Careers*. Berkeley and Los Angeles: University of California Press.

—————. 1981. *Women in Law*. New York: Basic Books.

Erikson, Erik H. 1963. *Childhood and Society*, 2nd ed. New York: Norton.

Estes, Robert, and Harold L. Wilensky. 1978. "Life Cycle Squeeze and the Morale Curve." *Social Problems* 25: 277–92.

Fabe, Marilyn, and Norma J. Wikler. 1979. *Up Against the Clock: Career Women Speak Out on the New Choice of Motherhood*. New York: Random House.

Fein, Robert A. 1978. "Research on Fathering: Social Policy and an Emergent Perspective." *Journal of Social Issues* 34 (1): 122–35.

Ferree, Myra M. 1976a. "Working-Class Feminism: A Study of Diffusion through

Social Networks." Paper presented at the annual meeting of the American Sociological Association, September.

———. 1976b. "Working Class Jobs: Housework and Paid Work as Sources of Satisfaction." *Social Problems* 23 (April): 431–41.

Fiedler, Leslie A. 1966. *Love and Death in the American Novel,* rev. ed. New York: Stein and Day.

Firestone, Shulamith. 1970. *The Dialectic of Sex: The Case for Feminist Revolution.* New York: Bantam Books.

Fogarty, Michael, Rhona Rapoport, and Robert Rapoport. 1971. *Sex, Career, and Family.* London: George Allen & Unwin.

Foner, Anne. 1978. "Age Stratification and the Changing Family." In *Turning Points: Historical and Sociological Essays on the Family,* edited by John Demos and Sarane S. Boocock. Chicago: University of Chicago Press.

Fox, Greer L., ed. 1982. *The Childbearing Decision: Fertility Attitudes and Behavior.* Beverly Hills, Calif.: Sage Publications.

Freeman, Jo, ed. 1979. *Women: A Feminist Perspective,* 2nd ed. Palo Alto, Calif.: Mayfield.

Friday, Nancy. 1977. *My Mother/My Self: The Daughter's Search for Identity.* New York: Delacorte Press.

Gavron, Hannah. 1966. *The Captive Wife: Conflicts of Housebound Mothers.* London: Routledge & Kegan Paul.

Gerson, Kathleen. 1981. "Models of Behavior and Women's Decision-Making Processes." *New England Sociologist* 3(Spring/Summer): 3–16.

———. 1982. "Mothers and Daughters: Reassessing the Impact of Childhood Experience on Women's Adult Behavior." Paper presented at the annual meeting of the Society for the Study of Social Problems, San Francisco, September.

———. 1983. "Changing Family Structure and the Position of Women: A Review of the Trends." *Journal of the American Planning Association* 49(2) (Spring):138–48.

———. 1984. "Explaining Patterns of Parenthood Among Young Adult Men." Proposal for Presidential Fellowship, New York University.

Gerth, Hans, and C. Wright Mills. 1953. *Character and Social Structure: The Psychology of Social Institutions.* New York: Harcourt, Brace & World.

Giddens, Anthony. 1976. *New Rules of Sociological Method: A Positive Critique of Interpretive Sociologies.* New York: Basic Books.

———. 1979. *Central Problems in Social Theory: Action, Structure, and Contradiction in Social Analysis.* Berkeley and Los Angeles: University of California Press.

Giele, Janet Z. 1971. "Changes in the Modern Family: Their Impact on Sex Roles." *American Journal of Orthopsychiatry* 41 (October): 757–66.

———. 1980. "Adulthood as Transcendence of Age and Sex." In *Themes of Work and Love in Adulthood,* edited by Neil J. Smelser and Erik H. Erikson. Cambridge: Harvard University Press.

Gillespie, Dair L. 1971. "Who's Got the Power? The Marital Struggle." *Journal of Marriage and the Family* 33 (August): 445–58.

Gilligan, Carol. 1982. *In a Different Voice: Psychological Theory and Women's Development.* Cambridge: Harvard University Press.

Glaser, Barney, and Anselm Strauss. 1967. *The Discovery of Grounded Theory.* Chicago: Aldine Press.

Glenn, Norval D., and Sara McLanahan. 1980. "The Effects of Offspring on the Psychological Well-Being of Older Adults." Photocopy.

Glick, Paul C., and Arthur J. Norton. 1974. "Perspectives on the Recent Upturn in Divorce and Remarriage." *Demography* 10 (August): 301–14.

———. 1977. "Marrying, Divorcing, and Living Together in the U. S. Today." *Population Bulletin* 32 (October): 2–39.

Glidewell, John C. 1970. *Choice Points: Essays on the Emotional Problems of Living with People.* Cambridge: MIT Press.

Goode, William J. 1963. *World Revolution and Family Patterns.* New York: Free Press.

———. 1982. "Why Men Resist." In *Rethinking the Family: Some Feminist Questions,* edited by Barrie Thorne. New York: Longman.

Gorden, Raymond L. 1975. *Interviewing: Strategies, Techniques, and Tactics.* Homewood, Ill.: Dorsey Press.

Gordon, Michael, ed. 1978. *The American Family in Social-Historical Perspective,* 2nd ed. New York: St. Martin's Press.

Gould, Roger L. 1978. *Transformations: Growth and Change in Adulthood.* New York: Simon & Schuster.

Hacker, Andrew. 1979. "Divorce a la Mode." *New York Review of Books* 26 (May 3): 23–27.

———. 1982. "Farewell to the Family?" *New York Review of Books* 29 (March 18): 37–44.

Hareven, Tamara. 1977. "Family Time and Historical Time." *Daedalus* 106 (Spring): 57–70.

Hartmann, Heidi I. 1976. "Capitalism, Patriarchy, and Job Segregation by Sex." *Signs: Journal of Women in Culture and Society* 1 (Spring): 137–69.

Held, Virginia. 1979. "The Equal Obligations of Mothers and Fathers." In *Having Children: Philosophical and Legal Reflections on Parenthood,* edited by Onora O'Neill and William Ruddick. New York: Oxford University Press.

Henning, Margaret, and Anne Jardim. 1977. *The Managerial Woman.* Garden City, N.Y.: Anchor Press/Doubleday.

Heyns, Barbara. 1982. "The Influence of Parents' Work on Children's School Achievement." In *Families That Work: Children in a Changing World,* edited by Sheila B. Kamerman and Cheryl Hayes. Washington, D.C.: National Academy Press.

Hirschhorn, Larry. 1977. "Social Policy and the Life Cycle: A Developmental Perspective." *Social Service Review* 51 (September): 434–50.

Hochschild, Arlie R. 1973. "A Review of Sex Role Research." In *Changing Women in a Changing Society,* edited by Joan Huber. Chicago: University of Chicago Press.

———. 1975. "Inside the Clockwork of Male Careers." In *Women and the Power to Change,* edited by Florence Howe. New York: McGraw-Hill.

———. 1980. "Emotion Work, Feeling Rules, and Social Structure." *American Journal of Sociology* 85: 551–75.

———. 1983. *The Managed Heart.* Berkeley and Los Angeles: University of California Press.

Hofferth, Sandra L., and Kristin A. Moore. 1979. "Women's Employment and Marriage." In *The Subtle Revolution: Women at Work*, edited by Ralph E. Smith. Washington, D.C.: Urban Institute.

Hoffman, Lois W. 1974. "Effects of Maternal Employment on the Child: A Review of the Research." *Developmental Psychology* 10: 204–28.

———. 1979. "Maternal Employment: 1979." *American Psychologist* 34 (10): 859–65.

Hoffman, Lois W., and Ivan F. Nye. 1979. *Working Mothers*. San Francisco: Jossey-Bass.

Horner, Matina. 1972. "Toward an Understanding of Achievement-Related Conflicts in Women." *Journal of Social Issues* 28:157–75.

Houseknecht, Sharon K. 1982. "Voluntary Childlessness: Toward a Theoretical Integration." Paper presented at the seventy-seventh annual meeting of the American Sociological Association, San Francisco, September.

Howe, Louise Kapp. 1977. *Pink Collar Workers: Inside the World of Women's Work*. New York: Putnam's.

Huber, Joan, and Glenna Spitze. 1980. "Considering Divorce: An Expansion of Becker's Theory of Marital Instability." *American Journal of Sociology* 86 (July): 75–89.

———. 1983. *Sex Stratification: Children, Housework, and Jobs*. New York: Academic Press.

Jackson, Robert M. 1984. *The Formation of Craft Labor Markets*. New York: Academic Press.

Joffe, Carole. 1972. "Child Care: Destroying the Family or Strengthening It?" In *The Future of the Family*, edited by Louise Kapp Howe. New York: Simon & Schuster.

———. 1977. *Friendly Intruders: Childcare Professionals and Family Life*. Berkeley and Los Angeles: University of California Press.

Kagan, Jerome. 1976. "The Psychological Requirements for Human Development." In *Raising Children in Modern America: Problems and Prospective Solutions*, edited by Nathan B. Talbot. Boston: Little, Brown.

Kahn, Alfred J., and Sheila B. Kamerman. 1975. *Not for the Poor Alone: European Social Services*. Philadelphia: Temple University Press.

Kahn Hut, Rachel, Arlene Kaplan Daniels, and Richard Colvard, eds. 1982. *Women and Work: Problems and Perspectives*. New York: Oxford University Press.

Kamerman, Sheila B., and Alfred J. Kahn. 1981. *Child Care, Family Benefits, and Working Parents: A Study in Comparative Policy*. New York: Columbia University Press.

Kanter, Rosabeth M. 1976. "The Impact of Hierarchical Structures on the Work Behavior of Women and Men." *Social Problems* 23: 415–30.

———. 1977a. *Men and Women of the Corporation*. New York: Basic Books.

———. 1977b. *Work and Family in the United States: A Critical Review and Agenda for Research and Policy*. New York: Russell Sage Foundation.

Karabel, Jerome. 1972. "Community Colleges and Social Stratification." *Harvard Educational Review* 42 (November): 521–62.

Kaufman, Debra R., and Barbara L. Richardson. 1982. *Achievement and Women: Challenging the Assumptions.* New York: Free Press.

Kessler-Harris, Alice. 1981. *Women Have Always Worked: A Historical Overview.* Old Westbury, N.Y.: Feminist Press.

Kett, Joseph F. 1977. *Rites of Passage: Adolescence in America, 1790 to the Present.* New York: Basic Books.

Kobrin, Frances. 1976. "The Fall in Household Size and the Rise of the Primary Individual in the United States." *Demography* 13 (February):127–38.

Komarovsky, Mirra. 1946. "Cultural Contradictions and Sex Roles." *American Journal of Sociology* 52 (November):184–89.

Ladner, Joyce. 1971. *Tomorrow's Tomorrow: The Black Woman.* Garden City, N.Y.: Doubleday.

Lamb, Michael E., ed. 1982. *The Role of the Father in Child Development.* New York: Wiley.

Land, Hilary. 1979. "The Changing Place of Women in Europe." *Daedalus* 108 (Spring): 73–94.

Lapidus, Gail. 1978. *Women in Soviet Society.* Berkeley and Los Angeles: University of California Press.

LaRossa, Ralph, and Maureen M. LaRossa. 1981. *Transition to Parenthood: How Infants Change Families.* Beverly Hills, Calif.: Sage Publications.

Lasch, Christopher. 1977. *Haven in a Heartless World: The Family Besieged.* New York: Basic Books.

———. 1980. "Life in the Therapeutic State." *New York Review of Books* 27 (June 12): 24–32.

Laslett, Barbara. 1973. "The Family as a Public and Private Institution: An Historical Perspective." *Journal of Marriage and the Family* 35: 480–92.

Laslett, Peter, ed. 1972. *Household and Family in Past Time.* London: Cambridge University Press.

Laws, Judith L. 1976. "Work Aspiration of Women: False Leads and New Starts." *Signs: Journal of Women in Culture and Society* 1 (Spring): 33–49.

Levinson, Daniel J. 1978. *The Seasons of a Man's Life.* New York: Ballantine Books.

Liebow, Elliot. 1967. *Tally's Corner: A Study of Negro Streetcorner Men.* Boston: Little, Brown.

Lipsky, Michael. 1980. *Street Level Bureaucracy: Dilemmas of the Individual in Public Services.* New York: Russell Sage Foundation.

Lloyd, Cynthia B. 1975. "The Division of Labor Between the Sexes: A Review." In *Sex, Discrimination, and the Division of Labor,* edited by Cynthia B. Lloyd. New York: Columbia University Press.

Lo, Clarence Y. H. 1982. "Countermovements and Conservative Movements in the Contemporary U.S." *Annual Review of Sociology* 8:107–34. Palo Alto, Calif.: Annual Reviews.

Lopata, Helena Z. 1971. *Occupation: Housewife.* New York: Oxford University Press.

Lorber, Judith. 1981. "On the Reproduction of Mothering: A Methodological Debate." *Signs: Journal of Women in Culture and Society* 6 (Spring): 482–86.

Lott, Bernice E. 1973. "Who Wants the Children? Some Relationships Among

Attitudes Toward Children, Parents, and the Liberation of Women." *American Psychologist* 28 (July): 573–82.

Luker, Kristin. 1975. *Taking Chances: Abortion and the Decision Not to Contracept.* Berkeley and Los Angeles: University of California Press.

———. 1984. *Abortion and the Politics of Motherhood.* Berkeley and Los Angeles: University of California Press.

Lynn, David B. 1974. *The Father: His Role in Child Development.* Belmont, Calif.: Wadsworth.

Maccoby, Eleanor E., ed. 1966. *The Development of Sex Differences.* Stanford, Calif.: Stanford University Press.

Maccoby, Eleanor E., and Carol Jacklin, eds. 1974. *The Psychology of Sex Differences.* Stanford, Calif.: Stanford University Press.

Malinowski, Bronislaw. 1930. "Parenthood, the Basis of Social Structure." In *The New Generation,* edited by V. F. Calverton and S. D. Schmalhausen. New York: Macauley.

Mannheim, Karl. 1936. *Ideology and Utopia.* New York: Harcourt, Brace.

Marris, Peter. 1974. *Loss and Change.* London: Routledge and Kegan Paul.

Masnick, George, and Mary Jo Bane. 1980. *The Nation's Families: 1960–1990.* Cambridge: Joint Center for Urban Studies of M.I.T. and Harvard University.

Mason, Karen O., John L. Czajka, and Sara Arker. 1976. "Change in U.S. Women's Sex-Role Attitudes, 1964–74." *American Sociological Review* 4 (August): 573–96.

Merton, Robert K. 1957. *Social Theory and Social Structure.* New York: Free Press.

Merton, Robert K., and Elinor Barber. 1963. "Sociological Ambivalence." In *Sociological Theory, Values, and Sociocultural Change,* edited by Edward A. Tiryakian. New York: Free Press.

Milkman, Ruth. 1980. "Organizing the Sexual Division of Labor: Historical Perspectives on 'Women's Work' and the American Labor Movement." *Socialist Review* 10 (January-February): 95–150.

Miller, Joanne, and Howard H. Garrison. 1982. "Sex Roles: The Division of Labor at Home and in the Workplace." *Annual Review of Sociology* 8: 237–62. Palo Alto, Calif.: Annual Reviews.

Miller, Joanne, Carmi Schooler, Melvin L. Kohn, and Karen A. Miller. 1979. "Women and Work: The Psychological Effects of Occupational Conditions." *American Journal of Sociology* 85 (July): 66–94.

Mills, C. Wright. 1959. *The Sociological Imagination.* New York: Oxford University Press.

Milne, Ann M., David E. Myers, Fran M. Ellman, and Alan Ginsburg. 1983. "Single Parents, Working Mothers, and the Educational Achievement of Elementary School Age Children." Photocopy.

Mitchell, Juliet. 1973. *Woman's Estate.* New York: Vintage Books.

———. 1974. *Psychoanalysis and Feminism: Freud, Reich, Laing, and Women.* New York: Vintage Books.

Mnookin, Robert H. 1979. "Foster Care–In Whose Best Interest?" In *Having Children: Philosophical and Legal Reflections on Parenthood,* edited by Onora O'Neill and William Ruddick. New York: Oxford University Press.

Modell, John, Frank F. Furstenberg, Jr., and Theodore Hershberg. 1976. "Social Change and Transitions to Adulthood in Historical Perspective." *Journal of Family History* 1 (Autumn): 7–32.

Modell, John, and Tamara K. Hareven. 1973. "Urbanization and the Malleable Household: An Examination of Boarding and Lodging in American Families." *Journal of Marriage and the Family* 35 (August): 467–79.

Moore, Kristin A., and Sandra L. Hofferth. 1979. "Women and Their Children." In *The Subtle Revolution: Women at Work*, edited by Ralph E. Smith. Washington, D. C.: Urban Institute.

National Advisory Council on Economic Opportunity. 1981. *The American Promise: Equal Justice and Economic Opportunity*. Washington, D.C.: National Advisory Council on Economic Opportunity, September.

National Center for Education Statistics. 1980. "First Professional Degrees Awarded to Women Up Ten-fold." *National Center for Education Statistics Bulletin* (October 17).

National Research Council for the National Science Foundation. 1983. *Doctorate Recipients from United States Universities, Summary Report 1982*. Washington, D.C.: National Academy Press.

Neugarten, Bernice L., and Nancy Datan. 1973. "Sociological Perspectives on the Life Cycle." In *Life-Span Developmental Psychology: Personality and Socialization*, edited by Paul B. Baltes and K. Warner Schaie. New York: Academic Press.

Norton, Arthur J., and Paul C. Glick. 1976. "Marital Instability: Past, Present, and Future." *Journal of Social Issues* 32: 5–20.

Nye, Ivan F., and Lois W. Hoffman, eds. 1963. *The Employed Mother in America*. Chicago: Rand McNally.

Oakley, Anne. 1974a. *The Sociology of Housework*. New York: Pantheon.

———. 1974b. *Woman's Work: The Housewife, Past and Present*. New York: Random House.

Oppenheimer, Valerie K. 1970. *The Female Labor Force in the United States: Demographic and Economic Factors Governing Its Growth and Changing Composition*. Berkeley: University of California, Institute of International Studies.

———. 1974. "The Life Cycle Squeeze: The Interaction of Men's Occupational and Family Cycles." *Demography* 11: 227–46.

———. 1982. *Work and the Family: A Study in Social Demography*. New York: Academic Press.

Papanek, Hanna. 1973. "Men, Women, and Work: Reflections on the Two-Person Career." In *Changing Women in a Changing Society*, edited by Joan Huber. Chicago: University of Chicago Press.

Parke, Ross D. 1981. *Fathers*. Cambridge: Harvard University Press.

Parsons, Talcott. 1942. "Age and Sex in the Social Structure of the United States." *American Sociological Review* 7: 604–16.

———. 1943. "The Kinship System of the Contemporary United States." *American Anthropologist* 45: 22–38.

———. 1950. "Psychoanalysis and the Social Structure." *Psychoanalytic Quarterly* 19: 371–84.

———. 1954. "The Incest Taboo in Relation to Social Structure and the Socialization of the Child." *British Journal of Sociology* 5:101–17.

————. 1958. "Social Structure and the Development of Personality: Freud's Contribution to the Integration of Psychology and Sociology." *Psychiatry* 21: 321–40.

————. 1959. "The School Class as a Social System: Some of Its Functions in American Society." *Harvard Educational Review* 29 (4): 297–318.

Parsons, Talcott, and Robert F. Bales. 1955. *Family, Socialization, and Interaction Process.* Glencoe, Ill.: Free Press.

Parsons, Talcott, and Edward A. Shils, eds. 1951. *Toward a General Theory of Action.* New York: Harper & Row.

Pedersen, Frank A., ed. 1980. *The Father-Infant Relationship: Observational Studies in the Family Setting.* New York: Praeger.

Pleck, Joseph H. 1975. "Work and Family Roles: From Sex Patterned Segregation to Integration." Paper presented at the annual meeting of the American Sociological Association, San Francisco, August.

————. 1979. "Men's Family Work: Three Perspectives and Some New Data." *Family Coordinator* 29 (4): 94–101.

————. 1981. *The Myth of Masculinity.* Cambridge: MIT Press.

————. 1982. "Husbands' Paid Work and Family Roles: Current Research Issues." In *Research in the Interweave of Social Roles: Women and Men,* vol. 3, edited by Helena Z. Lopata. Greenwich, Conn.: JAI Press.

Polatnik, Margaret. 1973. "Why Men Don't Rear Children: A Power Analysis." *Berkeley Journal of Sociology* 18: 45–86.

Pruett, Kyle D. 1983. "Infants of Primary Nurturing Fathers." *Psychoanalytic Study of the Child* 38: 257–77.

Rapoport, Rhona, and Robert Rapoport. 1976. *Dual-Career Families Re-examined: New Integrations of Work and Family.* New York: Harper & Row.

Rapoport, Rhona, Robert Rapoport, and Ziona Strelitz. 1977. *Fathers, Mothers, and Society: Towards New Alliances.* New York: Basic Books.

Rich, Adrienne. 1976. *Of Woman Born: Motherhood as Experience and Institution.* New York: Bantam Books.

————. 1980. "Compulsory Heterosexuality and Lesbian Existence." *Signs: Journal of Women in Culture and Society* 5 (Summer): 631–60.

Riley, Matilda W. 1971. "Social Gerontology and the Age Stratification of Society." *The Gerontologist* 11 (Spring): 79–87.

Rosaldo, Michelle Z. 1974. "Women, Culture, and Society: A Theoretical Overview." In *Woman, Culture and Society,* edited by Michelle Z. Rosaldo and Louise Lamphere. Stanford, Calif.: Stanford University Press.

Ross, Heather L., and Isabel V. Sawhill. 1975. *Time of Transition: The Growth of Families Headed by Women.* Washington, D.C.: Urban Institute.

Rossi, Alice S. 1968. "Transition to Parenthood." *Journal of Marriage and the Family* 30: 26–39.

————. 1977. "A Biosocial Perspective on Parenting." *Daedalus* 106 (Spring): 1–31.

————— 1980. "Life-Span Theories and Women's Lives." *Signs: Journal of Women in Culture and Society* 6 (Autumn): 4–32.

————. 1981. "On the Reproduction of Mothering: A Methodological Debate." *Signs: Journal of Women in Culture and Society* 6 (Spring): 492–500.

———. 1984. "Gender and Parenthood." *American Sociological Review* 49 (February):1–19.

Rowbotham, Sheila. 1973. *Woman's Consciousness, Man's World.* Baltimore: Penguin Books.

Rubin, Gayle. 1975. "The Traffic in Women." In *Toward an Anthropology of Women,* edited by Rayna R. Reiter. New York: Monthly Review Press.

Rubin, Lillian B. 1976. *Worlds of Pain: Life in the Working-Class Family.* New York: Basic Books.

———. 1979. *A Woman of a Certain Age.* New York: Basic Books.

Ruggie, Mary. 1982. "Explaining Social Policies for Women in Britain and Sweden." Paper presented at the seventy-seventh annual meeting of the American Sociological Association, San Francisco, September.

Ryan, Mary P. 1979. *Womanhood in America: From Colonial Times to the Present,* 2nd ed. New York: New Viewpoints.

———. 1981. *The Cradle of the Middle Class: The Family in Oneida County, New York, 1790–1865.* New York: Cambridge University Press.

Ryder, Norman B. 1965. "The Cohort as a Concept in the Study of Social Change." *American Sociological Review* 30 (December): 843–61.

———. 1979. "The Future of American Fertility." *Social Problems* 26 (February): 359–70.

Sawhill, Isabel V. 1977. "Economic Perspectives on the Family." *Daedalus* 106 (Spring):115–26.

Scanzoni, John. 1972. *Sexual Bargaining: Power Politics in the American Marriage.* Englewood Cliffs, N.J.: Prentice-Hall.

———. 1975. *Sex Roles, Lifestyles, and Childbearing.* New York: Free Press.

Scarf, Maggie. 1980. *Unfinished Business: Pressure Points in the Lives of Women.* Garden City, N.Y.: Doubleday.

Schur, Edwin M. 1984. *Labeling Women Deviant: Gender, Stigma, and Social Control.* New York: Random House.

Scientific Manpower Commission. 1981. *Professional Women and Minorities,* 2nd supplement. Washington, D.C.: Scientific Manpower Commission.

Scott, Hilda. 1974. *Does Socialism Liberate Women? Experiences from Eastern Europe.* Boston: Beacon Press.

Scott, Joan W., and Louise A. Tilly. 1975. "Women's Work and the Family in Nineteenth-Century Europe." *Comparative Studies in Society and History* 17 (January): 36–64.

Sheehy, Gail. 1974. *Passages: Predictable Crises of Adult Life.* New York: Dutton.

Shinn, Marybeth. 1983. "Well-Being and the Relationship Between Work and Family." In *New York City Area Study Proposal.* New York: Consortium for University Research.

Shorter, Edward. 1975. *The Making of the Modern Family.* New York: Basic Books.

Simmons, Roberta, and Jeylan Mortimer. 1978. "Adult Socialization." In *Annual Review of Sociology* 4: 421–54. Palo Alto, Calif.: Annual Reviews.

Slater, Phillip. 1970. *The Pursuit of Loneliness.* Boston: Beacon Press.

Smelser, Neil J. 1959. *Social Change in the Industrial Revolution.* Chicago: University of Chicago Press.

Smelser, Neil J., and Erik H. Erikson, eds. 1980. *Themes of Work and Love in Adulthood.* Cambridge: Harvard University Press.

Smelser, Neil J., and Sydney Halpern. 1978. "The Historical Triangulation of Family, Economy, and Education." In *Turning Points: Historical and Sociological Essays on the Family,* edited by John Demos and Sarane S. Boocock. Chicago: University of Chicago Press.

Smelser, Neil J., and William T. Smelser, eds. 1963. *Personality and Social Systems.* New York: Wiley.

Smith, Ralph E. 1979a. "The Movement of Women into the Labor Force." In *The Subtle Revolution: Women at Work,* edited by Ralph E. Smith. Washington, D.C.: Urban Institute.

——. 1979b. *Women in the Labor Force in 1990.* Washington, D.C.: Urban Institute.

Smuts, Robert W. 1979. *Women and Work in America.* New York: Columbia University Press.

Snitow, Ann, Christine Stansell, and Sharon Thompson. 1983. *Powers of Desire: The Politics of Sexuality.* New York: Monthly Review Press.

Sokoloff, Natalie J. 1980. *Between Money and Love: The Dialectics of Women's Home and Market Work.* New York: Praeger.

Spock, Benjamin. 1976. *Baby and Child Care,* rev. ed. New York: Pocket Books.

Stacey, Judith. 1983. *Patriarchy and Socialist Revolution in China.* Berkeley and Los Angeles: University of California Press.

Stack, Carol B. 1974. *All Our Kin: Strategies for Survival in a Black Community.* New York: Harper & Row.

Stasz, Clarice. 1982. "Room at the Bottom." *Working Papers for a New Society* 9 (1) (January-February): 28–41.

Steiner, Gilbert Y. 1981. *The Futility of Family Policy.* Washington, D.C.: Brookings Institution.

Sternlieb, George, James W. Hughes, and Connie O. Hughes. 1982. *Demographic Trends and Economic Reality: Planning and Markets in the '80's.* New Brunswick, N.J.: Rutgers Center for Urban Policy Research.

Stinchcombe, Arthur L. 1965. "Social Structure and Organizations." In *Handbook of Organizations,* edited by James G. March. Chicago: Rand McNally.

——. 1968. *Constructing Social Theories.* New York: Harcourt, Brace & World.

——. 1975. "Merton's Theory of Social Structure." In *The Idea of Social Structure: Papers in Honor of Robert K. Merton,* edited by Lewis Coser. New York: Harcourt Brace Jovanovich.

Strober, Myra. 1983. "Women Get a Ticket to Ride After Train Leaves the Station." *The Stanford Observer* 18 (October): 9.

Sullerot, Evelyne. 1971. *Woman, Society, and Change.* Translated by Margaret S. Archer. New York: McGraw-Hill.

Swidler, Ann. 1980. "Love and Adulthood in American Culture." In *Themes of Work and Love in Adulthood,* edited by Neil J. Smelser and Erik H. Erikson. Cambridge: Harvard University Press.

——. 1982. "Culture in Action: Symbols and Strategies." Paper presented at the seventy-seventh annual meeting of the American Sociological Association, San Francisco, September.

Szalai, Alexander. 1972. *The Use of Time*. The Hague: Mouton.

Tilly, Louise A., and Joan W. Scott. 1978. *Women, Work, and Family*. New York: Holt, Rinehart and Winston.

Treiman, Donald J., and Heidi I. Hartmann, eds. 1981. *Women, Work, and Wages: Equal Pay for Jobs of Equal Value*. Washington, D.C.: National Academy Press.

Tresemer, David. 1975. "Assumptions Made About Gender Roles." In *Another Voice: Feminist Perspectives on Social Life and Social Science*, edited by Marcia Millman and Rosabeth M. Kanter. Garden City, N.Y: Anchor Books.

―――. 1976. "The Cumulative Record of Research on 'Fear of Success.' " *Sex Roles* 2: 217–36.

Tuma, Nancy B., Michael T. Hannan, and Lyle P. Groenveld. 1979. "Dynamic Analysis of Event Histories." *American Journal of Sociology* 84 (4): 820–54.

U.S. Bureau of the Census. 1978. "Perspectives on American Husbands and Wives." *Current Population Reports*, Series P-23, No. 77. Washington, D.C.: U.S. Government Printing Office.

―――. 1979a. "Fertility of American Women: June 1978." *Current Population Reports*, Series P-20, No. 341. Washington, D.C.: U.S. Government Printing Office.

―――. 1979b. "Educational Attainment in the United States: March 1979 and 1978." *Current Population Reports*, Series P-20, No. 356. Washington, D.C.: U.S. Government Printing Office.

―――. 1980a. "Fertility of American Women: June 1979." *Current Population Reports*, Series P-20, No. 358. Washington, D.C.: U.S. Government Printing Office.

―――. 1980b. "Marital Status and Living Arrangements: March 1979." *Current Population Reports*, Series P-20, No. 349. Washington, D.C.: U.S. Government Printing Office.

―――. 1980c. "Money Income of Families and Persons in the United States: 1978." *Current Population Reports*, Series P-20, No. 123. Washington, D.C.: U.S. Government Printing Office.

―――. 1980d. "A Statistical Portrait of Women in the United States: 1978." *Current Population Reports*, Series P-23, No. 100. Washington, D.C.: U.S. Government Printing Office.

―――. 1981. "Household and Family Characteristics: March 1980." *Current Population Reports*, Series P-20, No. 336. Washington, D.C.: U.S. Government Printing Office.

U.S. Department of Health, Education and Welfare. 1976. "Fertility Tables for Birth Cohorts by Color: United States, 1917–1973." Publication No. 76-1152. Washington, D.C.: National Center for Health Statistics.

U.S. Department of Labor. 1975. *Manpower Report of the President* (April). Washington, D.C.: U.S. Government Printing Office.

―――. 1980. *Perspectives on Working Women: A Databook*. Bulletin 2080. Washington, D.C.: U.S. Government Printing Office.

Vanek, Joann. 1974. "Time Spent in Housework." *Scientific American* 231 (November):116–21.

Veevers, Jean E. 1980. *Childless by Choice*. Toronto: Butterworth.

Vickery, Clair. 1979. "Women's Economic Contribution to the Family." In *The Subtle Revolution: Women at Work*, edited by Ralph E. Smith. Washington, D.C.: Urban Institute.

Weiss, Robert S. 1975. *Marital Separation*. New York: Basic Books.

Weitzman, Lenore J. 1979. "Sex Role Socialization." In *Women: A Feminist Perspective*, 2nd ed., edited by Jo Freeman. Palo Alto, Calif.: Mayfield.

————. 1981. *The Marriage Contract: Spouses, Lovers, and the Law*. New York: Free Press.

Welter, Barbara. 1966. "The Cult of True Womanhood: 1820–1860." *American Quarterly* 18 (Summer):151–74.

Westoff, Charles F. 1978. "Some Speculations on the Future of Marriage and Fertility." *Family Planning Perspectives* 10 (March-April): 79–82.

Wikler, Norma. 1981. "Does Sex Make a Difference?" New York: N.O.W. Legal Defense and Education Fund.

Wilensky, Harold L. 1960. "Work, Careers, and Social Integration." *International Social Science Journal* 12 (Fall): 543–60.

————. 1968. "Women's Work: Economic Growth, Ideology, and Structure." *Industrial Relations* 7 (May): 235–48.

————. 1975. *The Welfare State and Equality: The Social and Ideological Roots of Public Expenditures*. Berkeley and Los Angeles: University of California Press.

————. 1981. "Family Life Cycle, Work, and the Quality of Life: Reflections on the Roots of Happiness, Despair, and Indifference in Modern Society." In *Working Life: A Social Science Contribution to Work Reform*, edited by B. Gardell and G. Johanssoon. New York: Wiley.

Wilensky, Harold L., and Hugh Edwards. 1959. "The Skidder: Ideological Adjustments of Downwardly Mobile Workers." *American Sociological Review* 24: 215–31.

Willis, Paul. 1977. *Learning to Labor: How Working Class Kids Get Working Class Jobs*. New York: Columbia University Press.

Wilson, William J. 1978. *The Declining Significance of Race: Blacks and Changing American Institutions*. Chicago: University of Chicago Press.

Wrong, Dennis H. 1961. "The Oversocialized Conception of Man in Modern Sociology." *American Sociological Review* 26 (April):183–93.

Zaretsky, Eli. 1976. *Capitalism, the Family, and Personal Life*. New York: Harper & Row.

————. 1982. "The Place of the Family in the Origins of the Welfare State." In *Rethinking the Family: Some Feminist Questions*, edited by Barrie Thorne. New York: Longman.

Zuckerman, M., and L. Wheeler. 1975. "To Dispel Fantasies About the Fantasy-Based Measure of Fear of Success." *Psychological Bulletin* 82: 932–46.

INDEX

78–79; cost-benefit analysis of, by
nondomestic women, 135–36;
"dilemma" of, and nondomestic
responses, 132–38; generational
transference of, 35; idealized
concept of, 4; and lack of universal
"mothering need," 199; and
maternal abuse of children, 199; as
occupation, 60–61, 110–12;
parental expectation of, 54–55;
premature, as cause of nondomestic
orientation, 62; as reluctant option,
1, 19, 92, 101, 159–84. *See also*
Childbearing; Reluctant mothers
Mothering: change in attitude toward,
7–8; in Chodorow's theory of
childhood socialization, 31–32, 33,
35n, 36n; "need," childbearing
unrelated to, 100–101, 199;
patterns of, 219–20; perceived
costs and benefits of, 195;
requirements of, 182–83; skills
required for, 152–53. *See also*
Childbearing; Child rearing;
Parenting

New Left, 228
Nondomestic beginnings: and career
attractiveness, 63–65; and nondomestic orientation, 59; and reaction against siblings, 61–63
Nondomestic choices, events triggering
movement toward, 117–19
Nondomestic orientation: and choice
of domestic life pattern, 92; and
domestic orientation, compared,
115–16
Nondomestic women, 132–38;
alternatives of, 218–20; career
consequences of childbearing
perceived by, 148–49; change in
orientation by, 216–17; childlessness chosen by, 138–57; choices
faced by, 124–27; consequences for
children of child rearing by,
149–52; costs and benefits of children for, 135–36; domestic women
assessed by, 186–90; fertility behavior of, 134; men's role in decisions
of, 137, 139–53; pressures confronted by, 123–27; range of mar-
riageable men for, 143; social
change promoted by, 125–26,
186–88; and work-career distinction, 136–37; work and motherhood combined by, 158–90
Nontraditional orientation: and
expanded work opportunities, 116;

and instability of relationships,
115–16; policies favoring, 237–32;
and stability and change in
adulthood, 117–21
Nursing: blocked job mobility in, 105,
209; as "traditional" profession,
11–12, 26
Nurturing, males excluded from, 32

Oakley, Anne: on frustrations of
domesticity, 195n; on rise of the
housewife, 4n; on structural
ambivalence, 123–24
Occupational equality, policies
favoring, 226–27
Occupations: educational background
and, 81; of fathers of sample
respondents, 252; of husbands or
partners of sample respondents,
253; of sample respondents, 41,
250; sex segregation in, 26–27,
103n, 209–11, 220–22, 225–26;
women as percentage of workforce
in selected, 238–39
Occupations, female-dominated,
26–27, 103n, 104–5, 209–11, 220;
changes suggested in, 225–26;
females employed in, 238–39;
income levels of, 209
Occupations, male-dominated, females
employed in, 9–11, 81–83, 238
One-child family, 14, 16, 167–69,
218–19
One-parent family, 8, 141n, 207n
One-paycheck family, 204, 207–9
"Overmothering," 179–80

Parental dynamics, and later life
choices, 66
Parental expectations: and childhood
socialization, 53–59; disagreement
with, 56–58; and mixed messages,
55–56, 198; reassessment of, over
time, 54, 58–59
Parental leave, paid, 226
Parenting: gender specialization for,
36; inequality in, and occupational
equality, 224–27; men's motivation
for, 144–46, 160–63; and
personality, 199–201; sexual
division of responsibility for,
146–47. *See also* Child rearing;
Fathers; Motherhood
Parsons, Talcott: and Parsonian
functionalism, 37; on role learning
and transfer of attachment, 31; and
socialization approach, 23–24,
30–31, 35n, 37

Designer: Sandy Drooker
Compositor: Graphic Typesetting Service
Text: 10/12 Baskerville
Display: Baskerville
Printer: Edwards Brothers
Binder: Edwards Brothers